You May Never See Us Again

You May Never See Us Again

The Barclay Dynasty: A Story of Survival, Secrecy and Succession

JANE MARTINSON

BUSINESS

PENGUIN BUSINESS

UK | USA | Canada | Ireland | Australia
India | New Zealand | South Africa

Penguin Business is part of the Penguin Random House group of companies
whose addresses can be found at global.penguinrandomhouse.com.

First published 2023
002

Copyright © Jane Martinson, 2023

The moral right of the author has been asserted

Set in 12/14.75 pt Dante MT Std
Typeset by Jouve (UK), Milton Keynes
Printed and bound in Great Britain by Clays Ltd, Elcograf S.p.A.

The authorized representative in the EEA is Penguin Random House Ireland,
Morrison Chambers, 32 Nassau Street, Dublin D02 YH68

A CIP catalogue record for this book is available from the British Library

ISBN: 978-0-241-66069-0

www.greenpenguin.co.uk

To Mum and Richard always

And, like the baseless fabric of this vision,
The cloud-capp'd towers, the gorgeous palaces,
The solemn temples, the great globe itself,
Yea, all which it inherit, shall dissolve.

—*The Tempest*, Act IV, Scene 1

Contents

No Man Is an Island

The island of Brecqhou is isolated and often dark, an unlikely Eden jutting out of waves sometimes so stormy they can bend steel, with winds that can make squalls out of dust. Around its coastline are the remains of old shipwrecks left to the will of the elements, and the sea creatures that occasionally rest on its craggy edges.

All other guests are invitation-only.

It was on this secluded isle, safe inside his vast neo-Gothic castle, that Sir David Barclay liked to withdraw from the world and its prying eyes. When COVID-19 came to Europe, the secretive billionaire hunkered down in the fortress he had built on the rocky outcrop in the middle of the English Channel. It was on Brecqhou that he and his wife found shelter from the pandemic.

David had built Fort Brecqhou with his twin brother, Sir Frederick, almost thirty years before, ordering 90,000 tons of concrete and steel, Spanish granite and Italian marble to be shipped across a choppy sea to their barren rock of an island. A Chinook helicopter airlifted cranes and diggers while thousands of men worked day and night – under floodlights stronger than any lighthouse – to build the 100-foot-high walls, gilded turrets, battlements and crenulated ramparts of the castle. At the time, it was the largest private house built in Britain for at least two centuries.[1]

Trespassers were not welcome.

The walls and towers stood as monuments to the success of the brothers, a paean to a career in which they had built one of Britain's most successful business empires from scratch. Inside the castle, no expense had been spared. Painted ceilings, marble columns – a grand rococo style with a personal touch. David liked to say that the island showed what could be done with 'barren rock, devoid of roads or any kind of infrastructure and little water supply'.[2] The brothers would spend many happy days with their families there.

Admission to Fort Brecqhou was through great oak doors as thick as ships' hulls, etched with the clan motto – *Aut agere aut mori*, 'Either do or die' – though the brothers' connection to their Scottish ancestry was slight. Inside their fortress, David and Frederick had branded everything – from the glistening tableware to the wrought-iron balustrade – with their specially designed coat of arms or their entwined initials, D&F. Yet by the time David sought refuge in this island hideaway, these engravings, once so symbolic of their symbiotic relationship, would only serve as a visual reminder of the fact that Frederick had not set foot on the island for more than five years. The twin he had shared his life with for eight decades haunted the fortress as a calligraphic ghost.

The great Gothic arches of the Royal Courts of Justice are older than those of Fort Brecqhou, and grander. Each day, the public go through security machines and sip liquids to prove they are safe, as they file in to watch justice be done at the biggest law courts in the land.

On an unusually hot Monday in the heatwave of July 2022, Sir Frederick Barclay, rarely seen in public and hardly ever alone, joined them.

Dressed in a well-tailored jacket with a polka-dot pocket square, a matching silk tie and sharply creased trousers, this octogenarian knight of the realm cut an unusual and solitary figure. After nearly fifty years together, thirty-four of them married, his wife had left him. A few years after he was banished from Brecqhou, she had simply upped and left him, walking out of their £30 million mansion a stone's throw from Buckingham Palace.

One half of Britain's most successful self-made business double acts was standing trial for failing to pay a penny of a £100 million divorce order.

Seated alone on the bench – apart from those he had paid to be there – Frederick told the judge that it wasn't that he wouldn't pay, but that he couldn't. Once one half of a partnership said to be worth £6 billion, he now had no money.

His wife could not have left him at a more difficult time. She had walked out in March 2019, never to return. Frederick had already split from his brother by then, but it was not until later that year that he discovered a far bigger betrayal: his nephews, his twin's sons, had been spying on him and his only child, a daughter, planting listening devices in a private room they used to talk in at the Ritz Hotel. And then they cut off his funds, he said.

At the start of 2020, after a career in which he and his brother had often turned to the law to protect their privacy, Frederick's response was to direct his legal firepower at his own blood. The ensuing courtroom drama would go on to rip open the curtain on this most private of families.

It wasn't meant to end like this.

Born just ten minutes apart in October 1934, identical twins David and Frederick had been inseparable as they went about building a multibillion-pound empire from nothing. They lived, worked and laughed together; their habit of dressing identically meant outsiders had to rely on the fact that they parted their hair on different sides to tell them apart. They were mirror twins, one left-handed and one right.

They had worked side by side, beginning as painters and decorators before going on to buy property, ships, shops and casinos, as well as some of the world's best-known luxury hotels and biggest-selling newspapers. The financial fortress they built around their complex array of businesses was almost as impregnable as the physical monument of Fort Brecqhou, and a complex administrative spider's web spun across several offshore islands meant that nobody could see inside anyway.

The brothers enjoyed decades of great success, building an

empire which would make them billions of pounds. Yet, as 2020 came around and the world entered a pandemic, that empire looked to be under attack from within, as a row over money and succession became public.

Family feuds, especially over inheritance, are as old as Cain and Abel, but the shock over this very public argument was intensified by the fact the two men and their families had once been so close, and entirely reclusive, employing phalanxes of lawyers to guard their privacy as fiercely as barons once guarded their fiefdoms. 'We are private about everything we do,' David once said. 'It stems from our philosophy of not talking about ourselves, or claiming how clever we are, or boasting about how successful we have been.'[3]

After a lifetime of secrecy, suddenly stories of family fallouts and crises filled the pages of the newspapers – all except their own *Daily Telegraph* – and their empire looked on the verge of collapse. More and more money lined the coffers of yet more lawyers, as the brothers refused to speak to one another.

Frederick's decision to sue his nephews was the start of what would prove to be an *annus horribilis* for the Barclay family, a year full of upheaval and change.

Towards the end of 2020, David accepted an invitation to a Christmas party at his son Howard's grand terraced house in Belgravia, presumably flying to London from Brecqhou in his private helicopter in order to attend. Long fearful of his health, there were unlikely to have been any strangers there. It is not known how many of his four sons or nine grandchildren attended the gathering, but it would be one of the last times that he would see many members of his family.

David's death was sudden and shocking, coming a few weeks later, on 10 January 2021. Despite the increasing isolation of his final months, the primary cause was pneumonia brought on by COVID-19.

In keeping with so much of his life, the details of David's passing were kept a secret. His first name was listed as 'Sir' on the death certificate and his sons even sought to keep the location of his burial out of the public domain. Having died at his home in Belgravia, David's body was flown back to Guernsey, and from there to a blustery Brecqhou, where he had long before overseen the creation of a beautiful chapel and filled it with the icons of his latterly acquired Catholic faith. The small funeral service was said to have been presided over by a leading cardinal.

Frederick did not attend. He took the unusual step of making a public statement instead: 'It was a great journey in everything that we did, the good, the bad, the ugly . . . We were twins from the beginning until the end. He was the right hand to my left and I was the left hand to his right. We'll meet again.'

1. Early Years

It all began in a small two-bedroom top-floor flat in Shepherd's Bush on 27 October 1934. It was the coldest October recorded in the twentieth century, a time when snow fell in the South of England and freezing fog turned London day to night.

By the time the twins were born, their parents, Beatrice and Frederick, already had three young children: Pauline, Lillian and Andrew. The family of seven squeezed into a home which today would be advertised as a small one-bedroom flat, just 700 square feet – a quarter of a tennis court – and so close to the railway line that the windows rattled every time a train passed by. Their parents went on to have three more boys, Douglas, Graham and Lawrence, with Beatrice caring for six boys under the age of fourteen by the end of the Second World War.

Beatrice Cecilia Barclay (née Taylor) loomed large in the life of her sons – they named their beloved yacht *Lady Beatrice* after her, and some of her grandchildren have her name – but she left very little by way of a public record. She was eighteen and pregnant when she married a thirty-three-year-old travelling salesman called Frederick Hugh Barclay in 1925. They both lied about their ages on the marriage certificate – she added a few years, he took some away. The bride's father, a solicitor's clerk called Henry Joseph Taylor, had died a few years before, and her only witness was a Louisa Jane Harris. The groom's younger brother, an earlier David Rowat Barclay, was the other witness.

Beatrice's new husband, the first Frederick Hugh Barclay, had been born in Glasgow in about 1891 and at some stage moved south with his family to Birmingham. According to the 1911 census, the then nineteen-year-old was living in a large house in

Moseley with his parents, older siblings, and two lodgers, including a journalist from London. But it was their father's earliest
years, spent in Scotland, that would form part of the treasured
Barclay family history.

These Scottish Barclays worked in 'markets', selling everything
from the relatively new product called margarine to confectionery. The twins' grandfather had previously been a master baker,
and their father would work selling cakes or sweets in one form or
another for most of his career.

A small man, even for the times, Frederick Sr was just five foot
three and weighed 114 pounds (just over eight stone) when he
enlisted in the British Army in 1916. A hernia and a speech impedi-
ment are mentioned on his sign-up papers, but neither were
enough to stop him being sent to France in August of that year,
where he survived the trenches for sixteen months. He was sent
home in December 1917, after which he spent a month in Glasgow general hospital being treated for gas poisoning. His request
for a pension on the grounds of ill health was rejected in March
1919, as many were in a post-war society without enough money
to pay for all its injured former servicemen. By the time his first
child, Pauline Frederica, was born in 1925, Frederick Sr had moved
the family south to London, where they would all more or less
remain.

Two more children – Lillian Rosetta and Andrew, known as
Roy – arrived before Beatrice found herself pregnant with the
twins in 1934, while the family were living in a flat on Sinclair
Road. Although this part of west London had been affluent before
the First World War, with residents able to afford live-in servants
for their four-storey white stucco houses, by the 1930s many of
those families had moved out of the city, avoiding the smog and
'pea-soupers' caused by coal-fired furnaces and the railways. As
the wealthier families left, most of the houses in the neighbour-
hood were divided up into flats or cheap lodging houses for a
more transient population. During the Great Depression in the

1930s, the area became home to many migrant workers – mostly Irish labourers – who needed cheap lodging.

Unemployment and hardship caused by the slump meant that a quarter of the British population were existing on a poor subsistence diet. Although London escaped the worst ravages of the Depression, life for the fast-growing Barclay family – supported by a man whose work was largely dependent on consumer spending – cannot have been easy.

At some point in 1939, an again-pregnant Beatrice took the children to Dorchester in Dorset, presumably for safety.[1] She gave birth to another son, Vivian, in September, just after the outbreak of the Second World War. Frederick Sr, who possessed an ability to turn his hand to many things, remained working in Hammersmith, this time as a pastry cook.

It wasn't long before the family returned to Shepherd's Bush, to a flat on the other side of the railway line, just as fears started to escalate that both the railway and the local Osram light bulb factory made the area a target for the German Luftwaffe. As such, the sound of bombs falling in London were among the twins' earliest memories – along with the time they saw a woman suspected of being a German spy being apprehended outside.

At some point, the twins – not yet five when the war started – joined the almost 1.5 million children evacuated from their city-centre homes to rural areas believed to be safer, in their case Coventry. Beatrice stayed in London, giving birth to two more sons and also suffering the loss of two-year-old Vivian in 1942. Though Beatrice is sometimes reported to have had ten children, only eight survived.

The twins were often unhappy as evacuees. Although they were unlikely to have been staying close to Coventry's city centre, Frederick recalled being 'bombed out of our beds', while David's obituary mentioned 'unpleasant experiences and the loneliness of being separated from his family'.[2] Being sent far away does not seem to have made them feel any safer. While Shepherd's Bush was hit when the Blitz began in earnest in 1940, its local pavilion destroyed by deadly doodlebug raids, Coventry was hit even harder. In October, the Luftwaffe launched forty-one raids on Coventry, mainly targeting the bicycle factories that had turned to manufacturing light aircraft and munitions.

The worst of it came on 14–15 November, with a ten-hour raid considered to be the most concentrated bombardment of an English city during the war. In one night, two-thirds of the city's buildings were destroyed or damaged – factories, offices, churches, and thousands of homes. Some 600 people were killed and more than 1,000 injured. All utilities were destroyed, including the water mains in the city centre, meaning that water had to be boiled for a long time after. The devastation was so bad that Hitler's sidekick Joseph Goebbels used the term *coventriert* to describe later vicious attacks on enemy cities. King George VI visited the city the day after this raid. He later wrote that the town which had once been one of the best-preserved medieval cities in Europe looked 'just like Ypres after the last war'.

There is much that is lost of the Barclays' early years, but what is certain is that the experience never left them. Eighty years later, Frederick still used the stress he had felt as a yardstick for measuring his suffering during his divorce; he would say he could survive anything because he had lived through the war.

There were, however, a few positive memories from life as evacuees. At one point they lived with an elderly Christian schoolteacher whom David, the son of a Wesleyan Methodist, subsequently credited for introducing him 'to a life of faith'.[3] Among the few stories to have survived their wartime experience was one in which the impoverished boys far from home discovered their entrepreneurial drive. The *Telegraph* obituary of David Barclay talks of the brothers 'earning a few pennies in a scheme looking after the bicycles of farmers going to market' in 1944, when they were nine. They could also be boisterous; a childhood neighbour called Shirley Hedges accused the twins of stealing her tortoise at some point. 'When the tortoise vanished someone said it was the Barclay twins so I went up there shouting. Their mum came out. There was talk about the tortoise having been sold for half a crown, but I got it back.'[4]

The Second World War ended on 2 September 1945, when the twins were almost eleven. The following year their uncle David Rowat died, aged just fifty-three; and then, a year later, their father died in traumatic circumstances. Still working as a com-mercial traveller, Frederick Sr was admitted to Hammersmith Hospital on 4 December 1947 for an appendectomy. According to the death certificate, signed just five days later after an inquest which would be considered unacceptably speedy today, the fifty-six-year-old died of respiratory failure following pentothal anaesthesia. He died while on the operating table waiting for rou-tine surgery after being given too big a dose of a drug similar to one subsequently used for euthanasia in the Netherlands. The word 'misadventure' was added to the cause of death.

The shock must have been awful for the thirteen-year-old twins and their siblings. Beatrice, having just turned forty, found herself in the ruins of post-war London, a single mother of eight children. Even though the boys helped out, their older sisters fell under the greatest pressure to support her – by 1950, Lillian had married Louis Barnham and had a son of her own, Gerald, who lived with the extended family until he was ten.

Like many large working-class families living in London at the time, the Barclays were incredibly close. Tracked down by *The Times* in 2004, Gerald described it as 'a loving family', before refusing to say more as he was 'worried about the consequences'.[5] The twins were particularly close to their brothers on either side, Roy and Douglas, but their early years were a time when identi-cal twins – even rarer than they are today – were treated almost as a single entity, like a two-headed hydra. It was common for twins to dress in the same clothes and they were most often con-sidered somewhat strange and interdependent.

It was also a time when music, dancing and movies meant that being a teenager, even a relatively poor one, had its benefits. According to Shirley Hedges, the Barclay twins acquired a reputation for snazzy dressing with matching jackets and Brylcreemed hair, and they shared a love of ballroom dancing. David later said that he had learned to dance in a school hall after work; in 1948 a future dance champion named Bob Burgess opened the Olympia Ballroom near Shepherd's Bush, where he gave lessons three times a week and demonstrations on Sundays. The twins were fourteen and had just started work, and Burgess later told the *Mail on Sunday* that they were among his first members: 'Their brothers and sisters came too, but the twins stuck at it.'

Although few people would be able to tell them apart, there were already differences between the brothers. 'Fred loved dancing. He still does,' said Burgess in 1992. 'David came for the social life.' While Frederick went on to win awards for ballroom dancing and danced regularly into his eighties (according to Burgess, who became a family friend, David met his first wife, a trained dancer and model, at a dance).[6]

The story of how the Barclay brothers made a fortune is not just a rags-to-riches success story, but the story of modern Britain.

A few years after their father died, when they were still teenagers, the twins left school and started work. One of their first jobs was at the General Electric Company (GEC), then still operating a lamp-making factory in Hammersmith; they also worked at Schweppes, the drinks company. The twins had always helped their mother with painting and decorating as they moved between flats in Shepherd's Bush – first on Sinclair Road and later Addison Gardens – and they used this experience as a springboard to work in property.

Born in time to take advantage of post-war reconstruction efforts meant to solve the desperate shortage of homes and offices, the Barclays were not alone in seeing property as the best and quickest way to make money. Like financial markets in the 1980s and technology at the turn of the twenty-first century, property was the get-rich-quick scheme of the age. It would define much of British society for generations to come.

The lives of the Barclays can often seem shrouded in mystery, as though covered with the pea-soup smog of their London child-hood, but their start in business – never spoken about, and with the actors and accounts lost or unclear – is possibly the murkiest period of them all. It was once said that their complex financial arrangements were 'like knitting fog', but stitching together their earliest forays into business is harder still.

They were more likely to mention their lack of much formal education rather than their start in business. In the 1980s, when an unsuccessful takeover bid for an establishment firm saw them take the unusual step of agreeing to publicity, David told the *Guardian*'s Geoff Gibbs that they had been educated 'in the school of adversity'. Frederick joked that they'd had to set up their own business because 'we are probably unemployable – we are the only people on the top floor not academically qualified'.[7] John Peyton, the Old Etonian member of the Hussars who became a Conservative peer and chair of the Barclay brothers' charitable foundation in the 1980s, traced their attitude to money back to their hard-scrabble start in life. 'They were once very poor themselves,' he told Bloomberg in 2004. 'They don't waste money; they spend it with care.'[8]

Their beginnings also made them hard-nosed, according to Frank Kane, a business journalist who got to know them well after they supported his seriously ill child for several years. In a positive profile, he wrote: 'It has to be understood at the outset that they are asset-traders, cost-cutters, tough negotiators and opportunity takers. In the hard-nosed business world the Bar-clays inhabit, these are compliments, and it is doubtful they would be where they are today – from humble origins in working-class west London – without these attributes.'[9] Yet the twins never talked much about how they went on to make so much money, a code of *omertà* combined with sparse public records helping to spark rumours and conspiracies as they became very successful men.

Peter Rivett, writing in a David Barclay-commissioned book about Brecqhou – a hagiography of the Barclay stewardship which at times reads as though Mr Collins is describing Lady Catherine de Bourgh – rebukes those who describe them as 'reclusive', an adjective which he says carries a 'slightly sinister air'. In a chapter titled 'But Who Are They?' he writes: 'The fact is that David and Frederick Barclay are private people who see neither need nor duty to parade themselves in public. As a result, little is known about them. This book cannot add much to that which is already in the public domain and this is how they wish it.'[10]

This desire for privacy, sinister or not, started early. Their *Who's Who* entry only offers 'former estate agent' for Frederick before starting with 'joint proprietors' of the Cadogan Hotel in 1968–78 for both men. Yet the twins had worked throughout the 1950s, running an array of businesses, nearly all in property, most with different names and addresses, which they never subsequently talked about.

After finding work at GEC and Schweppes 'rather tame', the twins 'went to work in the construction industry and learned a basic knowledge of all building trade experience which allowed them to build, restore and repair numerous properties over the following 40 years'. Then, just like that, they became estate agents and 'opened their own office in 1961' – even though, by then, Frederick and their younger brother Douglas had already been declared bankrupt.[11]

Frederick and Douglas had followed their father into the confectionery business at some point, by renting a shop called Candy Corner at 64 Richmond Way. By 1960, the two brothers found themselves unable to pay their landlord, a man named William

Davies, the several hundred pounds they owed him, breaching the terms of their lease. He seized the shop and issued bankruptcy proceedings on 10 October.[12] The reasons are unclear; the 'failure of a sub-lessor' has been mooted, as has other members of the family using the till like a source of ready cash. The only official notice found Frederick 'guilty of misconduct in relation to his property and affairs' but added no further details.[13]

At the time, there was no automatic discharge, and bankrupts could be saddled with the burden of insolvency for years – even for life. The official *London Gazette* notice which announced the bankruptcy lists several other ventures for the brothers, then still in their mid-twenties.[14] There was an eponymous building and decorating business called Barclay Brothers, as well as the Peter Howard Agency, a furnished accommodation bureau. Among their various ventures, Frederick is also understood to have worked for an alcoholic Polish estate agent and to have made him so much money that the man offered him a stake in his firm, though there is no record of either the man or the business.

David is not named in the notice, although Frederick and Douglas are described as having worked 'formerly in partnership with another' as the 'Barclay Brothers'. The business address for the firm of builders and decorators is 39 Addison Gardens;[15] we know for certain that David had lived at 39a Addison Gardens five years earlier, when he got married.[16] Frederick was also in partnership with 'unnamed others' in running the Peter Howard Agency, the address for which was given as 171 Holland Road, W14 – not only Douglas's address at the time, but also that of David's first wife back in February 1955. By 1960, Frederick had left Shepherd's Bush and was living in Holland Park, a twenty-minute walk away and possibly the furthest he would live from his twin brother until the split sixty years later.

So, while David's name was missing from the bankruptcy notice for the shop, his erstwhile home address and that of his wife were used for two other businesses linked to his brothers' enterprises. This brief paragraph was to provide the first clue to the use of interlinking companies based on home addresses – connected to close associates – that would continue to be a feature of the Barclay way of doing business. It would also not be the last time David's wife would be linked to his business affairs.

It's important to note that bankruptcies at the time were rare, and still carried the pre-entrepreneurial stigma that existed before the Thatcher government changed the law decades later and introduced a more forgiving, flexible approach. The stigma would have been particularly difficult for David, given the fact that by 1960 he was actually quite famous – or at least his wife was.

Zoe Margaret Newton had been born in Cornwall but moved to London soon after the war, where she trained as a dancer. Blonde, beautiful and just four foot eleven, she was eighteen when she was chosen as the National Dairy Council's milk girl, becoming the figurehead for the ubiquitous advertisements that encouraged ration-hit Britain to drink home-grown milk. When she married David in 1955 at Kensington's Anglo-Catholic St John the Baptist Church, the twenty-year-old David gave 'interior dec-orator' as his occupation, while Zoe, who had made the cover of the *Picture Post* magazine that year and could be seen on bill-boards across the whole of Britain, left her profession blank. Already known as the 'drinka pinta milka day' girl, Zoe's big blue eyes and elfin features had appeared on top of a huge tiger's head on the cover of the popular magazine. In the centre spread she toasted shelves of milk with a glass of red wine. Michael Cole, then a reporter at the *Acton Gazette*, remembered her as 'more famous than the Queen at the time'. There are pictures of the couple on their honeymoon, looking like Hollywood stars of the age. In one, David wears wide-legged trousers and a boxy double-breasted jacket while gazing up at a grinning Zoe. Both seem to be standing on a pile of rubble as workmen look on. In another, they are both happy and handsome, sitting by a fire.

The fame made David uncomfortable. Zoe gave a 'frank interview', according to the *Mail on Sunday*, in which she admitted Frederick was always with them and that she could not always tell the twins apart. The piece also mentioned that this most private of men slept in a circular bed with pink covers. Although Zoe was making enough money for them both, in his first public quotes David sighed: 'It's embarrassing. Very embarrassing, you know. It means that you cannot live comfortably in your own sphere of life when you are both so . . . famous.'[17]

Such fame meant that David must have been relieved not to have joined his twin brother in his first and most public misstep with the Candy Corner bankruptcy – an early venture into retailing they were not to repeat for decades. Instead, the brothers moved to focus entirely on property, doing so well that by June 1966 they were able to discharge Frederick's bankruptcy. How they did so is perhaps the true heart of their origin story.

It is no surprise that the wheeling-and-dealing Barclay brothers saw the local property market as the fastest way to make money in the 1950s – so did almost everyone else. London was full of buildings that had been either destroyed, damaged or left to decay in the years since the war. Some people made their fortunes and reputations largely by buying commercial property, but many more made money in a residential housing market that was undergoing enormous upheaval. Photos of North and West Kensington in the 1950s show once-grand terraced houses looking grubby and neglected. Many of the early Victorian properties had been given century-long leases due for renewal in the 1960s, which had discouraged renovation. Slum clearance often led to new office space rather than new houses, putting even more pressure on those who needed a home. And there were lots of people who did: the post-war servicemen looking to marry and raise a family, refugees from the war, and immigrants from the West Indies arriving to help with the post-war recovery efforts.

West London, home ground for the Barclays, was the epi-centre for this explosion in demand and desperate supply squeeze. Considered among the outer edges of respectability in the fifties, West and North Kensington now count among the city's most expensive real estate markets. One of those who made money at the time, Herbert Mortiboy, told the *Sunday Times* why Notting Hill was such a great place to start: 'I came in, like most property millionaires, after the war when the market was wide open and prices at the bottom . . . There's more money to be made in the dust-hole than there is in Piccadilly.'[18]

Homes in post-war London were largely owned by private landlords, but wartime legislation ensured security of tenure and a cap on rents. Conservative prime minister Harold Macmillan's Rent Act in 1957 ended these controls and allowed landlords to charge whatever they wanted to new tenants, believing this to be a way of resolving the problem of housing shortages by allowing more people to make money. Instead, almost overnight, slum landlords took over, using means fair and foul to evict protected tenants and replace them with those so desperate for somewhere to live that they would pay wildly inflated prices to share appall-ing living spaces – among them, black people suffering from racist 'no blacks' landlords, and prostitutes who had been kicked off the streets by different legislation. Even before the 1957 Act, however, only tenants of unfurnished accommodation enjoyed the benefits of cheap and stable rents and security of tenure. Ten-ants of furnished accommodation – most often those who had arrived with little more than the contents of a bag they could carry – enjoyed no such protection. With no rights and a market undergoing a revolution, these tenants could be charged as much as the landlord could get away with, and were evicted if they didn't pay. Prices skyrocketed, with slum landlords charging as much as £3 a week in 1960 – 60 per cent of an average working-class wage – for a double bedroom with a toilet and kitchen shared between as many as twenty people.[19]

The Peter Howard Agency – the furnished accommodation bureau run by Frederick 'in partnership with others' and listed at an address once used by his brother's wife Zoe – is the only evidence that the brothers operated at this less than salubrious end of the market. There is no evidence at all of any unlawful or even wrongful behaviour. What is clear is that financial institutions – and indeed anyone with cash to spare – were more than willing, in this rising market, to finance anyone improving properties and increasing profits. There were 100 per cent bank mortgages available for those able to turn rental accommodation that may have housed a few low-paying tenants into something closer to a human factory farm, where the chickens paid a fortune for the privilege of living in a shed. In the subsequent parliamentary debate on what became a housing scandal, the then Labour MP Harold Wilson read out an advert, in a tone of distaste, 'whereby a young man, who was clever enough to get into the property market, is to be a quarter-millionaire as a result of getting large loans from an insurance company'. He suggested exorbitant rents and desperate conditions were behind these riches.[20]

The Barclays were far from alone in looking to hit gold in a west London property scene that allowed anyone with an ability to do up houses and increase rents to make a fortune. A young Michael Heseltine was another of those who did. In his autobiography, *Life in the Jungle*, Heseltine records how he made his first fortune in the 1950s property boom before going on to become a Conservative cabinet minister and peer.[21] In the mid-1950s he used £1,000 from a Post Office Savings Account set up by his grandparents (worth about £29,000 today) and a small mortgage to buy a short thirteen-year lease on the Thurston Court Hotel in Notting Hill. Along with his business partner, Ian Josephs, he served notice to the existing tenants so that Josephs's father could renovate, after which they were able to charge some £2–3 per tenant per week, bringing in an agreeable £30 per week. A year later they sold the property for such a profit that they 'doubled their money'. 'It seemed too good to be true,' recalled the future Lord Heseltine. 'We seized the opportunity.' The profit allowed the pair to take out a £23,000 mortgage – worth some £670,000 today – which they used to buy a forty-five-bedroom cross between a boarding house and hotel which they called the New Court Hotel.

Heseltine's account offers a fascinating insight into the area around Bayswater, near Olympia, at almost the exact time and place when the Barclay brothers were also young men on the make. This model of turning large properties into many-roomed boarding houses or hotels proved a hugely successful one for the Barclays a short while after, by which time Heseltine had already started in politics. 'All human life was there,' Heseltine wrote of the small number of long-term residents, the smattering of com-mercial travellers, and the American serviceman who came for the weekend and at one point 'flung a naked prostitute' across the hallway. He managed to sell the New Court Hotel on almost immediately for a profit in 1957. By a strange twist of fate, it somehow ended up in the hands of a man whose career would become as notorious as Heseltine's became illustrious.

Perec (known as Peter) Rachman was a Polish Jew who had arrived in London just after the war. He built up a slum empire in the 1950s that proved the model for landlords who terrorized poor and vulnerable tenants while using a chain of companies to avoid any redress. 'Rachmanism' is a word defined as 'the exploit-ation and intimidation of tenants by unscrupulous landlords' by the *Oxford English Dictionary*. According to Shirley Green, whose biography of the slumlord is one of the best guides to the period, Rachman ran a 'perfectly respectable' gambling club in the New Court Hotel, which he bought in 1957 – the same year Heseltine is said to have sold it via Lieutenant Colonel George Sinclair.[22] In his autobiography, Heseltine mentions meeting Rachman at the time, although he mainly dealt with 'one of his managers'.[23]

A penniless refugee in 1946,[24] Rachman proved the adage that you did not need money to succeed in property – just access to people with money. Borrowing from banks, building societies and anyone with ready cash, Rachman bought run-down old houses, many of which were still governed by statutory controls, and used thugs known as 'the Heavy Glove Men' as well as Alsatian dogs to force out existing tenants. He also hired black men to threaten white residents and white ones to threaten the black ones, increasing tensions and feeding into the Notting Hill race riots of 1958.

Although his empire was mainly based around Paddington and Notting Hill, Rachman started as a flat-letting agent in Shepherd's Bush in 1954,[25] and it was his purchase of thirty slightly shabby end-of-lease houses on Shepherd's Bush Green that started him on his way to becoming a professional landlord. The fact that the most notorious landlord in Britain started his career and lived mostly within a thirty-minute walk of the Barclay brothers has served to sharpen the focus on the brothers' early years, but there is no evidence that the Barclays ever met him, let alone copied his dubious methods.

However, Rachman provides a well-documented example of how property speculators were able to exploit legislative loopholes that existed until the early 1960s. Under the Companies Act of the time, businessmen could set up a series of interlinked companies for as little as £19 each (about £500 today). Appointing close associates as nominee directors – easily controlled via undated letters of resignation – these companies could then be used both to conceal beneficial ownership and to borrow more money from banks or building society managers with set individual limits. This kind of web is still commonly found today with the use of offshore interests.

Rachman was not alone in spotting loopholes in the Companies Act. A *Sunday Times* investigation subsequently read out in parliament stated: 'As with most property concerns, Rachman operated through an interlocking chain of limited companies, usually with his own nominees as directors.' Companies were wound up and the properties reassigned to other companies, which meant that when officials wanted to serve notices – whether for sanitary problems, certificates of disrepair or even compulsory acquisition – they struggled to find the right people to serve it on. Nominee companies allowed the freehold to be separated from any leases, with the assets of some subsidiary companies 'an under-lease on one house or even of just one self-contained floor'.[26]

In 1959, the police uncovered a complex network of thirty-three companies Rachman had set up to control his property empire. He was also able to collect £10,000 a year in rent for a house that had previously been subject to rent control and had cost him just £1,500. By the time Rachman died of a heart attack in 1962, he had acquired more than 150 run-down mansion blocks and several nightclubs, and was said to have made a million pounds, which after the relaxation of exchange controls he had been able to send to Swiss bank accounts, thereby avoiding tax.

His empire had proved so successful he had caught the attention of two brothers prepared to benefit from illegal rather than legal means. Gangsters Ronnie and Reggie Kray used Rachman to branch out from their criminal stranglehold of east London. Through him they were able to buy a gambling club in Knightsbridge called Esmeralda's Barn.[27] Decades later, with the Krays long in prison, the club became part of the Berkeley Hotel.

In her biography of Rachman, Shirley Green argues that he was a scapegoat at a time of political crisis, pointing out that his behaviour as a slum landlord only caused a scandal after his involvement in what became known as the Profumo affair was made public. Christine Keeler and Mandy Rice-Davies were said to be two former mistresses of Rachman who had lived in one of his grander houses in Marylebone. They were at the centre of the affair, with Keeler accused of sleeping with both a Russian spy, Yevgeny Ivanov, and the cabinet minister John Profumo. The

Profumo scandal turned attention onto the housing scandal; a BBC documentary and several media reports highlighted the state of the housing market *ex post facto*. In July 1963, Harold Wilson started a debate in parliament on 'the consequences of the Rent Act 1957 and property profiteering' that was subsequently credited with helping elect him as prime minister, thereby ending thirteen years of Conservative rule.

Wilson's new Labour government passed a Rent Act, which offered both security and 'fair rents' to tenants. The new prime minister said of the Profumo scandal: 'Sometimes one turns over a stone in a garden or field and sees the slimy creatures which live under its protection.'[28]

Throughout this tumultuous period, the Barclay brothers' business continued to make money, first by turning rooms into boarding houses, then by turning those boarding houses into hotels. They did so with several different companies. On 23 May 1962, while Frederick was still banned by bankruptcy rules from acting as a director, David registered Hillgate Estate Agents. Hillgate's articles of association included twenty-one business objectives, ranging from estate and insurance agenting – with all the building, decorating and repair work that entailed – to mortgage brokering and moneylending, issuing loans 'with or without security'. As it happens, Hillgate still survives today, with David's two eldest sons as the sole directors,[29] although hundreds of other Barclay-owned companies have been folded, renamed or mothballed. A year after founding Hillgate, David founded Ilkent Properties and Ilkent Holdings. The Barclays were shrewd and hard-working, but they also benefited from the most astonishing boom in London property prices. A £5,000 investment in 1961, adjusted for nothing more than inflation, was worth just over £111,000 by 2019. David once told a journalist that a property he had bought in 1961 for £5,000 was valued at £25 million by 2019.[30]

Many of the people who worked with the brothers speak of them having a sharp sense of humour. One story is both funny and telling for what it says about their desire to do deals. Once, Frederick was working alone in the estate agency when a woman came in looking for a property, any property, on a particular road in Notting Hill, as she needed to live near her elderly father in order to look after him. Although there was nothing listed, Frederick immediately told her that he had the perfect place, and showed her a small property with no obvious sign it was up for sale. The woman was delighted and paid over the odds to be able to move in so quickly. Frederick had just sold his brother David's house without telling him first. Years later, when Frederick was asked if David had minded, he would say, 'Of course not, because the price was so good.'

Those with enough money, such as Heseltine years before this, soon discovered that even more money was to be made turning houses into hotels at a time when demand was booming. In 1964, David set up Primary Holdings Ltd and bought the leasehold for 3 Westbourne Terrace in London's Paddington,[31] a relatively seedy part of London at the time. The brothers renovated the house and turned it into the Hyde Park North Hotel, their first notable hotel launch. David and his wife Zoe then formed another company, Highgrange Investments, in the same year.

In 1966, while the brothers were still just thirty-one, Frederick's bankruptcy was discharged. But the public scandal over Candy Corner would irk the brothers for decades to come. It also seems to have exacerbated their liking for privacy. In 1967, after company law changed to require small private limited companies to make company accounts public, Hillgate was almost immediately re-registered as an unlimited company (such companies, common in the Barclay empire, are subject to more limited disclosure rules).

Meanwhile, Zoe had given up her high-profile modelling career and had had children. Aidan Stuart was born in early 1956, followed by Howard Myles in 1960, then Duncan Hugh less than fifteen months after that. One consequence of Frederick's bankruptcy discharge was that he replaced Zoe on the board of Hillgate Estate Agents.

The scale and speed of the Barclays' career growth as hoteliers is notable. From leaving school as teenagers, they bought, revamped, rented and sold houses before moving on to hotels. By the late 1970s, they had bought and sold fifteen hotels in little more than a decade. Their brush with bankruptcy had done little to slow them down, but their grand ambitions and need for cash to fuel them were about to lead them into their biggest scandal yet.

2.   A King's Ransom

The Crown Agents began in 1833, with two men in charge of a small team managing grants to what were then called the colonies.[1] By the start of the Second World War, almost 800 people were working in Westminster, a stone's throw from Big Ben, procuring goods and services – everything from paper clips to railway engines – for parts of the British empire.[2]

An 'emanation of the Crown', neither part of the civil service nor of the government, the agency was always a strange beast. When the dissolution of the empire led dozens of former colonies to declare independence after the war, the organization suffered an identity crisis. Having changed its name from the Crown Agents for the Colonies to the Crown Agents for Overseas Governments and Administrations in 1954, the Agents feared their role would become obsolete as newly independent nations developed their own staff and funds to find suppliers and agree contracts. It was then that the Crown Agents' management approved a new financial division, separate from its traditional role providing goods and services to 100 overseas governments – to make money on its own account and replenish lost reserves.

Thus began a tale of greed, hubris and mismanagement which ultimately cost the British taxpayer more than £175 million (some £1.2 billion today). It was the biggest financial scandal of the 1970s, and a precursor for many future financial failures, involving as it did a lack of oversight, and men who thought they could make a fortune using other people's money to invest in property, and more, around the world. Government and opposition ministers stood up in the House to call the scandal an 'enormous catastrophe' and 'one of the most serious betrayals of public accountability'.[3]

Their involvement with the Crown Agents – in which they played a relatively small part in a scandal which saw an investor like US property speculator William Stern declared Britain's biggest bankrupt – is by far the most obscure episode of the Barclay brothers' own corporate history. They were not censured in either of the two judge-led inquiries, despite defaulting on £9.5 million in loans, worth some £75 million today.

The scandal, played out against the property boom and then bust of the early 1970s, was the closest the twins came to financial ruin. The story of how this happened and how they survived – told largely through archive accounts and carefully preserved handwritten notes – gives an incredible insight into how they made a fortune. It also reveals unanswered questions about how they managed to avoid bankruptcy.[4]

By the time the Barclays were introduced to key players at the Crown Agents, the organization had undergone its own revolution. Senior staff had worried that jobs would have to be cut by the end of the 1950s, as more and more former colonies declared independence. Sir Stephen Luke, appointed as senior Crown Agent in 1959, described this period as 'traumatic'. Before he left in 1968, Luke sanctioned the abandonment of strict limits on how the Agents should make money and what they should invest in. It was to be a catastrophic mistake.

The organization was able to borrow money cheaply because it was considered a safe bet – no agent of the Queen could be allowed to go bust. In turn, huge numbers of developers flocked to borrow money from the agency at a slightly higher rate, at a time when the UK was cool for the first time since the war, with soaring demand not just for housing but hotel accommodation. The Crown Agents lent money not just to overseas governments wanting to build railways, but to property speculators wanting to make money, and made some for itself at the same time. Its lack of expertise in finance – there was only one qualified accountant in the whole operation until November 1970, for a start[5] – did not prevent the Crown Agents becoming the second biggest money market operation in the UK after the Bank of England. With more than £350 million to invest (over £5 billion today), the Crown Agents had no shortage of applicants eager to do business with them, especially as they developed a reputation as an easy touch. Or, as a self-satisfied internal note in December 1969 had it: 'As we become better known to property developers (and dealers) an increasing number of interesting properties find their way to us.'

Subsequent reports were less kind. 'These were quasi-civil servants at loose in the City jungle,' said one. Or, as one of the forty-six witnesses who gave evidence to the subsequent inquiry, said: 'We were all getting a little bit cocky. We were going round feeling we are as good as those people in the City . . . Now with dreadful hindsight we realise we were not as good.'

The lack of oversight is astonishing, even decades later. When the Finance Department Investment Account – Finvest – was set up to make money, there was no official meeting even to discuss it, just a one-line board minute of 23 May 1967. Investments were made in a wide range of new ventures, from silver mines to property in territories ranging from London to Australia and Singapore.

At the head of the finance department was a man called Alan Challis, whose charisma and ambition made up for his relatively limited financial experience. Described as 'adventurous' in the subsequent inquiry, Challis was part of the 'new look of competitive efficiency' that Luke had striven to give the Crown Agents – a look also adopted by Sir Claude Hayes, who replaced him as the head of the agency in 1968. Hayes was a senior civil servant mentioned in dispatches during the war, and was known for his fondness for overseas travel. His staff considered him unapproachable.

Under Challis, Finvest more than doubled its investments, from £58 million at the end of 1968 to £127 million a year later, with an ambition to increase that four-fold to £200 million within another nine months. The plan was mainly to invest in the property market, which like all boom markets seemed a surefire way to make money at the time. Government measures to encourage more bank lending and consumer spending accelerated a housing bubble that saw the average price of a home, which had risen from £2,000 to £5,000 between 1950 and 1970, double again in just three years.[6] With an aggressive target to meet, Challis lost no time promoting men with attitudes that made up for a lack of relevant financial experience, moving anyone with a knowledge of accountancy or risk sideways, or even out.

Bernard Wheatley, an ex-army officer who had joined the Crown Agents in 1947, was a key appointment, He was still a relatively junior employee when he was promoted to run the Crown Agents' money market operations in March 1967. He had no experience in the financial markets, but he had developed a taste for the booming London property market in the 1960s, when his job involved finding British embassies for overseas governments. His colleagues called him 'flamboyant' and 'dapper', and newspaper cuttings from the time show a handsome, thickset man with smooth, dark hair. One of his bosses wrote admiringly that 'his first concern was making money and nothing else'.

Although he was well regarded as 'one of best dealers in the city' by many of his colleagues, there were some warning signs over Wheatley's temperament. His ultimate boss, Challis, wrote of him: 'He thought guidelines irksome and unnecessary. Had tendency to like being seen as financial big boy, making instant decisions.' More worryingly, he was widely known to be a 'regular and habitual' gambler and frequenter of a gentleman's club in St James's called Crockford's. Before retiring in 1968, Sir Stephen raised this 'odd' membership with Challis,[7] who took it no further. In fact, none of Wheatley's seniors ever raised concerns about the fact that a man with a gambling habit had control of a fund amounting to £350 million. Subsequent reports suggest that he could lend up to £10 million, or £150 million today, without involving any of his colleagues at all.

Even this is less surprising than the blatant conflicts of interest by today's standards which went almost entirely unremarked at the time. Jack Walker and Henry Kaye were senior lawyers at Davies Arnold Cooper (DAC), appointed property solicitors for the Crown Agents. They took this as an invitation to introduce the law firm's other clients looking for a loan, including several on which they sat as either directors, or shareholders, or both. None of this was contrary to any professional regulations that existed at the time, and neither the firm nor any individual lawyer was singled out for criticism in the investigations that followed – even though the subsequent inquiry found that certain solicitors at DAC 'lapsed from professional standards of conduct'. Any later criticism was directed at the Crown Agents, and the 'haphazard' way in which connections were made between their clients and advisers.

At least two of these companies were owned by the Barclay brothers.

The sixties may have started with a brush with bankruptcy for the Barclays, but by the end of the decade they were fully fledged hoteliers with ambitions to do far more. Their initial success turning private flats at 3 Westbourne Terrace into the mid-priced Hyde Park North Hotel had led David and Frederick to launch several more companies to convert private houses or flats into hotels. Before the end of the sixties, they had added Primary Holdings, Highgrange Investments, Richwell, and Barclays Hotels. They had added Hyde Park West Hotel in 1966, followed by the renovated Cadogan Hotel in more upmarket Sloane Street, and the Lowndes Hotel. The last was in exclusive Belgravia, where the brothers now lived, still close to each other. They also bought three adjacent properties on Westbourne Terrace with plans to form a new 100-bed hotel called the Westminster Hotel.

By 1969, when they set up Barclays Hotels, they were thirty-five. David, who wrote all the official correspondence kept in the archives, was described as 'the director responsible for policy', while Frederick was the director 'responsible for finance and administration'. He signed no letters but was often called Fred or Freddy in the margins of notes. David was never referred to as Dave. Their younger brother Douglas, the only other relative named on the Candy Corner bankruptcy note from 1960, was not made a director but was listed as 'supervisor of all building works and conversions'. Despite – or perhaps because of – his brush with bankruptcy, he would stay with them for much of his working life, largely handling all renovations.

It was through Jack Walker that the twins were first introduced to the Crown Agents. Their original loan application to the agency, in 1968, was for about £300,000 to purchase the Cadogan Hotel in Chelsea. The application was made via Highgrange Investments Ltd. Jack Walker was listed as a director of Highgrange, while the more senior lawyer Henry Kaye was both a director and a shareholder. (Henry Kaye subsequently became a shareholder in Barclays Hotels when it bought the share capital of Highgrange.) This initial loan was agreed by Bernard Wheatley, who went on to approve all the money that was lent to the brothers.

Wheatley exists today in archived notes showing his bold, wildly looping handwriting. More often than not, he would add a few words and his initials to a typed facsimile sheet agreeing a loan. In one, he agreed to a loan of up to £2.5 million for the Barclays to buy a temperance hotel, which was one of their biggest successes of the decade. There are several letters between Wheatley and the lawyers acting for both the Crown Agents and the Barclays. The preferred means of communication between

Wheatley and David Barclay was the telephone, notes of which were jotted down in brief memoranda slips.

In January 1969, the lawyer Jack Walker was posted to Australia, a fact that did nothing to stop his involvement in the loan applications, but perhaps explains the lack of written correspondence left by him in the official files. Before emigrating, he invited Alan Challis, Wheatley's boss, and the Barclay brothers to a leaving dinner held at a restaurant called the Empress, around the same time that they were setting up Barclay Hotels and becoming more ambitious. In July of that year, he wrote to Challis, reminding him of the party and saying: 'I have the utmost faith in the Barclay Brothers and Henry Kaye and myself have, indeed, backed them financially. I would welcome the opportunity of introducing them to you again.' Solicitors are today barred from soliciting money for one client from another – especially one they have invested in – but in 1969, Walker implored 'Dear Bernard [Wheatley]' to lend the full amount of up to £2.5 million for the purchase of a hotel called MF North. The Barclays – practically teetotal themselves – had spotted the opportunity in buying this unloved temperance hotel without a liquor licence.

In August, Wheatley agreed to the loan, noting briefly that it was secured by both personal guarantees from the Barclays and, 'as additional security', their shares in Barclays Hotels, a newly formed company. He added a scrawl to the end of this letter: 'Please open a new commercial loan file for Barclays Hotels ltd'. For his part, Walker wrote that the new company would be listed on the stock exchange within a year. He also added that 'the total advance is not likely to be outstanding for more than 12 months'. In the event, the company was never listed – in fact, despite frequent suggestions they might be, no company ever owned by the Barclays has been listed – and rather than paying back their loan, the Barclays ended up borrowing far more.

By 1970, the Barclays' move into hotels had proved so successful that they decided to ask the Crown Agents for an even bigger loan, this time to buy Gestplan Hotels, owner of the Londonderry House Hotel, for £2.6 million. The site on Park Lane had served as the London residence of the Marquesses of Londonderry for many years before it was sold to a Lebanese bank in 1962, demolished and reopened as a 170-bedroom hotel in 1967.

On 22 May 1970, Jack Walker signed an effusive four-page memo in support of this proposal, extolling the virtues of both the historic location and the Barclays' track record, as well as forecasting high profits. This, he said, 'fully justifies the purchase price and as an addition to a hotel group anxious to invite public participation it becomes a good buy'. The proposed plan was no bargain, but the money to be made from a subsequent stock market flotation – allowing the Crown Agents an option to purchase shares – would make it all worthwhile, he indicated. Barclays Hotels Ltd, a holding company for both Highgrange Investments and Primary Holdings, authorized and issued share capital of £500,000, all of which was owned by both the Barclay brothers and the DAC and Crown Agents lawyer Henry Kaye.

Rather than raising any red flags, this conflict was apparently seen as a good thing by the team at the Crown Agents. Four days after the Walker memo, Wheatley's superior David Johns wrote in support of the loan application: 'BH have had a short but successful history so far (Henry Kaye of DAC is a shareholder and the approach has been prepared by Jack Walker)'. Relying on the fact that 'Walker has considerable experience in the field', the senior Crown Agent Johns urged speed: 'Unfortunately, there is a certain urgency as the deal for Londonderry has to be concluded in the near future.' There is no explanation as to why.

By 8 July 1970, Henry Kaye had told another agent that he was due to be appointed director of Gestplan Hotels Ltd after the deal. 'I have already spoken to Bernard Wheatley and have bespoken from him for tomorrow two bankers draft . . . for £1.1m combined and also a cheque to DAC for £320,000.' Thus it appears that the law firm received a fee for the introduction to a deal in which a company owned by one of its partners received a multimillion-pound loan.

That same month, the Crown Agents agreed to lend the Barclays the whole of the first instalment of £1.55 million, as well as four annual instalments totalling a further £1.4 million, for the Gestplan deal. In return, the agency gained an option to purchase between 17 and 29 per cent of the issued share capital in the event of the future flotation of the privately held Barclays Hotels. The loan was secured by a floating charge over the hotel group, including the Londonderry. This meant that in the event of a default, the Crown Agents were authorized to take ownership of the hotel – a bit like a defaulted mortgage allows a bank to seize a home. The charge was drafted by the lawyers at DAC, who were not only being paid by the Barclays but themselves part-owned the hotels.

When disaster struck and Barclays Hotels did indeed default on their loan, this charge, drawn up by lawyers acting for both sides, was found to be inadequate.

While the Barclays and others were pursuing the Crown Agents, Wheatley's lifestyle – including a lavish lunch account and a lucrative membership to the Curzon House group of clubs and casinos – was beginning to raise eyebrows.

Peter Nowers, the sole accountant among thousands employed at the Crown Agents, was the only one to ask questions about expense claims that dwarfed those of any other executive. Some of Wheatley's lunches in the early 1970s cost the equivalent of nearly £500 today, with wine going for as much as £125 a bottle. Nowers, described as a 'lone voice' in the subsequent reports, was heard to confront Challis over the excess, who 'instructed' him to foot the bill as Wheatley deserved to be 'indulged' – one argument given was that he wasn't earning what he could earn from commercial rivals. When Nowers continued to raise concerns about the exposure of the agency to the market, he was accused of crying wolf.

As for Wheatley, if any of his colleagues wondered how a man on a relatively modest salary owned three cars, including top-of-the-range Jaguars, and had built a swimming pool and sauna at his home in Aylesbury, Buckinghamshire, they thought he must have inherited money. A number of his colleagues suggested in subsequent evidence that, as one put it, 'what a chap does after hours is very much his own business'.

As boom went to bust, one other employee within Crown Agents showed signs of concern. George Towse, the controller of financial services, isn't even accorded a first name in most of the internal notes, and he certainly didn't get to enjoy the many 'good lunches' with clients that his senior colleagues did. Pages of his tall, spiky handwriting raising questions about accounting or financing – in the Barclays Hotels files at least – were either ignored or brushed aside by his more go-getting peers. When asked about shoddy financial management and acceptance of delays by the subsequent judge-led review, he practically sighed: 'Where on earth does one start? First of all, the management of the organisation regarded the accounts as a bore.'

Less than six months after the loan to the Barclays for Gestplan, there were already signs that the optimistic profit forecasts mentioned by Walker were way off beam.

To help them find a way to avoid a default on the first repayment, the Barclays appointed J. & A. Scrimgeour – the 'bluest of blue-blooded broking firms on the Stock Exchange'.[8] In December 1970, Viscount Garmoyle, acting for Scrimgeour, approached the Crown Agents, on behalf of the Barclays, with a proposal for the short-term loans to be replaced by longer-term ones, plus more equity finance which could be sold again after a much-dangled flotation. The situation was 'high risk' but 'could well prove extremely profitable for all parties', he added, urging the Crown Agents to appoint an accountant to check the accuracy of the profit forecasts.

Towse, his boss Johns, and Challis met and drew up a plan in which the original £3 million loan to the Barclays was fully drawn down, with £2 million converted to equity, 'provided profit forecasts were met'. In January 1971, Towse wrote to Johns that he was 'extremely uneasy' about the delay in accounts from the Barclays hotel group. No one else expressed any unease – indeed, the aristocratic Garmoyle seems to have been obsessed with the hospitality of the brothers. Just a month after this he wrote a note to Challis in which he told the Crown Agent 'Lunch with them today will be good!!'[9]

In a meeting at Scrimgeour, Towse raised concerns about the adequacy of the Barclays' accounting, pointing out that there was 'more judgement and less record than normal'. He pushed for a full report from external accountants at Cooper Brothers, but the Barclays objected to the inclusion of assumptions, calculations and figures that a fuller report would demand. The atmosphere was described as genial nonetheless. Besides, Towse needed a higher authority to agree a full certificate. Johns sided with 'Lord Garmoyle' and recommended a 'lesser' certificate that did not subject the Barclays' accounting to the same scrutiny. As further proof of the regard the Crown Agents men had for accountants, Johns expressed his doubts that Coopers Brothers, the accountancy firm that would go on to become PwC, 'would be fully competent to comment on the assumptions since they are not hoteliers'. In his subsequent evidence, the downtrodden Towse described this as 'a characteristic contempt for accountants'.

In their April 1971 report, Coopers were damning about the

Barclays' management accounting, which 'was so much in arrears that they did not in fact know the level of profitability of any of their hotels except for the Londonderry . . . the policy in respect of depreciation also appeared unsatisfactory'. The accountants also noted that the filing of the 1969/70 accounts for Highgrange Investments and Primary Holdings had been seriously delayed.

This report infuriated David Barclay, who fired off a letter to Coopers on 28 April accusing the accountants of being 'unnecessarily harsh and unfair'. 'I would remind you that this is a private company and the directors consider the information with which they are provided is sufficient for their purposes,' he added. There had been a high turnover among the eight people employed in the Barclays Hotels' accounts team, he admitted, but the chief accountant, one 'Miss Ryan', was a 'good bookkeeper with a long knowledge of accounts', if not a qualified accountant.

The tone in a subsequent letter to Challis, dated May 1971, was far more conciliatory, boasting that one of the accountants had referred to the hotel group as a 'first class plus company'. David, ever the salesman, also enclosed Barclays Hotels' first brochure – with a suite at the 170-room Londonderry House Hotel now among the most expensive in London at £22 a night. He invited Challis for lunch.[10]

In June, Garmoyle and Challis accepted the invitation and had lunch with the Barclays at the Londonderry. There they agreed a new loan, confirmed by the aristocrat in a subsequent note, which began: 'You can put it down to too good a lunch if I have got the following wrong'. In essence, the Barclays had committed to rectifying any accounting shortcomings in return for an additional loan of £500,000 from the Crown Agents to help them buy the lease for the hotel. Pencil strokes jotted down in the margins denote new interest rates. To one which reads 'Apparently Mr Challis agreed', Bernard Wheatley added his initials. In one note prior to the Londonderry deal, Wheatley had simply scratched out the amount of suggested loans and replaced them with higher ones.

Delays to extension works and Towse's continued doubts over the brothers' 'distinction between operating profit and net earnings' did not stop David Barclay inviting Challis to another lunch to discuss the brothers' interest in 'a hotel which overlooks the Thames a short distance from Savoy'. 'We intend to explore every possibility of purchasing or leasing a hotel . . . which will give the company the necessary growth in 1973/74,' he wrote in the letter, suggesting that a future pipeline of deals was a prerequisite for the still upcoming flotation. Perhaps anxious that Challis might listen to the accountants advising him, David ended with a telling line about the business habits of the brothers: 'If you feel at any time a little out of touch please do not hesitate to let me know as we are inclined to play our cards close to our chests as a matter of habit rather than for any other reason.'

This 'matter of habit' would never leave the Barclays.

In January 1972, Barclays Hotels reported a loss of £107,496, a number starkly opposed to the profit of £445,000 which had been predicted by Scrimgeour and others when they were looking to raise the money. In February, Towse sent a note to his boss: 'Forecasting is always difficult but I can not find any explanation of these huge discrepancies'. He called them 'recklessly optimistic assumptions'. Towse was in no doubt of his place in the chain of command, going as far as he could to push his boss to deal with the authoritarian entrepreneur. 'I feel that Crown Agents are entitled to greater frankness concerning accounting arrangement than has been the case so far. I am aware of the importance of personalities in this emergent company and recognise that attempts to obtain a more open approach may be counter productive. I feel that clarification of the relevant issues is more likely to follow from your initiative than mine, but would welcome your guidance.'

With £1.5 million due for repayment in the summer of 1972,

David Barclay called Bernard Wheatley and asked that the loan be renewed for a further year, according to a letter in the files signed by the Barclay company secretary, Stuart Brummer. 'I confirm a telephone conversation which Mr Barclay had earlier today with Mr Wheatley when he requested that this loan be renewed for a further year.' In a scrappy note in the margins to someone called 'Margaret', Wheatley wrote: 'We spoke. Interest shall not at present be taken on the following loans £1.2m, £340,000 and £60,000.' This support did not prevent Barclays Hotels Ltd missing its profit forecast by a wide margin and failing to repay the £1.5 million loan due to the Crown Agents.

Then the property bubble burst.

In September 1972, in a letter to the Crown Agents in which he also abandoned plans for the much-anticipated stock market flotation the following year, David Barclay blamed the miners' strike and conditions in the UK hotel business in general for profits 'considerably below forecasts'. 'So it is that we have to be a little more patient . . . In the meantime, I am arranging for the figures to be sent to you regularly in future.'

The following year, the Barclays repaid some of the outstanding loans and bought out the equity conversion rights, but simultaneously secured a new loan from the Crown Agents worth £3.5 million over three years, covered by a mortgage on Londonderry House Hotel. This deal was agreed with Challis and Wheatley, with both the repayment and new loan arranged on one day, 27 June 1973.

There were more calls between David Barclay and Bernard Wheatley during this time, all of which were recorded on slips of paper but not properly minuted. After agreeing the £3.5 million, a note in Wheatley's scrawl indicates that the total outstanding to the Barclays was now about £6.5 million. Mention is made of a very positive land valuation given by someone called Harold Caplan, a man who had also been introduced to the Crown Agents by Walker.

The subsequent inquiry report remarked on how property was accepted as security for millions of pounds' worth of loans without any attempt at an independent survey. As an example of the 'fortuitous' choice of associates, the report mentions 'Wheatley who meets Walker, who becomes property consultant and his firm the property solicitors. He introduces Caplan who becomes valuer.' The report notes how 'strange' it was that such a gilt-edged organization should allow a relatively junior official such as Wheatley 'to recruit from young men making their careers'.

While urging patience about the stock market listing that could have repaid their debt during this time, the Barclays asked for advice about the tax implications of buying property in France just as the UK property bubble was about to burst. There was a lot of discussion about the use of loans to avoid income tax before Towse declined with a sigh: 'I am afraid we do not share David Barclay's degree of optimism about the Paris office market.'

By early 1974, despite the issues with the earlier loan, the Crown Agents had lent a further £5.25 million to Ilkent Holdings and Ilkent Properties, which helped the Barclays fund the £5 million acquisition of the Kensington Palace Hotel and Prince of Wales Hotel from the Norfolk Capital hotel group.

With the plans for a flotation scotched and the accounts not as he would have liked them, George Towse started to lose patience – at least with some of his colleagues. On 5 April 1973, he demanded that Wheatley detail the outstanding loans to the Barclays, writing: 'I understand that the Barclays have been rolling over their interest for some time.'

At least five years after the brothers' introduction to Wheatley, Towse demanded that the money market manager obtain 'written confirmation before renewing or extending any loans' to companies controlled by the Barclay brothers, 'in order to avoid any possible misunderstanding on the subject'.

*

Alas, like all the Crown Agent measures to control excessive lending, Towse's note would come far too late. Doubts about the
agency's management – over far bigger fish than the Barclay
Brothers – had already surfaced. In August 1971, the *Guardian* ran
a front-page story and two inside pages headlined: 'How the
Crown Agents manage their £1,000m'. Among the questions
posed were: 'Do the developing countries for whom they act
know that their money is being used to buy parcels of London
property and is being put into banking and other enterprises thus
enabling a number of individuals to build up personal fortunes?'[11]
Questions were raised in the House of Commons.

Suddenly, the boom turned to bust. Chancellor Anthony Barber's 'dash-for-growth' budget in March 1972, with its unfunded
tax cuts, caused not just a short-lived 'Barber boom' but a wage-
price spiral and high inflation. Caught in a stagflationary trap of
high inflation and unemployment, the Bank of England asked
commercial banks to cut back their lending to property developers in September 1973. There was a secondary banking crash
following the miners' strikes, and an oil embargo that caused
power cuts and the introduction of the three-day week.

David Young, who went on to serve in Margaret Thatcher's
cabinet, later wrote about his struggle as an entrepreneur at the
end of 1973: 'The property market was dead. Sites and land had
no value; with no demand, investment property values and property company shares both continued to fall.'[12] It was a time of
misery and hardship for many consumers. Collapsing share and
property prices put pressure on the secondary banking market
and overextended property companies. Nowers, the 'lone voice'
accountant working at the Crown Agents, wrote a paper called
'What Went Wrong?' and sent it to senior officials at the end of
1973. He retired three years later.

In the run-up to this catastrophe, Sir Claude Hayes had spent
almost a whole month 'visiting principals in the Pacific'.[13] When
he left the Crown Agents in October 1974, he was replaced as

head of the agency by John Cuckney, a former Lazard banker and MI5 officer.

When the Crown Agents called in its loans, many of the property speculators once considered a sure thing defaulted. The new management, faced with a financial black hole worth some £212 million, launched an internal review. Then, as so many financial institutions have before and since, they turned to the government for help. After handing over £85 million, in April 1975 the government finally appointed a committee of inquiry, to be led by a Judge Fay.

A few months before this, as soon as Cuckney's review started to ask difficult questions, Bernard Wheatley had tendered his resignation. Alan Challis had left the agency at the end of 1973 for a job paying almost double the salary. He became joint managing director of First National Finance Corporation (FNFC), a company that the Crown Agents owned 5 per cent of, had lent millions to since 1969, and on the board of which he already sat.

The £9.5 million owed by the Barclays was a fraction of the total owed to the Crown Agents. Subsequent inquiries and reports focused on recipients such as William Stern, who was so grateful for his £54 million loan that he handed over a silver teapot worth £400 (or £3,000 today) to Challis, and gold pens, attaché cases and lighters to other Crown Agents. The agency had even lent money to the London Capital Group, the bank set up by Labour MP John Stonehouse in 1972, two years before he faked his own death and ran off to Australia.

That said, the 'serious defects' found in the legal agreements behind loans to Ilkent Properties drawn up by the lawyers at DAC prompted a new, chillier tone in correspondence written by the remaining Crown Agents staff to and about the Barclays. Seemingly undeterred, David Barclay continued to press his case that the market was to blame and the situation would improve. The new head of the Crown Agents, John Cuckney, appeared equally keen to stand his ground. He declared that he had made it 'harshly clear' to the Barclays that any promise of jam tomorrow 'was but of fleeting interest – not a basis for any reconsideration of their lending arrangements'. 'I said our problems here remained massive and urgent,' he wrote on 21 May 1975. The Barclays were given an extension of just a few months and put in a 'special situations' category along with other defaulters.

A committee was assembled to deal with these special situations, with weekly updates for all significant cases, including the Barclays. These were mainly written by a deputy head of banking, Eric Osgodby. It is clear from the updates how close the brothers were to going bust. Loans with other lenders, such as NatWest, had been secured with cross-guarantees from all their companies, while David and Frederick had also given personal guarantees for the debts.

In March 1976, the Crown Agents rejected the brothers' proposed repayment plan as both politically and commercially unacceptable, sensing it would attract complaints from competitors about the use of taxpayer money to subsidize a rival hotel group. In the same month, the special situations committee recommended the appointment of a receiver, and identified one at Turquand Youngs and Co. Osgodby noted that this appointment would 'bring down the whole Barclays Hotel group'. There was a sticking point, however, in the inadequacy of the security charge drawn up by DAC over the main hotel, Londonderry House. Osgodby admitted 'because our charge is faulty . . . a receiver will probably have no immediate control of the business'.

Despite the finger of blame for the faulty charge being firmly pointed at Davies Arnold Cooper, there were no sanctions. Testimony from the head of banking at the Crown Agents, Norman Hewins, said they 'had no reason to think that Davies Arnold and Coopers were not drawing up the legal charges in proper form'.

In retrospect, he admitted, they 'should have had independent advice'.

The inadequacy of the charge forced the Crown Agents to consider other options such as a sale. The brothers seemed keen: an unnamed 'Arab party' was said by them to have shown an interest in the group, as had Grand Metropolitan and Trafalgar House, in meetings during the spring of 1976.

The talks with Trafalgar House seemed particularly promising to Osgodby but, despite being spun out over several months in 1976, they ended without a deal being agreed. They would however introduce a man and a company who would be connected to the Barclays for some time to come.

At around the same time as talking to the Crown Agents, the two men at the top of Trafalgar House were in talks to buy the Ritz. An account of the hotel industry by one of the most successful hotel property agents of the time – the now out-of-print autobiography of Edward Erdman – offers a perfect vignette of not only the founders but the times.[14] Erdman was of the view that Nigel Broackes, the founder of Trafalgar House, was the right man to take over the Ritz – not just because of Trafalgar House's construction and tourism expertise but also because of the nature of the founder himself, who had turned a small legacy from his grandfather into a world-leading construction and engineering conglomerate. Broackes was not only a young and suave former Guards officer, he 'had a good family background' and 'was educated at Stowe'. The young tycoon also had a 'very good-looking wife,' wrote Erdman approvingly.

Erdman, a draper's son who had left school at sixteen, also admired Broacke's business partner – a former office boy from Islington in north London. Victor Matthews was a 'dynamic character' and 'a practical man of the building industry', according to Erdman. Another successful double act, Broackes was the front man and strategist while Matthews did much of the day-to-day running of the businesses for Trafalgar House. 'The amazing success of the Broakes/Matthews partnership may be due to the difference in character and style of the two individuals,' said Erdman, who could have been writing about the Barclays.

It was Matthews who talked to the Crown Agents about a potential purchase, in a series of discussions which at the very least gave them more time, and it was Matthews who would go on to have an unlikely relationship with the Barclays.

With interest on the outstanding £9.5 million loan to the Barclays accruing at a rate of more than £100,000 a month, the agency was keen to reach a speedy solution. Then, an offer came in from an entirely unknown and unexpected source. The Crown Agents agreed to sell Barclays Hotels' bad debts, rather than force the brothers into foreclosure. This not only allowed them to avoid the fate of most other Crown Agent borrowers – bankruptcy – but also somehow parked their responsibility to repay the loss of £6.5 million incurred by the Crown Agents. The story of how this happened has remained untold and is one of the most questionable aspects of the whole affair.

Their salvation came in the form of a £3 million offer made to Norman Barrington Cork of Cork Gully, an insolvency practice, for the debt of the hotels owned by the Barclays hotel group on 2 August 1976. The offer came from a new company, Trenport Investments Ltd, which had been set up that same year by two brothers, Leslie and Harold Bolsom, especially to buy the debt.

Little is known about the Bolsom brothers. Leslie Michael was born eighteen years before the twins, while his brother Harold Victor was a little closer in age. They had dabbled in a blinds business without huge success, and lived on the other side of Hyde Park to the Barclays in relatively modest flats. It is hard to tell where these unknown brothers found £3 million. We may never know.

Mired in controversy by this point, with highly political public inquiries and more to contend with, the Crown Agents appointed Morgan Grenfell, one of the most well-regarded merchant banks of the time, to negotiate with the Bolsoms. It failed to get a better deal, stymied as its bankers were by a floating charge held by another bank, as well as a series of unhelpful legal documents.

The subsequent arrangement was confirmed in its entirety by five paragraphs typed up and signed by Osgodby on 6 October 1976. This describes a declaration made in support of the offer by the Barclay brothers which showed their 'state of massive personal insolvency'. In order for the deal to go ahead, the Barclays confirmed that they had 'no present or future interest' in the equity of Trenport Investments.

These signed declarations allowed the deal to go ahead, but the last paragraph of Osgodby's official note suggests that the Barclays were not out of the woods. 'In view of the statutory declarations it may be purely a point of academic interest, but it is noteworthy that so far no mention has been made of the balance of the debt amounting to some £6.5 million (excluding interest) nor any release of the Barclays from their personal guarantees . . . In theory if these points remain unresolved, we should still be in a position to proceed against the Barclays as guarantors.' In essence, if these points did indeed remain unresolved, the Barclays were expected to pay off their debt to the British taxpayer, if they somehow survived the downturn of the mid-1970s.

The Crown Agents sold the Barclay brothers' debts for £3 million and wrote off the remaining £6.5 million as a loss, at a cost to the British taxpayer of some £44 million at today's prices. There is no public record of the Barclays ever making good on this debt.

When the Fay report was published at the end of 1977, three government departments – the Ministry of Overseas Development, the Treasury and the Bank of England – were criticized for failing to stop the Crown Agents' speculative financial dealings. Two men within the organization were censured: Sir Claude Hayes and Alan Challis. The latter was accused of 'unjustified risk-taking, lack of regulation and control, aversion to taking advice, secretiveness and a low standard of commercial ethics'. He resigned from the board of FNFC at the end of 1974.[15]

In the fallout, Bernard Wheatley, was charged with four corruption offences involving the awarding of more than £1.5 million in loans and the acceptance of more than £300,000 as 'gifts or consideration for granting Crown Agents loans'. The charges all related to a company called Big City Finance, nothing to do with the Barclay brothers. A second inquiry found 'serious criminal activity' and blamed Wheatley. 'It is an unfortunate fact that wherever the Crown Agents lost money, Mr Wheatley's hand could be seen behind the transactions.'[16] Having been released on £15,000 bail from Bow Street Magistrates' Court in London, Wheatley was found dead in a hotel in the New Forest on Friday, 1 July 1977. His death was marked by a paragraph in the business pages of the *Daily Telegraph* the following week.

Following the Fay report, politicians lined up to criticize the Crown Agents for 'incompetence', 'folly', 'euphoria' and 'low ethical standards' (despite its place as an institution meant to be held to a higher standard than most). Judith Hart, Minister of Overseas Development, called it an 'extraordinary idiosyncratic legacy of our colonial past'. Prime Minister Harold Wilson denounced the 'closing of the ranks' and 'cover-up' obvious from the scandal.[17] While parliamentarians spoke up in the House, the inquiries themselves were held in private – partly to avoid negative publicity overseas.

After the British empire crumbled in the 1950s, the decision of the Crown Agents management to replace the easy pickings of imperialism with a new money-making model based on soaring property prices ended in disaster. Yet the evidence of arrogance, greed and weak governance in the affair has featured in many corporate frauds since. It would also not be the last time that the bill was picked up by the British taxpayer rather than the perpetrators.

Having ignored any early warnings, the government had few options to recoup the money spent. It sued Wheatley's estate for £750,000 despite the fact he was heavily indebted when he died.[18] Probate was delayed for many years, and when it was published in the early 1980s, the value of his estate appeared to be just £9,575.

Despite acting as investor, borrower's solicitor and lenders' solicitor in several transactions, lawyers at DAC appeared to have escaped censure entirely.

The Crown Agents escaped closure but found a new purpose as a not-for-profit development agency with a new constitution. Since the outbreak of the COVID-19 pandemic in 2020, it has been involved in transporting medical equipment and vaccines to remote locations, including Ukraine.

William Stern lived through bankruptcy to become embroiled in other property scandals. He was excoriated by the media, especially after a company he had set up to raise money through property bonds meant that many private investors lost their life savings. This collapse prompted such an uproar it led to the creation of Britain's first Policyholders' Protection Act, which offered a safety net for savers by imposing a 1 per cent levy on premiums.[19] But the losses for an economy struggling with an oil crisis and the bursting of the property bubble were immense. In March 1976, as the Barclays faced insolvency, an editorial in the *Sun* newspaper summed up the whole scandal: 'Now they [the Crown Agents] are bankrupt. And the Overseas Development Ministry (that is, YOU the taxpayer) is picking up the pieces.'

The Barclays were not singled out for any criticism in the Fay report. One who was, Ramon Greene – a property developer involved with English and Continental Property who was left bankrupt in the wake of the scandal – knew the twins. In 2004, he told Bloomberg: 'The brothers were close to going broke, but they were cleverer than me . . . I don't know how they managed it.'[20]

Even during their darkest hour, when the Crown Agents were on the cusp of appointing receivers and insisting on repayment, the Barclays had continued to buy and sell hotels. In 1975, they bought the Howard Hotel on London's Embankment, the 'hotel which overlooks the Thames a short distance from Savoy' that David had mentioned to Alan Challis over lunch. In the ten years after they first approached the Crown Agents for a loan in 1968, they bought fifteen hotels.

The two Bolsom brothers remain a mystery and appear never to have done another significant deal, despite making a fortune from Trenport. In 1950 Harold married Eileen Marsh but has never been listed as a director at Companies House. Leslie was not listed as a director for another company until 2001, when he joined Houldsworth Business and Arts Centre,[21] before retiring in 2006.

After buying the £3 million debt, Trenport was able to sell some of the loans they took on in 1978 for £4.8 million. In that year's accounts, the Bolsoms paid themselves a dividend of £578,000 – more than £3 million today. Incredibly, in April 1979, an unusual restructuring of the share capital of Trenport Investments Ltd ended with the sale of the company to Gestplan, which had by then become a subsidiary of Barclays Hotels. This sale made a mockery of the promises made by the Barclay brothers less than three years before that they had no current or future interest in the company that had saved them from bankruptcy.

Accounts for 1979 show that Harold and Leslie Bolsom resigned as directors of Trenport on 3 April 1979 and were replaced by David and Frederick Barclay on the same day. The amount paid by Barclays Hotels to the Bolsoms was undisclosed, but based on existing mortgage loans and net cash when they bought it, the company could have been worth more than £4 million in 1979 – far more than the amount paid by the Bolsoms.

No one ever seems to have reminded the brothers of the declaration that allowed them to avoid bankruptcy in the first place. The agreement arrived at did not appear to release them from their obligations as personal guarantors, according to Crown Agent records. If this is so, there is no public record of them ever repaying the £6.5 million cost to the British taxpayer, worth more than £40 million today.

Trenport Investments Ltd is owned by Trenport Property Holdings Ltd, which is still owned by Shop Direct Holdings Ltd.[22] It is described as the Barclay group's property management company. At some point Frederick and David made way for David's son Aidan on the board, where he remained until June 2021.

As for the hotel behind much of the outstanding debt to the Crown Agents, Londonderry House, it was the gift that kept on giving for the Barclays, who bought it twice in thirteen years. It proved two of David's favourite sayings: 'Businesses are for buying and selling, and don't forget the selling' and 'It's never wrong to bank a profit'.

The Barclays sold the Londonderry in March 1980 to the Kuwait Investment Office (KIO) for a reported £9.5 million. This should have given them a healthy profit – likely to have been at least £5 million – having narrowly avoided bankruptcy in 1976. The Barclays bought the hotel again in 1985 from the KIO for £18 million and committed to spending a further £5 million refurbishing and redeveloping it. They then sold it for a second time, to Kennedy Brookes in 1987, for £45 million. They also received a further £19 million for the Howard Hotel.

In sum, they made tens of millions of pounds from the ownership of hotels they had come so close to losing in 1976.

The Crown Agents scandal confirmed the brothers' dislike of using public financing to finance their deals. Despite the frequent hints that they would do so, they have never listed a major company on the stock exchange, preferring to remain privately listed. Most of their subsequent deals relied on a small group of lenders such as the Edinburgh-based Bank of Scotland for financing. Their refusal to tap into public markets kept the details of their finances even more closely held. There were to be no more government inquiries in which files on their accounts were kept for future public consumption.

The brothers' involvement in the scandal must have hurt their reputation in the City. As Alex Brummer wrote in the *Guardian* in 1977: 'A run-down of the financial and property companies with which the Crown Agents dealt on their own account reads like a *Who's Who* of people to avoid in the financial world.' An article and broadcast discussing their involvement prompted their first significant libel action brought in both the UK and France against a journalist, John Sweeney, in 1995.[23]

The mid-1970s had undoubtedly been a difficult time for the Barclays. David, with his wife and three teenage boys, and Frederick, who had met and moved in with his future wife Hiroko in 1973, moved into smaller flats next to each other in Bolebec House on Lowndes Street, and holidayed together in the Channel Islands. By the end of the decade, however, they had not just weathered the financial storms of the decade, but had ended up in a far warmer place, both personally and politically. In 1979, just after the Winter of Discontent in Britain, with the coldest temperatures in sixteen years and industrial action that crippled many public services, a new Conservative government was elected – with a woman, Margaret Thatcher, the country's first female prime minister. In the same year, the brothers bought the Mirabeau Hotel, a luxury hotel on Monte Carlo's Avenue Princesse Grace, soon to be dubbed the world's most expensive street. They also rented large apartments on adjacent floors of the Roccabella tower on the same street and became resident overseas for tax purposes.

When the Barclays bought their first newspaper, a positive profile in the *Mail on Sunday* described Jack Walker, who had introduced them to the provider of most of their early capital, as the Barclays' 'big break'.[24] Walker, Ramon Greene and Challis were reported to be living in Monte Carlo after the scandal, before the principality garnered its reputation as a sunny place for shady people. Years later, Harold Bolsom and his wife Eileen would also be spotted with the Barclays while on holiday nearby.

3. Hitting the Big Time

An address in Monte Carlo was as much about business as pleasure for the Barclays. In Monaco, on neighbouring floors of the Roccabella, they got to know a woman who helped change both their fortunes and their lives.

Not much is now known about Lady Esther Ellerman, whose surname lives on in the financial world as the name of the management company belonging to the Barclay family, Ellerman Investments. But in the early 1980s, the name Ellerman was synonymous with a shipping company that had once been one of the biggest in the world.[1]

How the Barclays managed to buy the historic company for a song, snatching it from the clutches of other blue-chip buyers – and particularly what role their friendship with an ageing heiress in the final years of her life played – has been the subject of speculation ever since. Did they use their personal connections to gain an advantage? How exactly did they persuade the board and trustees of a once great company that had lost its way?

Whatever the truth, the Ellerman deal not only made them hundreds of millions of pounds, it showed all the hallmarks of a way of doing business that would stay with them for the next forty years: spotting an undervalued property; using back channels of communication to get involved in a sale; and, most important of all, keeping everything shrouded in secrecy. The Ellerman deal also showed how these somewhat unlikely hoteliers could blindside a bloated board full of self-satisfied men, as well as their inefficient advisers.

When the first John Reeves Ellerman died of a heart attack in 1933, he was Britain's richest man, with an estate valued at almost three times as much as the next largest estate. Secretive, buccaneering and hugely successful, Ellerman died a year before the Barclay brothers were born, yet he could almost be seen as a role model for the men who would go on to first buy and then break up his business, making their own vast fortune in the process.

Like the Barclays, John Ellerman did not come from money. Born in the gritty, bustling port town of Hull in 1862 to a German corn merchant father who died when he was nine, Ellerman went on to train as an accountant – a skill which, unusually for the time, he used to identify undervalued businesses.

By the time he was thirty he had bought an ailing shipping company from the estate of Frederick Leyland, which he then sold for a profit a few years later to the American financier John Pierpont Morgan. Awarded a baronetcy in 1905 for providing the government with ships during the Boer War, Ellerman was a financier who owned the world's biggest shipping fleet and then diversified into undervalued sectors such as breweries, coal mines, London property and, with the approach of the First World War, media companies. He became a major shareholder in *The Times*, *Daily Mail*, *Illustrated London News*, *Tatler* and *Financial Times*. William Rubinstein, an emeritus professor of history who wrote Ellerman's entry in the *Oxford Dictionary of National Biography*, believes Ellerman's love of secrecy may have had something to do with his heritage as well as his private life. 'He was afraid people would start picking on him because he was a German. He had an interesting solution to this and the press: he bought up most of Fleet Street.'[2]

Ellerman's private life was also unusual for the time. He began a relationship with a woman called Hannah Glover and they had a daughter, Annie Winifred Ellerman, in 1894, not long after he started buying ships. Scandalously for the time, they did not marry until 1909, just before their son – also John Reeves Ellerman – was born. Using the pen-name Bryher, Annie later moved to Paris and became a well-known feminist and supporter of artists such as James Joyce. She wrote of Ellerman's insistence that her mother remain practically hidden: 'Hannah was as if lifted out of nowhere.'[3]

Rubinstein, who wrote a study of the rich titled *Elites and the Wealthy in Modern British History*, said: 'Ellerman was not married, and lived openly with a woman, but nobody blew the whistle on him . . . their private lives were a closed book. The big newspaper owners were reluctant to expose them in case the same thing happened to them.'[4] To this day, the failure of newspapers owned by wealthy individuals to report on the peccadilloes of rivals is often attributed to something obliquely referred to as the 'proprietor's code'.

Ellerman was renowned for his hatred of publicity, another trait he shared with the Barclay brothers. Rubinstein, now living in Australia, says there is 'little in the records about this singularly secretive tycoon'.

Ellerman was an early example of a self-made man when the majority of Britain's wealthiest people were land-owning gentry. Like many of the super rich today, he also worked out ways to avoid paying tax. In the 1920s he started to distribute profits as capital gains rather than income, to avoid the increasing taxation introduced after the First World War. According to Rubenstein, 'He was probably the first successful British businessman to be trained as an accountant, and was a master of the art.'[5]

A study in August 2021 suggested that he avoided paying more than £2 million in tax this way – a fortune at the time, worth £100 million today. Then, just before he died in 1933, Sir John Ellerman transferred 'very large investments to Audley Estates Ltd, registered in Prince Edward Island, Canada', making him an early adopter of offshore funds.[6] The Inland Revenue at the time believed that Audley Estates was owned by members of his family.

When the first John Reeves Ellerman died, it took the Inland Revenue three years to assess his estate for probate purposes, valuing it at almost £37 million – equivalent to £2.8 billion today – the biggest estate in British history at the time. The vast bulk of this fortune, after £20 million in death duties, went to his then twenty-three-year-old son, while his older daughter was left just £900,000. The siblings provide further proof, if needed, that money alone does not bring happiness. Annie Winifred had a huge fight with her brother after their father's funeral – he threw a chair at her and she never spoke to him again despite living for another fifty years.[7]

A month after his disapproving father died, the second Sir John Ellerman married Esther Leopolda de Sola, the daughter of a banker from Montreal and descendent of a prominent Jewish family from Spain. It isn't known why Ellerman the elder had disapproved of Esther, who bonded with his artistic son over a shared love of amateur theatrics, notably Gilbert and Sullivan. When they married in August 1933, the *News of the World* head-lined the story: 'Romance of Britain's Richest Young Man'. When reporters tracked the young newlyweds down to a house in East-bourne, a seaside resort on the south coast, he was reported to have said, 'I can understand that there is some interest in our affairs, but I can't help wishing there wasn't.'[8]

Although markedly different to his self-made father, the second baronet shared his dislike of publicity, shunning society to research and write about the behaviour of rats, producing a three-volume, 1,500-page doorstopper called *The Families and Genera of Living Rodents*. At his funeral service in London, a friend from Malvern College, Dennis Martin-Jenkins, apparently blamed the shock of inheriting his father's enormous empire at the age of twenty-three for turning him into a recluse. 'He instantly became a celebrity and newspapers were after him all the time. He decided he didn't like this at all.'[9]

The younger Sir John died of a sudden heart attack, as his father had, while staying in his suite at the Dorchester Hotel in 1973. His estate of £53 million – while still the largest left at the time – was, after adjusting for inflation, around a half of his original inheritance.

Without heirs and increasingly worried about death duties, Ellerman had transferred 79 per cent of the shares in Ellerman Lines Ltd to two trusts, now known as the John Ellerman Foundation, shortly before his death. The rest of the company was owned by his wife, who as a trustee was involved in appointing Sir David Scott as both trustee and chairman of the board.

The best account of Ellerman Lines at the time and the story of its purchase by the Barclays appears in a now out-of-print memoir written by Scott, who took over as chairman of the board in 1982.[10] Scott was a distinguished diplomat who had been the British ambassador to South Africa, where he had worked on independence negotiations in what was then Rhodesia, so he was somewhat surprised to be asked to do the job. When he pointed out that he 'knew less than nothing about the technicalities of either shipping or brewing', he was told that his diplomatic experience and contacts would help 're-establish' Ellerman's image.

Scott's book offers a window into the norms of British business at the start of the 1980s, when old school friends and the 'right kind of chap' were even more likely to be appointed to run huge companies. It was a world unprepared for these strange twins with an unlikely fortune, prompting Scott to write: 'When I accepted this apparently undemanding job I had no idea what it would eventually involve me in.'

The shipping company had started declining well before the death of the founder's son in 1973, partly owing to increased competition from newly independent nations such as India after the war and Britain's declining role in world trade, but also due to unwise investments.

On becoming chairman, Scott launched a business review and discovered the 'extremely delicate state of the company's finances', as well as the fact that the previous chairman, a school friend of the younger John Ellerman, had appointed his two sons to the board, one of whom was the finance director. In July 1982 this man was replaced by Alan Chamberlain, his deputy, who 'had already demonstrated his ability to exercise tough financial discipline'.

In 1981, Ellerman Lines earned just £2.5 million on a turnover of nearly £217 million, a situation which worsened the following year, when it lost £8 million. The trustees decided that the dividends no longer reflected the value of the business, and so instructed Morgan Grenfell to approach prospective buyers.

Potential bidders included American cruise company Arisa and the British and Commonwealth group, but none made an offer or came close to the bank's valuation of some £77 million, which had already been set low to reflect continuing losses.

The Barclays were understood to be annoyed that they had not been approached formally about the deal. If the bankers had failed to take their interest seriously, it would hardly have been surprising given the fact that Barclay Hotels Ltd, their main UK registered company, reported sales of less than £5 million, while Ellerman's annual sales came in at £176 million. Doubts over how these hoteliers – with their accents suggestive of working-class London – could afford such an iconic shipping conglomerate drip from Scott's account.

As with many of the most important parts of their origin story, there are several versions of how the Barclays met Esther Ellerman and therefore the key to their biggest deal. One involves a man called James Grover, not just a friend of the Barclays but also a neighbour of Ellerman in Monaco. Another is that the Barclay wives – Zoe and Hiroko – met Esther Ellerman at a painting class put on by a club for the bored wives of wealthy men in the principality. (In fact, the art class was where Zoe met John Pelling, the ordained priest turned artist she started a long and happy relationship with after her marriage to David ended.)

In nearly all subsequent reports of the deal that made the Barclays, Lady Ellerman is often portrayed as a sort of grieving widow, unable to cope with the demands of business. While the latter may have been true, she had already been a widow for eight years when she decided in 1981, somewhat unexpectedly, to marry the Hon George Sandbach Borwick, the Old Etonian second son of a baronet, twelve years her junior.

It was Borwick who told the Ellerman board of an approach from two brothers with an interest in buying the group in July 1983. 'All he knew about them was that they owned a large hotel in Monaco, where they lived for much of the year,' recalled Scott, who struggled before their first proper meeting to find out much more about these secretive twins.

The lack of information did not deter him from agreeing to 'look in' on the brothers in Monte Carlo on his way back from a holiday in Tuscany that August. Staying with the Borwicks, he surprisingly did not tell the board about their subsequent meeting, as the Barclays had asked that their enquiry 'should not be discussed with the board until they had taken matters further with the trustees'. Scott later admitted he 'was not particularly happy with this', but felt he could not object. 'This was my introduction to the Barclays' obsession with secrecy which became such a feature of the subsequent negotiations.'

On the dot of 9 a.m. on 17 August 1983, the Barclay brothers arrived at Esther Ellerman's flat in Monte Carlo to discuss their interest in Ellerman Lines. Scott, a product of Charterhouse School and the Royal Artillery, could not hide his surprise at their appearance. Almost fifty, the brothers had adopted a sort of uniform. In the Riviera summer months, they would change their usual business attire of a suit, tie and pocket handkerchief for a stripy blazer and white trousers, often with matching tasselled blue shoes and a natty hat. Scott described them as 'two almost identical small men dressed as for yachting' and, referring to the popular musical pastiche based in the 1920s, 'looking for all the world like a pair of not-so-young juvenile leads from *The Boy Friend*'.

Anyone who remembers dealing with the Barclays in the 1980s

mentions their appearance, unusual not just because they were identical twins but because they dressed, in the words of one publicist, 'like wide boys and spies'. Known to have a fondness for cutaway collars and Windsor-knot ties, they kept to a relatively unchanging summer and winter wardrobe for years. One Monégasque neighbour said waspishly; 'It may have been fashionable in the 1980s but they were still wearing it 20 years later.'

Despite their appearance, the brothers always meant business. David Barclay, who led the negotiations as he did so many others, peppered the Ellerman chairman with questions about the firm's debt and finances – particularly the breweries, which he suggested might be a good fit for their existing hotels business. He flattered Scott by saying it was a 'pleasure to meet a non-executive chairman with such a detailed knowledge of the affairs of his company'. David then asked that his then twenty-seven-year-old son Aidan be given free rein to carry out an assessment of the company in which he could talk to the two key managers, in secret, without anyone else knowing.[11]

In his account of the negotiations, Scott doesn't really mention Esther Ellerman, despite her being described as 'crucial' in helping them secure the deal in David Barclay's obituary in the *Telegraph*. There was never any written agreement – the brothers by then had perfected their belief that all deals should be done with a handshake. Despite this, Scott was convinced that he had been promised the role of chairman after the takeover. Whether that made a difference to the process as it unfolded is hard to say. By the time Scott got back to the office on 30 August, 'detailed talks' were already taking place between Aidan Barclay and the Ellerman finance director, Alan Chamberlain.

David Barclay had stressed that their decision-making would be speedy and he was true to his word. By the end of the month the twins invited Scott to lunch at the Howard Hotel to discuss Aidan's preliminary report. David Barclay told Scott that, subject to a final audit of the accounts, they were prepared to make the trustees an offer. He also asked the chairman to stay on 'for a transitional period', according to Scott.

As Scott made to leave, David gave him an envelope, which he opened as soon as he got to his car. Inside was a formal letter addressed to the trustees offering £46 million for the group.

Scott was shocked that the brothers hadn't mentioned this over lunch – which had, after all, been arranged to discuss the deal. It was also remarkable, he thought, that the 'figure of £46m was almost exactly at the lower end of the range the trustees had privately agreed to accept. This led me to wonder whether they had had inside help in arriving at this figure, though it would have been virtually impossible to have proved that there had been a leak.'

The speed of the deal seems to have upset one board member, Anthony Cooke. The head of the shipping business had tabled a separate management buyout for the division before the Barclays, but on 20 September 1983 the Ellerman board voted in favour of entering exclusive negotiations with the Barclays as they were interested in the group as a whole.

Cooke was said by Scott to be 'deeply unhappy' that the trustees had granted the Barclays exclusivity. A few weeks before the deal was finalized, the *Financial Times* reported that the price had surprised the City as 'there had been other efforts to bid for the breweries for around £60m, with one major brewer ready to take a 15 per cent stake, the management itself around 30 per cent, and banks and institutions the rest'. As for the historic shipping division, 'management was ready with its own buy-out for some £5m'.[12] These figures were never confirmed.

Indeed, such was the level of secrecy around the deal that Scott remembered being taken to task by his own board and called himself 'increasingly embarrassed by [the Barclays'] demands for secrecy'.

Some of this was due to Scott's own sense of responsibility for a deal that he had been party to from the beginning. There were also the relatively new disclosure rules for public limited companies under the Companies Act 1979, which the previously private Ellerman Lines had signed up to when it registered as a PLC. In the face of the Barclays' refusal to furnish any information about how they were going to pay for Ellerman, board members grew concerned about their own liability if the bidders subsequently failed to raise the funds. Sir David Scott grew 'deeply frustrated at the constant stone-walling' he encountered in trying to get the Barclays to give him the necessary information to 'defend a deal which I had played some part in initiating and felt a sense of personal responsibility'.[13]

He wrote a letter demanding more information in order to reassure the board on 3 November 1983. This was ignored by the Barclays, and exactly a week later, on 11 November, the brothers became the new owners of the Ellerman shipping and breweries business, having paid £46 million for the privilege.[14]

Conscious that the deal had been done at speed and in secret, Scott asked David Barclay to meet the senior staff to assuage any fears that 'they were engaged in an asset-stripping exercise' and that their main intention was to sell off or close parts of the business. David 'firmly refused'.

Scott, confident that he would be staying on himself, told his team: 'The Barclay brothers are strongly finance-oriented and I believe their practice is to select and encourage managers who are prepared to accept their standards for improving profits and going for growth . . . those of us who can respond to stimuli will get on, and perhaps some of those who can't will have to get out.'

Scott was still keen for the Barclays to meet with the senior team, so the brothers threw a cocktail party at the Howard Hotel on 14 October for the board and 'a number of senior executives'. As no business was discussed, all it did was demonstrate to an anxious team that the brothers 'did not eat babies', said an increasingly 'embarrassed' Scott.

The board members' concerns over the Barclays' ability to

raise the necessary funds from private banks – again a hallmark of future deals – may have been misguided, but the fears of the staff over future sell-offs were not.

Within a few short months of the takeover, the brothers were in negotiations to sell JW Cameron to Scottish and Newcastle. They sold it for £44 million, almost the same amount as they had paid for the whole of Ellerman.

Even though this brewing deal was abandoned after a referral to the monopolies commission, the Barclays went on to sell the shipping division with its sixteen container ships for an undisclosed sum. David Barclay would later tell the *Spectator* that 'in and out is the trick with shipping'.[15]

After selling off the shipping business, the brothers sold the travel business for another £3.9 million. But the real money came in 1988 when they sold the breweries business with its 850 pubs to the Brent Walker Group for £239 million. That one sale earned the Barclays five times more than they had paid for the whole of Ellerman. The off-licences went in a separate deal.

Within five years the Barclays had sold every part of the business, keeping just the Ellerman name, perhaps in homage to their master stroke. A banker involved with the breweries deal told the *FT*: 'The Barclays have got the purchase of the year, if not the decade.'[16] Once, in early 1984, the brothers even allowed themselves to be publicly quoted saying that they had bought Ellerman for a 'snip'.[17]

David Scott was no longer embarrassed about any of this, however. On the day the deal was signed, instead of the large glass of something suitable he'd expected to celebrate the deal and his new role, he'd been handed a letter from David Barclay accusing him of a breach of confidence and asking for his immediate resignation. He was shell-shocked.

Years later, he reflected on the negotiations which had seen him caught between a fractious board, the trustees who were the majority owners, and the bidders insisting on secrecy above all else, and decided that a need for openness stopped being the way the world worked in the 1980s. 'One could only conclude that in the commercial, as in the political, field, gentlemanly behaviour could be a positive disadvantage,' he wrote somewhat despairingly.[18]

In his place, the Barclays appointed Victor Matthews – the Trafalgar House boss who had negotiated with the Crown Agents to buy their hotels while the brothers searched for a saviour – as non-executive chairman of Ellerman's shipping business in 1983, until it was sold four years later. A political favourite who had been made a baron in 1980, Matthews brought establishment respectability to a business owned by brothers whose public reputation still came with the taint of their involvement in the Crown Agents scandal.

Anthony Cooke carried on running Ellerman's shipping unit for the Barclays for two years, until it was sold to Trafalgar House in 1987, staying on when the conglomerate merged it with Cunard in 1987. After two more changes of ownership, the name Ellerman Lines disappeared in 2004.

In his eighties and living in Hampshire almost two decades later, Cooke had grown wary of being asked about the Barclays, citing some of the criticism they had attracted since the Ellerman deal. 'There's been a lot of criticism about the Barclays . . . after the time I was working for them. I don't want to get involved with that at all.'

A director at the Institute for Statecraft, a pro-democracy think tank, Cooke – like many who worked with them in the early years – is a fan of the Barclays. 'I have had and still have a high opinion of David and Frederick Barclay and working for them . . . I thought they were very good bosses. Very honest, very straight, dealt very well with people . . . They trusted me and they were very competent. That also was a fairly nice thing to have in your bosses that they . . . were very, very competent. They worked together very well.'

When asked if he was still angry about not getting a chance to bid for the company, he said: 'I'm very happy about it all. It all was fine. Nothing untoward anywhere.'[19]

Alan Chamberlain, the finance director who had impressed David Scott with his acumen, ended up as a key executive for the Barclays. He had worked with them for thirteen years in a variety of roles, from running offshore diamond mines to acting as an early spokesman, when he told Bloomberg in 2004: 'Even though they're identical twins, they're different. David Barclay was more attuned to taking a risk, and Frederick was generally willing to have a look but would never bet the farm. It worked very well.'[20]

Their behaviour during the Ellerman deal – in which they refused to answer questions even from board members, and behaved in a less than open fashion – gave the brothers a reputation as secretive asset-strippers that never really went away.

'They were break-up merchants really. Obsessed with trying to pick up £5 notes for £2. And they loved distressed sellers and squeezing the last drop out of them,' said one associate. Another, who remained a fan, said that Ellerman showed the outside world that the brothers could carry out better due diligence than anyone else and were able to spot a hugely undervalued and undermanaged company. Both views have prevailed.

It was also the first deal where David's eldest son, Aidan, tasked with spending a week going through the books, showed evidence he had some business nous of his own.

When the brothers bought the *Telegraph*, an accusation that they had somehow taken advantage of an 'owner in distress to pick up assets on the cheap' prompted them to sue *The Times*. The subsequent clarification, published on page 61 of *The Times* more than two years (and an astonishing criminal libel hearing in France) later, stated that *The Times* had not meant that 'the Barclays frequently exploit vulnerable people in financial difficulty in an underhand and unfair way for commercial gain or to impugn their business ethics or integrity'. The Murdoch-owned title, which did not pay any damages, stated: 'We are happy to make the position clear and regret any distress caused.'[21] In return, the Barclays dropped the case.

There is no record of what Esther Borwick Ellerman thought of the sale, which could have earned her much more money. She died aged seventy-four in March 1985, not long after the Barclays bought Ellerman. George Borwick never remarried and lived on in Ellerman House on the Cape until he died aged seventy-two in November 1994. He is buried in Cape Town cemetery.

The behaviour of the board members and trustees, who owned by far the largest share of Ellerman and should have been experienced businessmen (no women of course), has rarely been challenged. Yet they appear to have been entirely outmanoeuvred by brothers who were able to bring the eminent chairman onside with only the merest hint of information, while holding out the carrot of a future role. It is a tale which does little to assuage the sense that the newlywed heiress merely facilitated a meeting with company managers who were not as effective as they should have been in realizing the company's true value.

The money they made from buying Ellerman Lines took the Barclays' finances into another league. They moved out of their rented accommodation to buy two neighbouring white-stuccoed six-storey houses, with a floor for live-in staff, in the heart of London's Belgravia. Chester Square is one of the loveliest and most exclusive garden squares in London. Close to Buckingham Palace, its residents included famous singers such as Mick Jagger in the 1960s and '70s, and oligarchs such as Roman Abramovich much later.

The twins and their families lived and holidayed together throughout the 1980s, when David's three sons – Aidan, Howard and Duncan – were all in their twenties, a few years older than Frederick's stepson Ko. His daughter, Amanda, born in 1978, was still a child when he started to spend most of the year in the South of France.

Their mother Beatrice lived to see her twins become hugely rich, residing in a house in leafy Richmond that at one point was owned by one of their companies, Hillgate Estate Agents. In 1987 her sons had bought their first yacht, the forty-eight-metre *Klementine*. After she died in July 1989 they bought a new, far bigger yacht and called her the *Lady Beatrice*.

The last decade of Beatrice's life, the 1980s, saw Britain change dramatically. A bonfire of regulations governing corporations and the City not only changed the way business operated, but also led to a fundamental change in society in which making money – lots of it – was increasingly celebrated rather than looked down on. The decade was marked by a new breed of industrialist, corporate raiders who borrowed huge amounts of money to buy under-performing companies before slashing costs to pay it back. Unemployment soared while research and development budgets were cut. Short-term profits trumped longer-term ambitions. Supporters saw this as buying companies that were worth less than the sum of their parts; detractors saw people putting quick profits above working conditions and future prosperity.

It was in the middle of the decade, just as a flurry of deregulation known as 'the Big Bang' revolutionized the City's fortunes and turned it into a financial capital to rival New York, that the Barclays would attempt a takeover that pitched them against the heart of the British establishment.

Flush from their biggest success and keen to do ever more deals, it soon became apparent that the City of London was still a bastion of old school ties and snobbery. Throughout this time, the Ellerman head office was a hive of deal-making. Members of the team quipped that they never had board meetings, just the one they had every morning and every afternoon. The brothers had become partners in a US investment company called Boston

Ventures, which typically took stakes in media companies before selling them for a profit soon after. It was through this company that the Barclays became the unlikely – if indirect – shareholders of the gossipy US newspaper the *National Enquirer* as well as Motown Records. Billionaire and philanthropist Charles Clore had also been a neighbour in Monaco, and when he died in 1979 his only son, Alan, fought the Inland Revenue over his estate and lost. In 1985, the brothers bought Alan Clore's controlling stake in a loss-making US-based energy and fertilizer business, the Gulf Resources and Chemical Corporation. This meant the Barclays were not just hoteliers and shipowners, but also shareholders in American oil and gas fields, coal mining operations in Pennsylvania, and fertilizer and salt operations in Utah.

Never enough, they wanted to diversify further. They used Gulf as a bid vehicle to quietly buy an 11 per cent stake in the Imperial Continental Gas Association, an oil and gas explorer established under an Act of Parliament in 1824 and the provider of Calor gas.

Known as IC Gas, the company with roots in Victorian exploration attracted directors from the very heart of the establishment. One of them, Philip de Zulueta, had been private secretary to not one but three prime ministers – Eden, Macmillan and Douglas-Home – before he left to become a merchant banker. The company's long history and links with international trading partners meant it was known in the City as a sort of 'velcro for spooks'.

Meanwhile the Barclays' acquiring vehicle, Gulf Resources, was a largely unknown US company with shareholders' funds of £118 million and lower annual revenues than IC Gas. Undeterred by this, just as they had been with Ellerman, Gulf launched a £750 million hostile takeover bid for IC Gas in October 1986.

Eight banks had agreed to lend Gulf Resources £670 million – 90 per cent of the purchase price – according to the offer document. One of these lenders was the Bank of Scotland, which would go on to back nearly all of the Barclays' big deals over the next decade. A substantial portion of the loan had to be repaid within the first nine months, and the Barclays suggested this would mainly come from 'revitalizing' Calor, whose portable heaters were popular in many households but regarded as unglamorous and unloved by the company itself.

The Times called the highly leveraged plan a 'bid in the American style', which in those days was no plaudit. IC Gas and its blue-chip directors instantly rejected the offer, pointing out quite correctly that Gulf's management had no experience in running a business like IC Gas. They also criticized the financing as unconventional and unsound. It was to be the start of an unusually public battle that saw the bid discussed in parliament before being referred to the Monopolies and Mergers Commission.

Someone who saw this battle close up was Brian Basham, the veteran PR man who acted for the Barclays. 'It was pretty clear that we were up against the might of the establishment,' he says.[22] Not only were there continuing questions about their past, about which they refused to talk, but the Barclays, with their cutaway collars, large Windsor knots and London accents, looked and sounded like very few City advisers and financiers at the time. According to Basham, 'They were regarded as spivs.'

Thirty-five years later, he still remembers his first meeting with the twins. 'I've got such a vivid picture in my mind of David and Fred, because they were bizarre. They were Tweedledum and Tweedledee, you know, they really did finish each other's sentences.'

One exchange stands out, when David Barclay quibbled over Basham's fees of some £30,000. 'David said to Fred, "Fred, do you remember that bloke who stole 30,000 pounds from me?" So Fred said: "Yes, I do David." So he said: "So, what did I do?" And he said, "You did nothing, David." "Yes, that's right. I did nothing . . . I did nothing until I completely destroyed him."' Years later, the memory is still vivid in Basham's mind: 'I thought,

"What a gangster." I'd grown up in South London and seen all those threats.'

He continued to work for the brothers on the IC Gas deal, during which they also took the highly unusual step of speaking to the *Guardian*. In the interview, conducted at the City HQ they had renamed Ellerman House, the brothers suggested that they would do a better job of running Calor Gas than its then management, and 'threw their hands up with horror' at the suggestion that, as II per cent shareholders, they were merely trying to flush out a rival bidder in order to make a quick profit.

They refused to talk about their earlier business ventures or to allow a photographer to be present, but they did provide some rare quotes.

'Privacy is a valuable commodity,' David Barclay said. 'People accuse us of being secretive but you can't think of people with a lower profile than IC Gas over the years.'

'When,' added Frederick Barclay somewhat cryptically, 'did you last see a Calor Gas advertisement?'[23]

This PR campaign wavered in the face of increasing political and public concerns over hostile takeovers for companies considered important national assets. This was epitomized by a separate takeover which didn't involve the Barclays.

James Hanson and Gordon White had started in business together with a greetings card company, before expanding into everything from batteries to bricks. Their company, Hanson, was worth more than £II billion in the 1980s. Hanson himself was against nationalized industries and the European Union and a supporter of low taxes and Margaret Thatcher – he became one of the Conservative Party's biggest donors of the time.

In 1986, he finally pulled off his most audacious but controversial takeover with the purchase of Imperial Tobacco, a conglomerate with huge tobacco, brewing and food divisions and a fat pension pot. After the pension trustees closed the scheme the day before the deal went through, it became apparent that Hanson was hoping to use the money set aside for future pensioners to pay off the purchase price, something that has been outlawed since. Instead he paid for the deal by selling off all Imperial's subsidiaries, leaving him with a business that made an operating profit margin of nearly 50 per cent.

This sort of behaviour was making parliamentarians nervous. 'It would be a tragedy if an international firm were taken over by one with a short-term future,' said MP Doug Hoyle to parliament. 'The Government have a duty to ensure that that does not happen.'[24]

Ahead of these very public concerns, both the IC Gas board and Westminster appeared to be moving against the Barclays and their highly leveraged way of doing business. Eventually, eighty MPs would sign an Early Day Motion opposing what they called the 'Wall Street-style leveraged breakup' of Imperial Continental Gas. Another 120 members demanded a review of the offer by the UK Monopolies and Mergers Commission (MMC), which ruled on antitrust issues.

A furious David Barclay wrote a rare official note to parliament following the Early Day Motion on 20 November. 'It is regrettable that Early Day Motions are now being used for the commercial and financial benefit of certain people and professional organisations,' he stormed, going on to accuse several signatories of being 'retained' by the group's political lobbyists Ian Greer Associates and its bankers Morgan Grenfell.

'It is an abuse of the Parliamentary system which has been used in an attempt to discredit the bid by Gulf Resources for IC Gas. What is equally alarming is the amount of fear and anxiety which has been orchestrated which cannot be substantiated by the same people and organisations with which they are connected and I sincerely hope that steps will be taken to curtail this abuse of the system.'[25]

When the bid was referred to the MMC in December, the Barclays threw in the towel. Gulf Resources dropped its offer.

Two months later, IC Gas agreed to split itself up, a move which boosted its share price and handed the Barclays a paper profit of £27 million from their stake.

They would never be so devoid of political support again.

In the summer of 1985, a few months before their bid for IC Gas, the Barclays were invited to lunch by Alistair McAlpine, the treasurer of the Conservative Party for fifteen years under prime minister Margaret Thatcher, at his art gallery in Mayfair's Cork Street. Whatever whispers were made of them in the City, the brothers' newfound riches had put them on the invite list for fundraisers and other gatherings of the rich and powerful. Lord McAlpine's lunches, usually held at the Garrick in Covent Garden – a men-only club whose tie he often wore – or his own offices, were generally considered jolly affairs. Nothing as déclassé as money was ever mentioned; typically a follow-up letter after the lunch would point out the rival Labour Party's damaging policies over taxation and other business *bêtes noires*.

The Barclays – particularly David – hit it off with McAlpine immediately, and they became lifelong friends. Before he died in 2014, McAlpine was reported to be writing David's biography. Other friends of the Barclays – most of whom orbited around Britain's first female prime minister – included Gordon Reece, the political strategist who helped Thatcher to victory in 1979 and spent time on *Lady Beatrice* in the 1990s.

They met other significant politicians at the same lunch. John Peyton, a Conservative who had stood against Thatcher in the leadership election and had moved to the House of Lords in 1983, was there. He had also just been appointed treasurer of the Zoological Society of London; and, over lunch, the Barclays proposed a £500,000 donation to London Zoo. This sum was almost twice as much as was given to the fundraising zoo by oil companies Esso, Shell and BP combined. Peyton, who would go on to head the Barclays' charitable foundation, said: 'I never had such an offer before or since.' The zoo's central plaza is still called Barclay Court.

Throughout their lives, the Barclays preferred to give money to charitable causes they had chosen themselves rather than to a nation's coffers via what they considered unnecessary taxation. It was a trait they shared with many billionaires at the time.

It was McAlpine who introduced the twins to Margaret Thatcher, a woman whose belief in a small state and low taxes chimed with that of the billionaires who supported her. The twins had always been natural Conservatives: they hated red tape, bureaucracy, and someone else telling them what to do with their money or trying to take any of it away in taxation. Brian Basham, who worked for them during this time, recalled: 'They were always talking about rules. They hated regulations.'[26]

Thatcher is most often remembered for the financial reforms that ushered in the so-called Big Bang deregulation in the City in 1986, but she had made many changes before then to loosen the rules for global corporations. She opposed her own Chancellor's proposals to scrap the non-domicile rules that allowed anyone mainly living outside the UK to avoid paying British taxes.[27] But it was one of her first acts after coming to power in 1979 that really changed Britain – specifically who owned it. The first Thatcher government got rid of restrictions on the amount of money that could be moved abroad.

The huge growth of offshore tax havens since is partly due to this change. Offshore registration tends to avoid much of the taxation domestic homeowners pay such as inheritance tax, stamp duty and capital gains tax. As John Christensen of the Tax Justice Network has said: 'A company doesn't die. If a person dies the property has to be passed on to someone else – obviously this is not the case with a company.'[28] Especially if the company in question is owned by unknown beneficiaries and any subsequent sale is swapped with another offshore company.

Although their admiration for the former grocer's daughter

who became Britain's first female prime minister was profound, there are no publicly available photos taken of the Barclays with her. The best-known fact of their relationship is that Lady Thatcher spent her last months living in a suite at the Ritz Hotel as a guest of the Barclay brothers. She had also stayed on their private island Brecqhou and on their best-known yacht, *Lady Beatrice*.[29]

It is perhaps their support in providing her last home in London that shows the extent of their regard. However, it is a tale, as with so many about the Barclay brothers, which remains mysterious.

. After she was ousted as prime minister in November 1990, Thatcher, with 'no money at all in the bank', according to her closest adviser,[30] was desperate for a home big enough to entertain in and house her new charitable foundation. Her home in Dulwich was too far from Westminster – and besides, any journey would have to pass through the badlands of Labour-supporting south London.

The sort of property she needed did not come cheap, even in the London of 1991. When the Barclays heard that she had not yet found anything suitable from Alistair McAlpine, they offered her 73 Chester Square, a former home of David's – and at one time of the singer Shirley Bassey – which graced a corner of the leafy square.[31] With several other properties in London, and still resident in Monte Carlo, the brothers had already agreed to sell the lease on number 73, the freehold of which was owned by the Duke of Westminster. As soon as he heard about Thatcher's predicament, David Barclay withdrew from this deal and instead arranged to sell it to a trust established for her son Mark's children, according to an interview he gave to Thatcher's biographer Charles Moore. David also gave them two paintings for the drawing room as a housewarming gift.[32]

In May 1991, Margaret and her husband, Denis, moved into one of London's most expensive squares as tenants of the trust, and she lived there more or less until she died twenty-two years later.

There were repeated rumours that the Thatchers lived in Chester Square courtesy of a wealthy benefactor who did not want to be identified, but few details emerged until years later. In 2002, as part of an investigation into property taxes, the *Guardian* discovered that the Thatchers did not own their own home. Instead, in 1991, when she moved in, a Jersey-based company called Bakeland Property Ltd bought the thirty-nine-year under-lease of the house at 73 Chester Square for a reported £290,000, a peppercorn amount even at the time and for a relatively short lease. The lease was then extended in 1996 to last for just under sixty years.

The Jersey-based company's shares were held by Hugh Thurston and Leonard Day, Thatcher's friends and financial advisers who were acting as nominees for a trust with concealed beneficiaries. When asked in 2002 why the prime minister who had done more to promote home ownership than any other did not in fact own her own home, Day said: 'No one's going to tell you about that.'[33]

No one did, and four years later, in 2006, the lease was sold for £2.4 million to a firm with the same name, Bakeland Property Ltd, but this time based in the British Virgin Islands (BVI), where disclosure rules were more limited than in Jersey. A Liechtenstein trust replaced men associated with Margaret Thatcher as the nominee directors. It was reported that the title deeds also specified that the property should not be sold 'without the consent of the previous owner', a stipulation normally inserted to avoid a new owner flipping the home.[34]

In December 2012, the then Lady Thatcher was diagnosed with advanced bladder cancer and spent a week in hospital over Christmas. As soon as she was discharged, the Barclays offered her a suite at the Ritz, where she stayed as their guest in rooms costing £3,660 a night until she died aged eighty-seven on 8 April 2013. Although she made a five-figure contribution to the cost of her stay, according to Charles Moore, the Barclays paid for the rest of a bill which ran into six figures.[35] A bronze bust of the Iron Lady was placed just inside the Ritz to commemorate the final resting place of the then owners' favourite prime minister.

It was only after her death that the tax advantages of the ownership structure were partly revealed. The gross value of Lady Thatcher's estate, unveiled by her will in 2013, revealed that she had left some £4,768,795, split between her two children and their children. The Belgravia mansion, then valued at £12.4 million, was not included, thereby avoiding the taxes accruing on death. The lease on the Belgravia mansion was sold in September 2013 to 73 CS ltd (a Guernsey-based company owned by a developer, Leconfield Property Group) for £4.2 million.

The fact that Thatcher's final home was owned by an offshore company that avoided British taxes raised eyebrows. 'It has always been strange that Margaret Thatcher, that most British of prime ministers, enjoyed the benefits of a property registered in the British Virgin Islands,' Richard Murphy, who founded the Tax Justice Network, told the *Daily Mirror*.[36]

In 2001, a land registry review called on the Lord Chancellor to outlaw loopholes that allowed homeowners to register their property as belonging to offshore trusts with concealed beneficiaries, calling out such behaviour as an abuse, adding 'it flies in the face of the principle [that] ownership . . . of all properties should be in the public domain'.[37]

Nothing really happened. The ownership of property registered offshore, particularly prime residential homes in the most expensive parts of London, became practically endemic among the wealthy, and even politicians on all sides of the House – including former prime minister Tony Blair, who owned multiple homes registered offshore.

The relaxation of ownership rules that the Barclays and the

Thatcher government had either pioneered or encouraged eventually grew to dominate the UK property market. By 2022, the year after David died, more than 40,000 London properties were owned by the anonymous owners of companies in tax havens from Liechtenstein to the BVI, according to an investigation by the Wealth Chain Project.[38] One in ten of all properties in the City of London and Westminster were owned by offshore trusts, according to an analysis of Land Registry data.[39]

After 2013, the lease on 73 Chester Square was extended, and major renovation works included a new basement and more. It was put on the market for £30 million.

There is a neat circularity perhaps in the fact that men who had Thatcher to thank for many tax and business reforms during their careers were able to thank her by providing her with a tax-efficient home for the last two decades of her life.

By all accounts, the 'Greed is Good' decade in the City and Wall Street was an exciting time to be working for the Barclay brothers. The failure of IC Gas had done little to blunt their enthusiasm for buying and selling, and a flurry of deals were ongoing.

In 1988, they paid $670 million for shipping group Gotaas-Larsen, expanding it through the purchase of huge supertankers until it became at one point the largest independent liquid natural-gas carrier in the world. When they sold it to Osprey Maritime nine years later for $750 million, they made a paper profit of $80 million. The then Osprey chairman Tim Cottew spoke admiringly of the Barclays, calling them 'straightforward and uncomplicated'.[40]

At this stage, the twins had grown friendly with Tim Bell, Margaret Thatcher's favourite PR man, and when he needed investors to help him finance the buyout of his PR agency from a bigger company, they stepped in. The experience with IC Gas must have convinced them of the value of PR advice to an extent, and they paid £600,000 for a 10 per cent stake in his new PR company, Chime Communications.

The brothers backed a management buyout of casino operator London Clubs International in 1989. They had met Max Kingsley, the clubs' managing director, on Cunard's *Queen Elizabeth 2*, the world's largest ocean liner at the time, when London Clubs ran the onboard casinos. 'Why do they go on? It's the thrill of the chase, the thrill of doing a deal,' Kingsley said years later. 'That's where they got their buzz and still get their buzz. It would eat up most people's adrenaline, doing deals the size of theirs.'[41]

After the success of Ellerman, the Barclays had gone on to buy several other companies from supremely keen – some would say desperate – sellers. In the early 1990s, the man who introduced Nissan cars to the UK and built up one of the country's biggest motor dealership groups was living as a fugitive in the Swiss mountains, while the Inland Revenue sought his arrest over one of the UK's largest cases of tax fraud.[42] Octav Botnar, a Conservative Party donor and philanthropist, had hidden the ultimate ownership of his businesses in entities registered in Panama and the Bahamas, but the investigation into overstated profits led to two of his closest associates being jailed in 1993 for their part in the fraud.[43]

In November 1994, the Barclays, with no known experience of car dealerships, offered £200 million for Automotive Financial Group Holdings via a company called Caledonia Motor Group. By the time Botnar agreed a £59 million no-guilt settlement with the Inland Revenue before his death in 1998, the Barclays had started to sell off the company to other dealers such as Reg Vardy.

Despite being little remarked upon in any account of their career, their treatment over IC Gas had marked a seminal moment for the Barclays. Brian Basham, who has worked with many billionaires including Robert Maxwell and Mohammed Al Fayed, says: 'I believe that IC Gas was why they went and bought respectability by buying the *Telegraph* and the *Spectator*.'

IC Gas was a rare failure in a decade – the 1980s – which

brought the Barclay brothers huge success and political connections. They would never appear so blindsided by politics again.
The brothers did make a stab at buying the house bible of the
Conservative Party soon after, but they had another dream acquisition to do first. Extreme wealth had only exacerbated their
desire for secrecy and security – and where better to find both
than their own private island?

4. How to Buy an Island

On 26 August 1993, *Country Life* magazine carried an unusual advertisement for 'an impressive small private island'. Beneath a full-page picture of a dark rock jutting up from crashing waves, topped with a large lawn, there were details of a stone manor house, a private harbour and a helipad, on an island just ten minutes' flight from Guernsey. The words 'Tax Free Status' were highlighted in bold.[1]

Channel Islands such as Guernsey, located in the sea between the United Kingdom and France, have long enjoyed a special legal status: they are official dependencies and subjects of the British Crown, but politically and financially they remain independent. In practice, this has made them havens for those who want to avoid mainland taxation – which was an attractive proposition for the increasingly wealthy Barclays. The brothers snapped up the seventy-four-acre Channel Island called Brecqhou just a few weeks after the ad appeared.

There was one complication. In advertising Brecqhou, *Country Life* had failed to mention a neighbouring island – separated from the Barclays' new home by the Gouliot Passage, a small strait with a cruel riptide – which, at just three miles long and a mile and a half wide, was the smallest of all the Crown dependencies. In 1993, Sark was the last bastion of feudalism in Europe – and crucially, it claimed its neighbouring rock as part of its domain. Eventually, this would put the Barclays at loggerheads with their nearest neighbours, igniting a conflict that would last for decades.

In 1993, however, the brothers were more focused on transforming their barren rock into an island idyll: private, secure and magnificent. The purchase price of Brecqhou – even at the asking price at £2.33 million – would be dwarfed by what the brothers spent building their own fortress on the island. By 2021, when it became the subject of court proceedings, the cost of building their hideaway was valued at between £80 million and £120 million.[2]

The brothers called the castle they built there Fort Brecqhou, and invited royals and heads of state – including Margaret Thatcher, Tony Blair and David Cameron – to stay, as well as family, friends and specially favoured employees. From the very start they took a tough line with anyone trying to enter without an invitation, patrolling the border with guards and suing the first journalist who landed without permission. David's obituary in his own newspaper, the *Daily Telegraph*, said this 'fortress-like neo-Gothic mansion . . . came to symbolise their preference for privacy and fiscal independence'.[3] Trespassers were strictly forbidden.

The twins bought Brecqhou from the heir of Leonard Matchan, a millionaire businessman who had paid £44,000 for the island in 1966. He had moved to nearby Jersey a few years earlier, telling a local paper that he wanted to avoid death duties.[4]

This plan did not prevent years of legal wrangling over his estate when he died in 1987, however. Matchan, who had made his money from lipstick cases and cosmetics, had separated from his wife and the mother of his two children in the 1950s, and had been living ever since with a woman twenty-nine years his junior called Sue Groves. She was described as his secretary, house-keeper and long-term companion in reports of the time, the fact of their long relationship undisputed; her claim to Brecqhou was anything but.

Matchan left no will but, before he died, he was alleged to have transferred the lease of Brecqhou to a Jersey trust called Solaria Investments and asked his son Peter to sign away his right to inheritance under the local laws of primogeniture. This was all to allow Groves to continue living there, she later claimed. Peter, a year older than Groves and living on the mainland with his mother and older sister, refused.

The case ended up in court as well as in the papers. As Peter Matchan had refused to relinquish his rights as the nearest male relative – and, as Matchan had neither told nor got permission from the feudal overlord – Sue Groves was forced to leave the island.

The battle over Leonard Matchan's estate was said to weigh heavily on David Barclay in particular.

As soon as they bought Brecqhou, the Barclay twins hired Quinlan Terry – an architect described as the 'high priest of the classical tradition' who had just been appointed by the then Prince Charles to help create Poundbury, his vision of a new town.

Terry later described how David produced a sketch of the castle exactly as he wanted it at their very first meeting. 'The design was, of course, developed in a number of ways, but the general principles remain exactly as were made clear to me at our first meeting.'[5]

With its square shape and turrets, high grey walls and neo-Gothic grandeur, Fort Brecqhou would become a sort of pastiche of the most famous of royal palaces, Windsor Castle. It was almost like a child's drawing of a castle. In *Brecqhou: A Very Private Island*, author Peter Rivett compares the fortress design, built around the four sides of a huge internal courtyard, to the 'open land surrounded by four castellated walls' made famous in *The Adventures of Robin Hood*, a somewhat unexpected analogy to the legendary outlaw who robbed from the rich to give to the poor.

The scale of the Barclay brothers' ambitions would match any storybook excesses. After generations in which the increasing democratization of wealth had diminished the kingdom's grand estates, it was the largest private home built in Britain for 200 years. By the time David died, one associate said it was neither environmentally friendly, nor cheap, costing some £5–10 million a year in running costs.

Rivett describes the Barclay brothers as modern-day 'earls', suggesting that they could trace their ancestry to an island just thirty miles from France via Roger de Berchelai, who came to England in 1066 with William of Normandy.[6] Not only was this favourite of the king awarded a chunk of Gloucestershire, he is credited with founding a Scottish clan, the branch of the family said to be responsible for the Quaker movement, a banking dynasty, and one which defeated Napoleon in Russia. 'Thus the two brothers who arrived on Brecqhou in 1993 were of Normandy descent, albeit distantly,' writes Rivett, without much in the way of historical evidence.

It was on Brecqhou that David's love of genealogy and interest in his own ancestry came to the fore. The brothers adapted the vaguely nautical coat of arms created for Leonard Matchan, with waves and an anchor, by adding two identical shields and Celtic crosses in homage to their Scottish roots. A new motto was placed above the castle's entrance: *Aut agere aut mori* ('Either do or die').

If an Englishman's home is his castle, Fort Brecqhou was perhaps the Barclays' homecoming, a visual reminder of what they had become in which they could tell their own history – in this case as far back as 1066 – rather than the far more recent and somewhat seedier past.

Conscious of their grand ambitions, Rivett ends his purple paean to the Barclays and their achievements on Brecqhou by quoting the ancient poet Horace:

I have raised a monument more lasting than bronze,
loftier than the Royal pile of pyramids, that neither biting rain,
nor the powerfully raging north wind can destroy,
nor the innumerable files of years, nor the flight of time.

*

The Barclays' transformation of Brecqhou was undoubtedly a tremendous feat of engineering. They installed a new water treatment plant and a waste disposal system, new pipes, sewage and refuge collection, as well as postal, fire and medical facilities and an underground power station. The plan was called 'Project 95' to remind all working on it of the planned completion date. In the end, Fort Brecqhou was completed in just under three years despite its immense scale. Rivett credits the 'vast building experience' of the brothers' early lives for getting it done so quickly.

They razed the old island manor house to the ground and hired a huge Chinook helicopter from Norway to help lift machinery such as cranes, JCB diggers, dumper and forklift trucks. Thousands of boat crossings were needed to transport at least 90,000 tons of concrete, steel, lead piping, and two types of granite from Spain – crema champagne from near Madrid and Silvestre from the north-west – as well as different coloured marbles from Italy for the rococo decor inside. An army of 1,500 builders, almost a third of whom stayed in specially built accommodation on-site, worked round the clock. The all-night floodlights looked like an emergency or an alien invasion to the residents of Sark, an island with so few lights it would later be designated a 'dark sky' island.

During Project 95, some twenty-one on-site managers maintained discipline over the hundreds of men living and working together in challenging conditions, largely by imposing instant dismissal in case of any minor incidents. The brothers thought about making Brecqhou a totally dry island, but eventually gave each man vouchers for two pints of beer a day in a specially built pub that was called the Dog and Duck (a portrait of Lady Thatcher was given pride of place above the bar).

Hills were formed and gulleys dug, not just to protect the castle and its gardens from the wind but to make it difficult to spot, despite its vast size. Security cameras were everywhere and secrecy was paramount. Built before Google Maps allowed aerial shots, photographs were forbidden and employees were asked to sign non-disclosure agreements. A firm called Adams and Palmer, which had helped with the transformation of some of the Barclay hotels, was used, overseen at times by the twins' younger brother Douglas. Rivett states that his own 'probably unrivalled access' to the island was awarded on the understanding that no unauthorized photographs were taken, in order to 'respect the owners' wishes to preserve their privacy'.

By February 1995, the first concrete harbour was ready. The Barclays moved into the castle in August 1996.

Invited guests would be greeted, either at the harbour or helipad, by monogrammed-uniformed staff in golf buggies. The brothers had transformed the poor soil along the drive up to the castle entrance when they bought the island, and eventually they planted an olive grove, (poorly performing) vineyards, an organic market garden, and a carp pond with a bridge modelled on Monet's Giverny.

However grand the outside, no expense was spared on the inside. The eighty-metre-long banqueting room was decorated in gold leaf; there was a red dining room and a library with a hand-painted ceiling based on the Sistine Chapel. The design was inspired by Robert Adam and his brothers, the eighteenth-century neo-classicists who hailed from Scotland but created the London home of the Dukes of Northumberland, Syon House, which is still said to be one of the last great houses of England. There were huge Chinese vases and gold sconces and lots of paintings.

The front doors of Fort Brecqhou opened onto a vast circular entrance hall with Corinthian columns in green marble and a sweeping staircase made from the same. A huge urn stood in the middle of the classic black-and-white-tiled floors and, at the height of their success, two huge, full-length oil paintings of Sir David and Sir Frederick wearing matching formal Scottish dress – with bow tie, tight jacket and tartan trousers – adorned the walls on either side. Frederick was painted near a cannon with the castle façade behind him, while David held some kind of huge document like a map or drawing under one arm. A green crucifix shone from an alcove.

There were several portraits of the twins and their families throughout the castle, but there were also two matching Cana-lettos above the two grand fireplaces in the central meeting room and, at one point, a huge portrait of Wellington. There was also a decompression chamber for the health-obsessed twins, who once offered it to local divers.

Although grand like a luxury hotel, the plan was for a huge estate that was both private and large enough for separate quar-ters for their growing families. It was a desire to avoid family members having to brave bad weather to gather together which led to the Barclays putting their own twist on the classic castle design, placing a giant glass roof over the central atrium. It was in this vast chamber, which became known as the Winter Garden and which looks like the glasshouses at Kew Gardens from above, that the brothers would be brought their morning cigars when in residence and where the family members socialized. Inside it were more matching portraits, some painted by John Ward, the celebrated English portrait artist whose subjects included royalty, cabinet ministers and celebrities.[7]

Public rooms included a large office containing models of the ships and gas containers from the company that had made the Barclay brothers' fortune, Ellerman Lines. There were other homages to their lives and careers to date – the huge working chimneys were said to be based on the grandest pubs from the Tolly Cobbold chain they had sold for a fortune in 1990, while a tall cupola with gilded weathervane was said to be inspired by the police station in Monte Carlo. Gates from a bakery where their father had once worked were said to have been brought over from the mainland. Although the brothers were publicity-shy, guests mentioned seeing photographs of them with Thatcher, De Gaulle and Nelson Mandela.

As well as a specially designed stamp for the island, the brothers had insignia printed, etched and featured on most of their fixtures and fittings, from the glassware to the drainpipes and the uniform of their waiting staff. This insignia, featuring their initials – D and F – was everywhere.

Few guests forgot their first impressions of Fort Brecqhou. The reviews, despite its grandeur and cost, were mixed. Some raved about its beauty. Sark resident Paul Armogie said: 'The only other building I've been in like it was the Palace of Versailles'. David Leigh, a *Guardian* journalist invited to the island by David, described the interior decor of the castle as 'like a Trust House Forte hotel . . . which isn't a compliment'. One local resident who, like most, preferred not to be named, said the heavy drapes and pink tones were like 'a cross between Barbara Cartland and Ceaucescu's Palace'. The ever-attentive butlers, who brought the twins their favourites cigars, reminded another of Nick Nack in the James Bond movie *The Man with the Golden Gun*.

The mysterious and identical twins also attracted nicknames and fictional comparisons. Their matching and always coiffed exteriors prompted sarcastic monikers such as Pinky and Perky or Sirs Tweedledum and Tweedledee in the satirical magazine *Private Eye*.

They were so close that their decisions were always jointly taken; so identical they were rarely differentiated. Yet to the people who knew them well – and they engendered long-serving loyalty from many of their employees and associates – David was nearly always described as the dominant ideas man, the strategic visionary for most projects and particularly Brecqhou, while

Frederick had control of the detail, the twin who would sign off the expenses with an eye for the smallest amount.

Although David is credited with the vision for the castle, Frederick is most often credited with having got it built. 'When Frederick and David worked together there was a fairly clear split on who did what,' said someone who worked for them. 'Frederick was and remains a far more precise person and he did the majority of all the day-to-day administration and coordination of the property.'

Rivett wrote that architects and builders were 'answerable to Sir Frederick on matters of minute detail concerning design quality and choice of material – everything had to have his approval'.[8]

'You have to understand the twins,' said someone else who knew them both. 'Frederick was the doer in the relationship. David was the ideas man, the dreamer . . . And that's something that Frederick never had time for. He was never interested in that . . . He would always think, "What should we do next?" . . . All he was concerned about was dealing with stuff on a day-to-day basis.'

The most successful of the Barclay consiglieres tried to make sure they talked to both brothers at once. 'You need both brains on any particular issue,' said one.

While the brothers appeared always as a united front, insisting on joint decisions, the whole family was close. As well as holidaying together on the yacht and later in their chalet in Gstaad, they would all spend part of the year on the island, often at Christmas. Frederick's wife, Hiroko, described the island and its castle as 'beautiful', especially in the summer, if 'quite isolated'. It was perfect for large family gatherings, she said. 'We had Christmas together when we were all in the same happy family.'[9]

Each adult child had separate quarters in the castle, as did Douglas, the twins' younger brother who also played a key role in helping to design and build Fort Brecqhou. By the 1990s, David's older sons were starting families of their own. In 1991

Aidan had two young children, his son Andrew born almost two years after his stepbrother.

Long used to owning a complex web of companies, the twins restructured their finances as soon as they made serious money in the 1980s. Years later, Aidan Barclay would say in court that this was when his father and uncle 'decided to give everything away. They didn't want to own anything.'[10]

It stands to reason that the Barclay brothers would start thinking of their legacy at this point, not just in business terms but the one they would leave their children. Many people do in their fifties, even without extreme wealth. They were fifty-nine when they bought Brecqhou in 1993, and David had been suffering from bouts of ill health for some time. He had separated from Zoe in Monaco and had married a woman called Reyna Oropeza Jimenez. Beautiful, of Mexican origin and about twenty years younger than David, she gave birth to their only child, Alistair, in October 1989. He was David's fourth son, while Frederick's daughter Amanda was fifteen when they bought the island.

The twins' intense relationship had its fault lines, as most do.

Hiroko, who had four sisters she adored, said the brothers were 'extremely close' but also highly competitive, with each other as well as with outsiders. Still largely resident in the Roccabella, the brothers would holiday together on the *Lady Beatrice*. It was on this yacht in the 1990s that they came to blows over their succession plans, according to subsequent court testimony.[11] David, suffering from a flare-up of a condition similar to ME as well as heart palpitations, had been unable to get out of bed and wanted his brother to agree a succession plan there and then, on the yacht. He pushed for his sons' greater involvement in the business to be recognized before he died.

Although always close to his nephews, Frederick was obviously concerned about giving up a half share in the family business he had built jointly with his brother. Having never been seen to argue in public, there was evidence of tension. Hiroko said later that, during one particularly fraught episode and despite David's ill health, the two brothers started 'punching each other'.

Out of sympathy for his ailing brother as much as in recognition of the greater role his older nephews were playing in the family firm, Frederick eventually agreed to give David's side of the family half of his 50 per cent share when they settled their empire into a series of trusts. This division was to leave his only child, Amanda, with 25 per cent of the family fortune, while David's sons would share 75 per cent between them. Hiroko's son, Ko, who was a few years old when his mother met Frederick, had taken his stepfather's name but was not regarded as a fully entitled member of the family and was excluded from the succession plans.[12]

A desire to control their own destiny, their fortune and their family was a hallmark of the brothers. So much so that it became a rare source of tension between them. So it should come as no surprise that they would object to the idea of oversight by a parish potentate. Rows over succession and taxation would be the first of many fights the brothers had with their nearest neighbours to Brecqhou.

Sark takes some explaining to the modern reader. In 1565, when the first Queen Elizabeth of England wanted to stop an island close to the French coast being taken over by pirates or (worse) the French, she awarded the royal fief of Sark to a Jersey-based nobleman, Helier de Carteret, who became the island's first Seigneur. In return, he had to protect the island with a garrison of forty musket-wielding men.

Sark continued to be owned by the monarch but with its own government and rules. With the island on lease from the Crown, rather than part of the UK, the seigneur still pays an annual rent to the monarch worth a twentieth part of a knight's service – some £1.79 today.

In the sixteenth century, in order to entice his armed men to come and live on a windy if 'rapturous' island, de Carteret gave them each a parcel of land so they could be self-sufficient, and a seat on the local governing body, which they called Chief Pleas.[13] With a language derived from medieval Norman, ownership of one of the forty parcels, or tenements, of land remained the basis for the island's feudal governance until the new millennium.

Although Guernsey, its much bigger neighbour, provided a criminal justice system, Sark's ministers still managed to take full advantage of their uniquely powerful status with a series of anti-quated laws, which ranged from the significant to the quaint (some of which are still in force). Cars were banned, as were divorces, while only the Seigneur could own an unspayed bitch or fly pigeons. They banned aircraft from flying less than 2,000 feet above the island in order to preserve its 'tranquillity', an exception not afforded to anyone in the UK – not even the monarch, whose castle at Windsor lies directly below the flight path to Heathrow. Sark was an anachronistic land of almost 600 souls with no welfare state, and no significant taxation to pay for it either – at least no charge based on income, inheritance or capital gains. There was only a property tax and a small forfait for those who did not want to declare assets held in other parts of the world.

When the Barclay brothers bought Brecqhou, they found themselves awarded a single seat on Chief Pleas as landowners, but were also subject to a system of governance that had remained largely unchanged for 450 years.

Although advertised as 'tax free', this meant they were subject to a local tax. As part of his feudal dues, Sark's Seigneur was able to demand a 'treizieme' from all new homeowners equal to one-thirteenth of any sales price, or 7.69 per cent. The property sales tax was one of very few taxes on the island and it went straight into the pocket of the local potentate.

When the Barclays were sent a £179,000 bill for the treizieme soon after buying Brecqhou, they paid it, but were so unhappy about Sark's powers that, in March 1996, they issued a summons on the Seigneur claiming that Sark had no jurisdiction over Brecqhou at all, a fight not just against the treizieme but for their own independence. The resulting legal battle went on for more than four years and was eventually taken all the way to the Privy Council, then the highest court in the land. By the time the brothers demanded this tax back, after they had built Fort Brecqhou, the Seigneur had spent the money, some say on a luxury holiday.

It seems fair to say that Michael Beaumont, a former aircraft engineer who had been the island's 22nd Seigneur for more than twenty almost entirely uneventful years by the time the Barclays moved onto Brecqhou, was completely unprepared for the onslaught that followed.

By most accounts, Beaumont was an amiable if ineffective man who doesn't seem to have upset many of his subjects with his anachronistic powers. In his book *Offshore: In Search of an Island of My Own*, Ben Fogle describes him as 'a gentle mild-mannered man more intent on wielding a pair of garden shears than his bizarre constitutional rights'.[14] Along with his wife, Diana, Beaumont spent the last ten of his almost forty-two-year reign living in a small cottage, while supportive neighbours, the Synnotts, moved into the grand but dilapidated seventeenth-century manor house with its clock tower, dovecote and huge walled garden, in exchange for free rent, because they could afford the extensive renovation work needed.

The Beaumont family was unrelated to the original sixteenth-century Seigneur, Helier de Carteret; they had simply taken possession of the island in payment for a bad debt in 1852, as although the title is hereditary it may be mortgaged or sold with the permission of the British Crown. This fact would not be forgotten by David Barclay.

The Barclays liked to point out that the fully functioning cannons they had installed on Brecqhou could reach the Seigneurie, but it soon became apparent that their armed militia of choice wore wigs and gowns.

In 1997, the brothers started a campaign over Sark's laws of inheritance – notably that of primogeniture, which insisted that only male heirs could inherit. Within two years, they had not only petitioned the UK government but also complained to the European Court of Human Rights about it. In a statement to support the case, they said: 'The rights of primogeniture inevitably tend to disrupt a harmonious family life.'

One associate said the brothers were 'as close as they ever were' at the time, and described the fight with Sark as 'all about trying to do something for the interest of a female'. For years afterwards, most outsiders believed it was Frederick leading the charge, given the fact that he had one female heir, but almost from the start it was David who was most incensed by what he regarded as the injustice of feudalism.

The story of the Barclays versus the people of Sark is not a simple tale of good and evil. Few could argue that some of the legal battles waged by the Barclays, especially the early ones, had history on their side – and, by rights, the Barclays should have been lauded for their attempt to change Sark's anachronistic ways. Many of Sark's laws, which gave the Seigneur the right to say who could buy property and muddied legal and governmental powers, failed to meet post-Enlightenment norms, let alone those regarding more recent human rights.

As an island, it was best known before the arrival of the Barclays for a system of tax dodging which had been nicknamed the 'Sark Lark'. In June 1999, David wrote about the horrors of primogeniture and feudalism for the *Guardian*. Even then he was furious. The headline was: 'I have spent £1.75m trying to change this repugnant medieval system, akin to ethnic cleansing.'

In the article, David wrote: 'Sark is used as a haven for international tax evasion, subterfuge and fraud. It has been an accommodation address for nearly 40 years for people avoiding tax in the country of which they are resident, but they never set foot on the island of Sark. In addition, it has been used by companies all over the world in what is now known as the "Sark lark".'[15]

In a scheme which first gained notoriety in the 1980s, local residents on Sark were registered as nominee directors for offshore companies, thereby getting paid for their own 'services' and allowing non-resident companies to claim tax-free status. The Edwards report into the scandal in 1998 discovered that an island of just 575 souls was home to 15,000 directorships. Three residents had between 1,600 and 3,000 directorships each, prompting rumours of nonagenarians acting as finance directors, and a resident's garden shed burning down and affecting thousands of companies.

The report found that companies were combining 'secrecy and tax-free status by forming non-resident companies ... in Sark (where there is no legislation or regulation of companies or Directors)'.[16] In his *Guardian* article, David Barclay accused the Seigneur and his wife of sitting on 200 boards.

Jennifer McDermott, who had first come to the Barclays' attention when she was an articled tax clerk in the early 1980s, worked on many of their biggest cases on the island. 'They didn't want to be part of Sark because Sark had feudal laws, which were repugnant,' she recalls. 'David really wanted to change this feudal system and make it more into a modern democracy. And it took a lot of time and money, but he did achieve it.'[17]

For many of the most significant reforms, the brothers were pushing at an open door. Before 2000, Sark's government had voted to abolish primogeniture – allowing a man or a woman

to inherit equally. Then it set up a constitutional reform committee to consider the end of feudalism and the introduction of
democracy.

Unravelling centuries of feudal rules took time, however.
During that time, the Barclays refused to take up their seat on
Chief Pleas, sending in sick notes via their lawyers, who sat in
their place.

Meanwhile, Drs Richard and Marie Axton, fellows at Cambridge University who would retire to Sark and become its de
facto historians, dug through ancient archives to help prove that
Brecqhou did indeed fall under Sark's jurisdiction.

The Seigneur's lawyers argued that, as Sark was held on a lease
from the monarch, the case for independence needed to involve
the Crown. The result of this was that the Queen's lawyers submitted a counterclaim in support of the status of Brecqhou as
part of Sark.

On Friday, 30 June 2000, the day the case was due in the Royal
Court in Guernsey, the Barclays unexpectedly withdrew their bid
for independence. Islanders cheered the Seigneur and the work
done by the Axtons. They also wondered if the counterclaim had
prompted concerns that the alternative to some governance by
Sark – control by a much larger island such as Guernsey or even
the UK itself, with their far stricter rules over building regulations
and taxation – had put the Barclays off.

One long-time resident said the attempt to end all governance
by Sark was always doomed to fail. 'It would have created a situation where Brecqhou was effectively an independent jurisdiction
just floating in the channel . . . It would have been completely
lawless.'

In his still-unpublished autobiography, Beaumont describes
the Barclay brothers as 'the neighbours from hell'. Darkly, he
writes that his grandmother Sibyl Hathaway, the former Dame
of Sark, warned the Queen after the island's wartime occupation
by the Nazis that she feared her island was vulnerable to control

by 'wealthy men' because of its largely voluntary system of governance.

When, just a few months after dropping the case, on 31 October, the twins were knighted by the Queen in the first 'double dubbing' in modern times,[18] some wondered if there had been another reason for them to drop the lawsuit. Although awarded for charitable services – they had donated £40 million, largely to medical foundations – the honour would have been awkward during a court battle involving the Queen's own Privy Council.

Peace had broken out, in the short term at least. Just a few weeks after dropping their bid for independence, in July 2000, David and Frederick had changed the ownership structure of the island, the consequences of which would not become clear for some time. In contravention of Sark law, the Barclays granted a 150-year lease of the island to a Guernsey-registered company called Brecqhou Developments Ltd (BDL). BDL had two half-owners – the Island Trust and Amelia Island Trust – which were eventually said to have been set up for Alistair and Amanda as well as the twins. Both were based in the British Virgin Islands.

Richard Axton, an energetic, stocky man with a head full of white hair and a huge enthusiasm for life, had grown weary of the outside world seeing only the bad things about feudalism and not recognizing one significant factor at odds with the way the world was moving. Before he died aged eighty in 2021, he said: 'What defined [the feudal system] is that everybody is in a personal relation to somebody else, the Crown, the Seigneurs and the tenants and sub tenants. It's not a corporate thing, it's an individual personal thing . . . But that's all been blurred now because of allowing corporations and trusts to own property. Once you begin to undo the responsibility from an individual, then the whole thing begins to unravel.'[19]

Feudalism, with its anachronistic rules and whiff of knights in shining armour, was on its last legs. New knights of the realm, from humble origins and with a brand-new and bespoke castle, were about to enter a golden age.

Although the brothers liked to point out that the Brecqhou cannon were trained on the Sark Seigneurie, on 12 July 2001 they were fired for the first time. The twenty-one-gun salute commemorated Queen Elizabeth II's visit to Guernsey.

5. Ritz and Glamour

The Ritz Hotel was founded by a self-made man whose name had already become a byword for glamour and style when the twins were born. César Ritz, the thirteenth child of a Swiss peasant, had started in the business as a lowly wine waiter. He worked his way up through the ranks, not without criticism, but his first Hôtel Ritz, in Paris, changed the hotel industry for ever. After Ritz, king-size beds, wall-to-wall carpeting and indirect lighting all became de rigueur.

When he opened a London namesake in 1906, its neo-classical Belle Époque façade more typical of the Rue de Rivoli than London's Piccadilly, he was dubbed the 'king of hoteliers, hotelier to kings' partly because of his association with the English monarchy. The playboy Prince of Wales, the eldest son of Queen Victoria, was rumoured to have got stuck in a bathtub in the Hôtel Ritz in Paris with his mistress; as King Edward VII, he favoured the hotel within walking distance of Buckingham Palace and is credited, by the hotel itself at least, with the saying: 'Where Ritz goes, I go'.[1]

The Irving Berlin song 'Puttin' on the Ritz', from the 1930 musical of the same name, played on the fact that 'ritzy' had become a byword for expensive, fashionable and showy. The dance-loving Barclay brothers could hardly have avoided either the song or the name of one of the world's most famous hotels.

A sprinkling of stardust added to the gilt-edged decor. Guests included socialites, writers and stars, as well as heads of state. Early pictures show Charlie Chaplin, Anna Pavlova, Noël Coward, Jackie Onassis, the Aga Khan, Benazir Bhutto and J. Paul Getty outside the Ritz. Michael Cole is a former journalist who worked for many years for Mohamed Al-Fayed when he owned the Ritz in Paris. He recalls: 'Before César Ritz, a hotel was somewhere you stayed on your way to somewhere else. With the advent of Ritz, the hotel . . . was the destination. People went there for the sheer delight of being there. They resorted to it; it was a resort.'[2]

By the Second World War, while the Barclay brothers were being bombed in Coventry, the Ritz was hosting glamorous 'blackout balls' for anyone who could afford to ignore the Blitz bombers. Historically important meetings were also held there, with Winston Churchill, Charles de Gaulle and Dwight Eisenhower meeting in the Marie Antoinette Suite to hammer out strategy.

Ritz had died in 1918, at the end of the Great War. His widow and son managed the hotel in Paris, but in London, a former teacher from Yorkshire called Bracewell Smith, who had made his fortune turning a bomb site into the Park Lane Hotel in the 1920s, bought the hotel.

Smith – entrepreneur, Conservative Party donor, member of parliament and London mayor – was knighted in 1945, and became a major shareholder in and chairman of Arsenal Football Club, a fact that would remain relevant to the Barclay story.[3]

When Smith died in 1966, his son and heir, George – by then in his fifties – took over. Perhaps in homage to his father, and in recognition perhaps that his status deserved a double-barrelled name, he adopted a new surname. Like the second John Ellerman before him, he was far less successful than his entrepreneurial father in running the family business. Known as Guy, George Bracewell-Smith's *Who's Who* entry lists as many club memberships – including the Royal Automobile Club and the Royal and Ancient Golf Club of St Andrews – as boardroom seats.

The Barclays, as ever, spotted an opportunity, and invited Guy to lunch sometime in the early 1970s. Always on the lookout for bargains, there was nonetheless something special about the Ritz – so special, in fact, that their dream of owning it became part of their folklore.

There were several versions of the story of how badly the brothers wanted to own the Ritz. One version had the still-teenage twins earning money as window cleaners working nearby and gawping at the glamorous guests until someone, either staff or guest, threw things at them to shoo them away. Another had the unmarried Frederick insisting on taking women to the Ritz for their first date. He would order two glasses of champagne, but if the woman asked for another, he would have to take a sympathetic barman to one side and come back a few days later with some more money. While both stories ended with the brothers promising to one day buy the hotel, the latter also saw the helpful barman working at the Ritz until he retired, for the Barclays even then liked to reward loyal employees.

The third and most enduring story involved their mother, Beatrice. Early on in their careers, once they had a few successful property deals under their belt, the twins started taking Beatrice to the hotel's Palm Court for a weekly glass of wine. One of them (in most tales David) vowed to buy it one day, and Beatrice, who comes across as tough and strong-willed in most of these stories, scoffed at the very idea.

The twins tried to prove her wrong twice before she died in July 1989.[4] When they first approached Guy Bracewell-Smith, in the 1970s, he was not ready to sell. Fresh from the Crown Agents scandal, it is not known how close they were to being able to buy it.

By 1975, Guy Bracewell-Smith's American wife, Helene, had died. This 'charming man' had 'become lonely and depressed', according to Edward Erdman in his previously mentioned autobiography.[5]

By early 1976, the hotel was losing money every week, hit not just by the economic collapse prompted by the oil crisis, but the fact that it was terribly outdated, its rooms without air conditioning or double glazing. The occupancy rate was just 45 per cent. The Grill Room, once one of the most glamorous parts of the hotel, was 'empty and derelict'. There were abortive plans to sell it to a casino operator.

Sir Charles Clore, a minority shareholder in the Ritz and another man who had built a huge empire from humble beginnings as an estate agent before the war, told Erdman that he feared Bracewell-Smith no longer had his heart in the business. He was right: Bracewell-Smith told Erdman he wanted out.

The agent called on London's leading hoteliers, 'all of whom expressed interest in acquiring the Ritz'. His autobiography fails to mention the Barclays.

The Ritz had fallen into a general state of disrepair; potential purchasers needed cash to improve it, cash that few buyers had in the middle of a recession. Enter Nigel Broackes and Victor Matthews, the duo at the head of one of the fastest-growing conglomerates of the age, Trafalgar House, and soon to be favourites of Margaret Thatcher.

Bracewell-Smith was pleased as 'he had been concerned that the Ritz – as part of the establishment of this country – should pass into the hands of hoteliers of good standing'.[6] In the wake of the Crown Agents scandal, few would have been happy with the Barclays' standing in 1976.

Intriguingly, after the Ritz board agreed the Trafalgar House deal but before it could be announced to the stock exchange, Erdman received an 'unsolicited enquiry from solicitors on behalf of undisclosed clients who wished to inspect the hotel'. Although Erdman is long dead and no one is able to confirm the identities of the two men, it isn't beyond the realm of imagination to think that these mystery buyers might have been the Barclays, who had not let their hiccup with taxpayers' money stop their penchant for buying more hotels, having bought the Howard Hotel in 1975.

Prohibited by stock exchange rules from telling these unsolicited purchasers about the deal that had already been agreed, Erdman tried to put them off but could not. So he found himself, three days later on 5 April 1976, ushering 'the gentlemen' into the

Marie Antoinette Suite at the Ritz, where he 'swamped' them with coffee while checking on the status of the announcement. When he told them that the hotel had been sold to Trafalgar House for £2.75 million, they were understandably cross and left.

Within months of the sale, both Guy Bracewell-Smith and the founder's son, Charles César Ritz – who had a small residual stake in his father's legacy and who had long hated the use of 'ritzy' for its suggestion of ostentation – had died.

A short while after, in June 1977, 'Trafs' as it became known, at least by the bankers making a fortune out of its advisory fees, also bought the three newspaper titles once owned by Lord Beaverbrook: the *Daily Express*, the *Sunday Express* and the London *Evening Standard*. Victor Matthews, who became 'star struck' by the newspapers and the access they gave him to the rich and famous, according to some accounts, started to focus on what was then one of Britain's biggest-selling newspapers.[7] 'The editors will have complete freedom as long as they agree with the policy I have laid down,' Matthews told the *New York Times*. 'This is: Believe in Britain and look for the good things.'[8]

While Matthews was busy with the newspaper business, his co-founder at Trafalgar House, Nigel Broackes, was put in charge of the huge redevelopment of the London Docklands. At this point, the Barclays spotted another opportunity to achieve their dream, according to some close to them. Broackes rebuffed their latest bid but kept in touch with these twins who were obviously terribly keen on buying his hotel. In the end it was taken out of his hands.

Having bought Cunard, the owner of the *QE2* luxury cruise ship, a few years before the Ritz, Trafalgar House planned to open up the exclusive hotel to a different market – or as the *New York Times* put it, 'a wider clientele'.[9] Hotel rooms started to fill up in the 1980s after tax-cutting governments on both sides of the Atlantic prompted a consumer spending boom. Trafalgar House introduced package tours for guests of the *QE2*, which saw them whisked onto a train from the harbour in Southampton straight to the Ritz. By 1990, the hotel was reported to be worth seventy times what Broackes had paid for it.[10]

The expansion programme, coupled with the lack of investment, had started to tarnish the brand, however. 'The effect of it all was you got the sort of Americans with white belts, plaid trousers and loud voices and it was not the Ritz of old,' says Michael Cole. 'Although it clung to its status as much as possible the glamour was wearing thin. The film stars, the great people of the past era, they weren't going to the Ritz.'[11]

Growth was all, and Trafalgar House continued to buy more businesses, spending £750 million on commercial property alone in the last two years of the 1980s. Questions were raised, however, after it was discovered that interest payments were being moved from the profit and loss account to the balance sheet. An investigation by the Financial Reporting Review Panel saw £142.5 million wiped from the Trafalgar House accounts in 1990–91, turning a declared £112.5 million profit into a £30 million loss in one year. Losses ballooned to more than £800 million over four years in the early 1990s. The ensuing scandal turned this predator of the Thatcher era into prey.

Among those circling was Hong Kong Land, part of the huge conglomerate Jardine Matheson, which had already bought a 15 per cent stake in the company and removed Broackes from the board, even as the company he had built from next to nothing reported a £347 million loss. While Broackes continued to be involved as an investor, the Hong Kong-based conglomerate eventually built its stake to 25 per cent and installed a new chairman, Simon Keswick.

The Ritz was put up for sale, but this once iconic hotel failed to attract many serious offers. Not only had it been starved of serious investment but it was considered to have too few rooms to ever be properly profitable, despite its history and prestigious location. By April 1994, having slashed the value of the hotel in its books from £120 million to just £30 million, the hotel was ready for a fire sale. And the return of the Barclays.

Anyone who has ever worked for the Barclays attests to the speed of their decision-making. Devoid of many boards or even many senior executives outside a handful of trusted executives, the brothers bought properties, especially those they had long coveted, with the speed with which most people buy coffee. As soon as Frederick heard the Ritz was up for sale, he went to see it. People who worked for him at the time say that the brothers put an offer on the hotel the very next day. They had not even waited for a survey or an in-depth look at the accounts.

Frederick wanted the hotel so badly he later said he had paid for 10 per cent of it out of his own pocket, having 'personally' written a £7.5 million cheque as down payment.[12]

On Friday, 6 October 1995, Ellerman Investments bought the Ritz for £75 million. The brothers were so proud of their achievement they sanctioned a spokesman to say that buying the Ritz fulfilled a thirty-year ambition. Beatrice had died six years before.

The brothers may have been spending tens of millions of pounds on Project 95, their fortress in Brecqhou, at the time, but the Ritz was a bargain. The price was good – not just because of the mess Trafalgar House was in, but also because of the state the Ritz was in. One of the hotel's then employees said: 'The beds were all rickety. The carpets were frayed and the curtains were literally hanging on a thread.' The signs of neglect and parsimony were so great that there were stories that the management would leave the lights off in the less public areas to try to save electricity.

The Barclays invested £40 million over the next eight years, restoring the Ritz to what they considered its former glory. David suffered several bouts of ill health in the 1990s and spent time convalescing in Switzerland while Frederick largely managed the Ritz rebuild. Workmen for Adams and Palmer, the construction firm from Essex, started at the top of the hotel and worked their way down, gutting each room, so it was said, stripping out the electrics, plumbing and walls.

As always, the Barclays surrounded themselves with loyal employees and family members. Douglas Barclay, the twins' younger brother felt to have a flair for design, was put in charge of Adams and Palmer. He was responsible for choosing the fabrics, the new light fittings, the chandeliers and anything else that stayed in keeping with the pre-revolutionary style of Louis XVI. Ornate wallpaper, often in pinkish tones, heavily swagged curtains, and gilt or inlaid furniture multiplied.

Kevin Delaney was a former Dagenham factory worker turned director of Adams and Palmer. The Barclays were so impressed by the work of this Essex-born son of an Irish Catholic family that they sent him over to Brecqhou to complete the work on their new fortress. He would continue to work for them for more than twenty-five years.

The brothers appointed Michael Patrick Day as acting general manager of the hotel on 27 October 1995. Well-dressed and usually to be found with a Havana cigar before they were banned outside the smoking room, Day stayed for 17 years, until 2012. A devout Catholic, he eventually followed the tertiary orders of the Franciscan friars before his death in January 2018.[13] The brothers, whose father was Wesleyan, increasingly turned to Catholicism as they got older.

New senior staff members were typically vetted by Day, but David's son Aidan – taking an increasingly hands-on role after Ellerman – had a say in appointments. Over them all was Frederick, who from the beginning was described by staff as a 'perfectionist', patrolling the hotel corridors whenever he visited to report on patches of threadbare carpet or broken light bulbs. Even when money seemed tight, with staff numbers cut, Frederick would insist that an expensive rug be replaced if it had started to look shabby.

★

As well as its access to prestige and power, the Ritz was also useful financially. Indeed, the hotel's accounts offer a case study in how the Barclays used physical assets in the UK to shift money offshore.

A short while after buying the hotel, the brothers opened a casino in the basement where the wartime dances had once been held, which helped in terms of revenues. More so than the hotel's use as a location for the film *Notting Hill*, in which Julia Roberts as a famous film star stays in one of its suites.

As the Ritz name had been famous long before the arrival of effective intellectual copyright laws, there was little money to be made suing the makers of Ritz crackers or indeed Ritz-Carlton hotels.

Banks were always happy to lend money to a prestigious property in a good location, however, and the Barclays used this to the full. First, they revalued the Ritz in the same way less wealthy families revalue their homes to re-mortgage them. So in 2001, six years after the Barclays bought the Ritz for £75 million, but after the £40 million refurbishment programme, Jones Lang LaSalle, the chartered surveyors, declared that the hotel's value had doubled to £150 million, based on the standard accounting procedure of what buyers were willing to pay on the 'open market'.

By 2007, accounts for Ellerman Investments show that the directors believed this estimate seriously undervalued the hotel. Due to 'unsolicited bids', the book value of the Ritz was increased fourfold to 'in excess of £600m'. A further £25 million was added for the Ritz Club casino lease, after its directors put a value of more than £125 million on the casino itself.[14]

These unsolicited bids, which never materialized as public offers, continued to increase the book value of the Ritz Hotel for years, using rule FRS 15 of 2000, a common accounting practice which offered an exemption so that properties could be revalued at their 'open market value' – that is, prices offered by these unnamed, unsolicited offers.

The revaluations made a difference when it came to the way money and ownership was moved around within the Barclays' internal structure.

In 2008, Ellerman Investments, which was registered in the UK, sold the Ritz Hotel and various subsidiary companies – the Ritz Hotel Casino, Ritz Fine Jewellery, even the newly acquired Cavendish Hotel – to a similarly named company, Ellerman Holdings Ltd, also owned by the Barclays but based in offshore Jersey. The consideration was £730 million, almost ten times what they had paid for the Ritz Hotel thirteen years before.

No actual cash was paid to the UK company for this 'sale' to a company whose ultimate holding company, B.UK Ltd, is registered in Bermuda. Instead, an IOU for the Ritz was offered from the offshore business to its UK sister company.

What the revaluations and 'sale' had done simply meant that the Ritz Hotel, an asset deemed to be worth more than £700 million, was owned by an offshore company rather than a UK-based one following an inter-company process which began in 2008. The £707 million IOU continued to sit as one of several large interest-free inter-company loans between on- and offshore parts of the Barclay empire for years.

It is not clear what the benefit to the Barclay family was in doing this, unlike the way they used the Ritz to reduce their tax burden and send more money offshore. This was done by borrowing money from banks, secured on the Ritz Hotel, and then making interest-free loans from the UK company to its holding company (initially Ellerman Investments Ltd and then subsequently Ellerman Holdings Ltd).

In 2006, the Ritz Hotel Ltd increased its bank debt by £84.6 million. At the same time, the company paid £54.3 million to the UK parent, Ellerman Investments, partly to repay a parent company loan and partly to lend some more money.

The initial investment, added to the high interest costs of servicing its bank debt, lowered the hotel's profits. This meant that in fourteen of the first sixteen years of their ownership of the Ritz, the Barclay brothers recorded no corporation tax. By 2011, they had reported just two charges – £56,000 in 2005 and £114,000 in 2008, or £170,000 in total.

After 2006, when the cost of borrowing started to fall, and before 2018, bank debt secured against the prized asset of the Ritz Hotel increased by £242.3 million. At the same time, the Ritz Hotel Ltd lent some £224.5 million in unsecured loans to its now offshore parent company.

There is nothing unusual in the practice of borrowing money to reduce a corporate tax bill – the revenue practically encourages it as a way of boosting investment. Essentially, money comes in from the bank, not to fund onshore investment but to be offered to offshore parent companies without any interest or security – or indeed time limit. The practice underlines how UK-based businesses with physical assets and workforces can be used by offshore entities with neither to extract cash. Many multilayered companies enjoy the benefits of moving money offshore, where it can be managed without much involvement from the British tax authorities. It was the scale of this process that was unusual at the Ritz. Accounts for the Ritz Hotel show that the company paid tax of £1–2 million a year after 2012, coincidentally the same year a BBC documentary on the brothers called *The Tax Haven Twins* was broadcast. Presented by John Sweeney, the journalist the twins had successfully sued after he had landed on Brecqhou and then given an interview about it to BBC Guernsey, the programme focused on the fact that one of the best-known hotels in the world was able to borrow millions as a going concern without paying a huge amount in tax.

Aidan Barclay pointed out that the hotel had not paid dividends to its shareholders and said profits had been reinvested into the business. The question of which part of the business was never answered. In a statement, he said: 'The Barclay family members and their companies abide by the law and pay the taxes required by UK law and the laws of other relevant countries.'[15]

Stephen Boxall, then managing director of the Ritz, said that the £50 million or so spent on refurbishment were costs which were 'lawfully off-settable against trading profits'.[16] Between 2012 and 2018, the Ritz – a five-star hotel valued at more than £700 million – reported a total corporation tax charge of £15.5 million to HM Revenue and Customs (HMRC).

Although a classic takeover in many ways, the Ritz – bought at speed after being a target for years – was always something more for the Barclays. It was a passport and a prize. Frederick spent far more time there, but both men loved it. They lived and often worked in its gilded rooms when they were in London, and used it as an entrée to the sort of high society that included political leaders and royalty – people at the opposite end of the social and political scale from where they had begun. As well as regular lunches at the hotel with friends such as Lord McAlpine, they dined there in the early years with British prime ministers and the editors of all the newspapers they owned. They also maintained and even strengthened the hotel's royal connections.

After buying the Ritz, a stone's throw from Ellerman's head-quarters in St James's, the brothers fell into a sort of routine when in London, meeting at the hotel to drink coffee and study the morning's papers, as they did when in Monte Carlo. Although they were never big drinkers, known only to have the occasional glass of something, they always had a cigar on the go.

Staff grew to recognize how long they would be sitting together by the size of the cigars they ordered. With a liking for Churchills (the bigger the better) as well as Cohibas, they would smoke a cheroot if in a hurry. 'If they took a small one, it was probably because the meeting wasn't going to take a long time and they had other things to do,' said one employee. 'A nice long cigar? They would be there for the duration.'

Always sticklers for a dress code, the brothers still dressed identically but with increasingly well-cut suits and matching silk pocket handkerchiefs, and they loved the old-world formality at the Ritz. Frederick could not abide the liveried waiters and braided porters, their white gloves tucked under their epaulettes, showing a wrinkle out of place. The brothers took the same approach on Brecqhou when it was finished. Male guests at the Ritz had to wear a jacket (or rather 'coat', as a Ritz view was that 'only potatoes wear jackets') as well as a tie. Jeans, trainers and T-shirts were banned. Again this formality was continued at home with guests on *Lady Beatrice* surprised to be asked to wear ties, even in the height of summer.

If they ate outside their private rooms, the twins would always eat at Table Nine in the far right-hand corner of the restaurant, by the floor-to-ceiling windows with a view over the terrace and into Green Park beyond. Politicians, including Margaret Thatcher and other heads of state, tended to favour Table One in the opposite corner by the window, as did Aidan and Howard eventually. Table Nine, however, could only be reserved by two families: the Barclays and the Windsors. The table was a favourite of Queen Elizabeth, the Queen Mother, when she came in. Staff talked of having to move other diners from her table if ever she arrived unexpectedly.

The royal family had a history with the hotel, dating back to its inception and the son of Queen Victoria. Under the Barclay ownership, it was the eldest son of an even longer-serving British Queen who grew particularly attached to the Ritz. The then Prince Charles first went public with his relationship with an old friend, Camilla Parker Bowles, at the hotel, two years after the death of his first wife, Diana, Princess of Wales.

On 28 January 1999, in a carefully stage-managed event dubbed 'Operation Ritz' by the Palace and the media, the couple attended the fiftieth birthday party of Camilla's sister, Annabel Elliot, at the hotel. As they left, hundreds of cameras happened to be waiting to take the first picture of the pair attending an event as a couple.

By 2002, the Prince of Wales was regularly holding parties for his household staff there, where the young princes would fire off party poppers and entertain the grown-ups. In the same year, two years after the Barclay brothers had been knighted, the Ritz became the first and only hotel to be awarded a royal warrant for services to banqueting and catering. The quest for standing, with their self-made crest and motto, was delivered in spades by the hotel in London's Piccadilly.

Their relationship with the heir to the throne and his partner would only become closer. After Frederick bought *Leander*, a yacht many considered his most desirable, Camilla – by then Duchess of Cornwall – would spend a week at the end of the summer, usually in September, staying on her, as well as using the private jet whenever she needed.

As a private holiday, the trips never needed to be declared, but they provide an example of how much owning the Ritz, and buying famous yachts, changed the Barclays' standing in the world. Once enmeshed in a scandal involving agents of the Crown, they could now provide services for the man who would be King.

6. Bing-Bang-Bong

As well as luxury hotels, grand properties and their own island, as the twentieth century came to a close the Barclays owned businesses that ranged from gas transportation to car financing, Japanese luncheon vouchers to diamond mines. But not since the collapse of Candy Corner, half a century before, had they owned much of a shop.

That was all to change after an encounter with a man who would go on to become infamous for his deal-making and catastrophic fall from grace. As so often with the Barclays, the deal involved a struggling seller and a neighbour in Monaco.

Philip Green, with his penchant for open-necked shirts, love of lavish parties and enthusiasm for talking to journalists, was as loud as the Barclays were silent; the yin to their yang, apart from a shared love of the principality and of a deal.

In 1998, with Green's attempts to buy the UK's fifth-largest clothing retailer written up in the financial press, he found himself in a 'little tiny restaurant' in France. 'I was having a coffee with somebody,' Green later told a television crew. 'And the guy I was having a coffee with says, "Do you know the guy over there? That's one of the Barclay twins."'

'So we go out on the street and he taps me on the shoulder and says, "Hello."'

'So, I said, "Are you Freddie or David?"'

' "I'm Freddie," he said. "I've been watching what you've been doing. Why don't you come and see me?" '[1]

Green had been struggling to raise the money he needed to make a bid for Sears, which owned high street chains such as Miss Selfridge and Wallis, as well as mail-order catalogue business

Freemans. Several years earlier, he had been forced out of a listed retail company called Amber Day, in a row over corporate governance and missed financial targets. The affair had made investors wary of backing Green, and Green wary of using public markets to raise money. 'Floats are for milkmen,' he would say of listing on the stock exchange, a view he shared with the Barclays.

When he bumped into Frederick, Green had already made one failed bid for Sears. This failed bid had been backed by Tom Hunter, a Scottish entrepreneur who had worked with Green on a shoe shop deal, and Jack 'Black Jack' Dellal, a colourful property tycoon and former deputy chairman of the Keyser Ullman bank – which, like the Barclays, had been caught up in the Crown Agents scandal.[2]

When Green flew out to meet the Barclay brothers at the Hôtel de Paris in Monte Carlo, he took Hunter with him. At this first proper meeting, Green sketched out his plans for buying and then selling off the Sears retail brands. When Frederick had asked the younger man to meet him, he'd told him to whittle down his large dossier of information to a handful of pages, a sign not that the brothers disliked details but that they had already largely worked them out. It was the sort of asset-strip the brothers had employed with Ellerman, but Green had the potential partners for offloading the various parts of Sears more or less lined up. A further attraction was that the businesses could be sold on, leaving the undervalued properties for the new owners.

Ever since hitting the big time, the brothers had shown increasing pride in their Scottish heritage, adding Celtic crosses to their coat of arms and wearing kilts for their official portraits. Earlier in 1998 the twins had been delighted to have been awarded honorary degrees by the University of Glasgow, despite having never lived in Scotland and leaving school before the age of sixteen. The citation called them 'outstanding examples of the modern Scottish ability to combine geographical mobility with fidelity to Scotland'.[3]

The brothers appeared to take a shine to Hunter. Sitting across from the two younger men, Frederick leaned across the table and offered 'Young Tom' some advice. 'Never do business with arse-holes,' he reportedly said, a line that made both Barclay brothers roar with laughter. As they left, Green turned to Hunter and called his unlikely potential partners 'fucking weirdos', according to his biography.[4] He wouldn't be the first or the last to find the identical twins in matching outfits a little odd, even though he went on to make a fortune with them.

The Barclays agreed to invest £100 million.

Eyes twinkling at the memory, Green still sounded as though he could hardly believe his luck in a TV interview more than a decade later. 'Bing-bang-bong, off you go, you've got the money,' he hooted. 'We hostile it the following Thursday.'[5]

Frederick had spotted an opportunity in both the business and Green's lack of financing. Once a successful retail empire founded by John Sears and developed by Charles Clore, by 1998 Sears was a 107-year-old shadow of its former self, beset by poor perform-ance and a much-maligned management. A series of failed disposals and more had dented its share price, which by October 1999 was trading at a big discount to the sum of its parts.

Richard Ratner, a well-regarded retail analyst, described the company's share price performance as a 'sad indictment of the Sears management'.[6] Investor discontent focused on the role of its chairman, Sir Bob Reid, who was running the business after the departure of the chief executive despite sitting on several other boards as a non-executive director.

While shareholders were less than supportive of the Sears management, however, they doubted Green's ability to come up with the cash.

The Barclays had recognized the value in a company which its existing management and owners had not. They had also spotted an opportunity to buy something cheap and flip it. Sears, an undermanaged, unloved conglomerate, represented a classic break-up opportunity and, as always, the Barclays acted with astonishing speed.

Or 'bing-bang-bong', as Green put it.

Having met just before Christmas, the new and unlikely team set up a shell company, January Investments Ltd, and launched a £519 million hostile bid for Sears on 14 January 1999. The brothers' £100 million gave them about 80 per cent of the business, while Green – or rather his wife, Tina, who had already bought 1.7 million shares in the company – contributed £20 million for a 20 per cent stake. Tom Hunter also invested an undisclosed sum.

The rest of the purchase price came from loans from two banks. Robertson Stephens, a US group focused on offering loans to entrepreneurs collateralized by their illiquid private company holdings, contributed £300 million, while Bank of Scotland provided less than half that at £115 million.

Scotland's second-biggest bank, a venerable old Edinburgh institution, had already financed some of the Barclays' purchases. Still two years away from the merger with the UK's biggest mortgage lender which would turn it into HBOS, the Sears investment was its biggest yet, but would eventually be dwarfed by others – nearly all signed off by Peter Cummings, who ran the bank's leveraged lending team.

In *Hubris: How HBOS Wrecked the Best Bank in Britain*, journalist and executive Ray Perman describes Cummings as quiet, thoughtful and unshowy, a rather unremarkable man who ended up with a remarkable career.[7] Born and brought up in Dumbarton, Cummings continued to live in the commuter town outside Glasgow even after he had been dubbed 'banker to the stars'.

The decision of Bank of Scotland's corporate lending department to back entrepreneurs such as Green, whose big ideas were often larger than the size of their bank balances, would go on to transform the reputation of the traditional, almost staid, bank.

The unlikely Sears team – Green, Tom Hunter and the Barclays – became some of the bank's best clients. Cummings would say of his methods, 'I just make sure I don't lend to idiots.'[8]

The £115 million the bank provided to the Sears bid consortium was embarrassing for the target's chairman Bob Reid, whose many non-executive roles included deputy governor of Bank of Scotland.

Sears had several hallmarks of a classic Barclays' deal. For a start, their reputation as canny dealmakers in the wake of Ellerman made the arrangement of two private bank loans relatively straightforward. Without the need to issue shares or use any public markets they could avoid sharing too much information with potential rivals or the media and move fast. Not only had the financing been completed in a matter of days, but January Investments, the new shell company – led by Green as chief executive – had already won the backing of the target's biggest shareholder, Phillips and Drew Fund Management, by the time it launched the hostile bid.

Having launched the offer in just a few short weeks, even the usual sixty-day period following the publication of an offer document was more than halved to twenty-four days. Green said speed was of the essence in a 'people business' like Sears, because staff needed the reassurance. The speed also put pressure on the beleaguered management, of course, with little time to find a white-knight rival bidder. In the event, the board rolled over quite quickly.

On 21 January, just a week after the surprise bid was launched and a short while after it was increased slightly to £548 million, Sears agreed to the bid.

The Barclays had turbo-charged Green's long-held ambition to buy a significant part of the British high street at a time when he was a pariah to others. Sears' shareholders took the Barclay-enabled cash now rather than wait for a better offer later. 'The Barclays are happy with my understanding of shops, and they have expertise in financial services and property,' said Green. Privately, the Barclays said that they had made Phillip Green when few other people wanted to work with him.

What's more, the price was a steal. Even newspaper reports at the time spoke of the takeover as 'one of the biggest January sales bonanzas ever'.[9]

The previous management had already started talks to sell Freemans catalogue as well as the financial services arm, and before the month was out, Green had sealed the deal for a combined £291 million. The Adams childrenswear brand was sold to its management for £87 million, while the womenswear division went to arch-rival Arcadia for £151 million. After just six months, all the Sears trading businesses had been sold and the company broken up, an asset-stripping operation which returned some £550 million – roughly what they had paid for the whole business before the property was included. In total, the deal made the Barclays and Green some £250 million in less than a year, more than double the £120 million they had invested.

In July 1999, six months after the takeover, Green told the *Financial Times* that the new dream team were 'actively looking at other opportunities in the marketplace', with a potential war chest of about £1 billion. He joked that his next bidding company might be named August or September Investments.[10]

There were to be no more deals. The Barclays and Philip Green did go on to enjoy an unlikely friendship over the next few years, however. For Green's fiftieth birthday, in March 2002, David and Frederick sent a pre-recorded video message in which they fired a six-gun salute from Brecqhou. In doing so, they looked like 'looney pensioners' to the guests at the lavish party in Cyprus, according to Oliver Shah's biography of Green.[11] Frederick even made a rare appearance at the bar mitzvah for Green's teenage son at the Grand-Hôtel du Cap-Ferrat in the South of France in May 2005. Entertainment during the three-day extravaganza included blind tenor Andrea Bocelli and Beyoncé. A little while

later, Green and his wife moved into a penthouse flat in the Roccabella, above the Barclay brothers on the seventeenth and
eighteenth floors.

It seems surprising that these arch deal-makers never worked
together again, despite Green's talk of a war chest and the Barclays' name being linked to several of his future deals. There
were rumours – never substantiated – that they had fallen out
over a missing payment, but perhaps friendship with a man who
seemed to seek out publicity, with a penchant for talking to – and
even shouting at – journalists, was simply always going to be
unlikely for the brothers.

'I think Phillip thought they were really close,' says Jeff Randall, the editor of the Barclays-owned *Sunday Business* at the time,
who got to know both Green and the Barclays. 'But I'm not sure
anyone gets really close to the Barclays. As the famous statesman
said: "We don't have allies, we have interests." And I think that's
how the Barclays are. They have perpetual interests and their
allies come and go.'[12]

The Sears deal kick-started Philip Green's journey to becoming the controversial, self-styled 'King of the High Street'. His
success meant that when he went looking for funding for his
£850 million acquisition of Arcadia in 2002, Cummings lent the
money on the basis of one phone call – a call which reportedly
made the newly merged HBOS bank £96 million.[13]

Ambitious men at financial institutions keen to take advantage of
the booming property sector would be of huge help to the Barclay family's way of doing business. The next few years saw a
complete transformation of their business into a holding company for retail, property and media businesses.

And there was one retail property they had been stalking for
some time.

Back in the mid-1980s, not long after the Ellerman takeover,
the brothers had made their first approach to the family of Sir

John Moores – owners of Littlewoods, the football betting and retail group and largest family-owned business in the UK. But with the domineering founder still alive, albeit semi-retired, their approach went nowhere. Twenty years later, sometime after the death of Sir John at the age of ninety-seven, Littlewoods was riven by its own succession drama.

John Moores was one of eight children born to a Lancastrian bricklayer at the turn of the century. He had started the Little-woods pools business alongside his brother Cecil and others in 1923, taking advantage of both a growing passion for football and an age-old enthusiasm for gambling. The Littlewoods Mail Order Store was launched nine years later in January 1932, when many families in Liverpool and other big cities were suffering from Depression-era levels of unemployment.

Difficult working conditions and need were behind new financing operations popular in the North of England, which allowed the poor to pay for things in instalments. At the same time, the retailing success of big American mail order firms such as Sears, Roebuck and Co. inspired the production of mass-produced catalogues to tempt consumers – mainly women – to buy stuff they needed and to pay in small amounts over an agreed period of time. A 'turn club', in which members would club together to pay money into a kitty before taking a 'turn' to buy something, offered cash-strapped families fair credit terms while also encouraging them to spend. Unusually for the time, the Littlewoods businesses offered this easy credit for ordinary house-hold goods like blankets and pans.

In these days before data protection, Moores hit on the genius idea of writing to the 20,000 subscribers of his pools betting business in a bid not just to find agents who would collect the payments and distribute the goods but also to market his new catalogue without having to pay for advertising.

Littlewoods was a huge and almost immediate success. Sales grew to £4 million within just four years and, in 1937, the company opened its first department store. Post-war prosperity and a period of full employment saw the company switch from turn clubs to interest-free credit – a system which delivered goods immediately on the first part-payment and which has helped to fuel spending booms ever since. The post-war baby boom and consumer spending spike led Littlewoods to add pages of essential items for newborns and homeware in their increasingly popular catalogues. Between 1957 and 1961 the sales of mail order houses such as Littlewoods, which offered extended payment terms, increased by 87 per cent.[14] It isn't difficult to imagine Beatrice Barclay, whose youngest child was a teenager in 1960, using such cheap credit to buy goods from catalogue companies such as Littlewoods.

Enthusiasm for his products made Moores one of Britain's richest men as well as one of its biggest post-war benefactors. He was particularly revered in Liverpool, for working conditions that included relatively high wages but also for a paternalistic approach that included staff trips to the seaside. By the 1970s, his increasing involvement in two local football rivals, Liverpool and particularly Everton, and increased competition from high street retailers saw sales start to flag. Declining returns, as so often for family-owned businesses, exacerbated existing tensions. The autocratic patriarch, so desperate for his business to stay in family hands, failed to find an obvious successor among the next generation or two, despite living into his nineties.

His eldest son, John Jr, had quit as an executive director in 1971 after a disagreement with his father, who did not stand down as chairman until 1977, at the age of eighty-one. His second son, Peter, then spent three years in charge – during which time profits fell – only to be humiliatingly sacked by his octogenarian father, who took charge again in 1980. By then, the business was owned by thirty-two family members, with several members of the second and third generations on either the main or subsidiary board. A significant minority of them were keen to sell out completely. A stock market listing or outright sale was mooted.

Among those keen to sell was one of the biggest individual shareholders: the patriarch's grandson John Moores III, who lived in Monaco.

The elderly Sir John rejected both the listing and the sale. Without an obvious successor, he eventually appointed an outsider to run the business for the first time in 1982, a period that coincided with the first expression of interest from the Barclays.

Sir John rewrote his will to make it tax-efficient in 1988. By the time of his death in 1993, the founder owned just 0.0013 per cent of the Littlewood shares, with the rest shared between his descendants and those of his brother.[15]

Almost immediately after his death, feuds that had remained private for years broke into the open. In an increasingly bitter atmosphere, there were reports of such a breakdown of trust between members of the family and senior employees that they hired private detectives to investigate each other. Newspaper reports at the time compared the saga being played out among the Moores family to the popular soap opera also set in Liverpool, *Brookside*.[16]

The Barclays must have looked at this internecine family rivalry and drawn-out saga and been grateful that they had an obvious successor to take over the family business in the shape of Aidan, David's capable and hard-working eldest son. Aidan would go on to act as chairman of the family business and, along with his younger brother Howard, could control the entire empire with a majority share.

By the turn of the century, the Littlewoods pools business was struggling to compete with the National Lottery, introduced six years earlier. It was sold off in 2000 for £161 million, a fraction of its former value.

The retail business was left to be managed by Barry Gibson, a company lifer who had started there as a trainee. Plummeting sales and a disastrous new stock management system led to headlines such as 'Catalogue of disasters'. Disgruntled staff and shareholders even took issue with an incentive plan that awarded a new car to the three best store managers. 'In 1982, when Sir John Moores made redundancies for the first time, he gave up his Rolls Royce and people in Littlewoods felt sorry for him,' said one insider. 'Now staff would happily set fire to both Barry Gibson and his chauffeur-driven car.'[17]

In January 2002, the Barclays made their first approach to the board for the company's 120 department stores, 69 stand-alone Index catalogue stores, and a business responsible for almost one-third of the UK's mail order sales. David Simons, the Littlewoods chairman, took this – along with other approaches for parts rather than the whole of the company – to the Moores family shareholders.

By October, the Barclays had set up not one but three inter-locking shell companies to buy Littlewoods, a sign of what would become one of the most complicated wings of a madly compli-cated corporate financial structure. Within two decades, there would be at least thirty-five different companies based on or linked to the original Littlewoods purchase. It was LW Corpor-ation, a new Jersey-based company, that bought Littlewoods for £750 million through its UK subsidiary, LW Investments. There was also an intermediary holding company called LW Finance. This pattern of using almost identically named companies like a series of blank-faced Russian dolls was a typical feature of the Barclays' way of doing business.

The £776 million offer was £115 million less than Littlewoods' net assets, recorded earlier that year.[18] This discount to assets reflected shareholder irritation at the performance of the existing management, as well as the company's sensitivity to consumer spending and lacklustre profits. Only the Barclays, it seemed, could see the upside.

They offered £376 million in cash up front, satisfying the desire of some members of the Moores family for ready money, and £400 million in a loan note repayable by 2012, guaranteed by

Bank of Scotland.[19] The purchase ended eighty years of the Moores family's ownership of Littlewoods.

The scale of the acquisition even appears to have given those buccaneering lenders at Bank of Scotland some pause. In providing some of the cash for the Littlewoods deal, the Edinburgh-based bank took a 5 per cent stake in LW Finance, the shelf investment company that still operates as a UK headquarters between LW Investments and LW Corporation, the Jersey-based parent company.[20] This stake must have made money as the bank set up a series of subsidiary companies, all bearing the name from the old Bank of Scotland Latin motto *Tanto uberior*, 'So much the more plentiful'.[21]

The Littlewoods takeover surprised a City which had started to think of the Barclays as hotel and property owners. Charles Sherwood, a partner at Permira, a private equity group that had also expressed an interest in Littlewoods, called the Barclays 'very effective stealth buyers . . . They come out of nowhere and move quickly.'[22]

The surprise was not so well received in Liverpool itself, where the names Littlewoods and Moores were considered key parts of the city's financial, social and philanthropic history. Local politicians and trade unions raised concerns about the future of some 22,000 Littlewoods staff, as well as the plans of a family regarded as asset strippers post-Ellerman.

In a bid to squash these concerns, David Simons said: 'We are pleased that Littlewoods is being acquired by another private, family company with similar values.'[23] As part of the agreement, the Barclays had committed to retaining the Littlewoods brand, its HQ in Liverpool and the executive board. They kept to the letter of these promises but, by the following February, had split the group into seven different business units, sacked more than 200 people, and relocated the head office out of the city centre to the suburb of Speke. The historic headquarters in the city centre was sold.

The new management team withdrew from the Ethical Trading Initiative (ETI), which monitored working conditions among developing world suppliers, prompting Christian Aid supporters to send more than 1,000 emails urging the company to reconsider.[24]

The Barclays had also scrapped Littlewoods' automatic donation of 1 per cent of company profits to charity almost immediately, saying that they preferred to back their own causes, often involving medical issues rather than the arts and education, which had been a focus of the Moores Foundation's giving.

In the face of growing criticism in Liverpool, Jeff Randall, who had left the Barclays-owned *Sunday Business* to become the BBC's first business editor, felt moved to write in support of the brothers in the *Liverpool Echo* in February 2003. 'Scan some of the more hysterical headlines that have accompanied reports about the Barclay family's purchase of Littlewoods, and you . . . might infer that the paternalistic Moores family had been manoeuvred out by a bunch of slash-and-burn merchants whose sole intention was to eliminate the charitable work for which Littlewoods' founders were renowned.'[25]

Randall then recounted an act of charity to a former colleague that showed their ability to be personally generous to others. Not long after buying the *Sunday Business*, the news editor Frank Kane's baby son had fallen seriously ill, eventually losing some fingers and part of his lower leg. The new team were understandably upset by the tragedy, which Randall mentioned to Aidan Barclay. A short while later, David Barclay called Kane and offered to help with expensive prosthetics not available on the NHS. He continued to support the young boy's prosthetic care for years, even after Kane stopped working for them. In the early noughties, when he was at the *Observer*, the sort of liberal newspaper the brothers disliked, Kane and his son, who was a similar age to Alistair, were even invited to Brecqhou in the private helicopter.

Randall remained fond of the family, saying, 'The Barclays always treated me with courtesy and respect.'

At the time, he sought to assuage fears about the Barclays' asset-stripping reputation. 'I called Aidan [Barclay] and put it to him that critics claim that his intentions are to smash up Little-woods for a quick profit. He told me: "We have no plans to sell the principal businesses, namely retail, catalogue shopping, delivery, property and financial services." His word would be good enough for me.'

Aidan Barclay was true to his word, up to a point. The retail business formerly known as Littlewoods was still the biggest Barclay-owned business, both in terms of value and employees, when David died in 2021. The acquisition had shown how the Barclays did their homework and then took risks to make money. In the first accounts for the business under their ownership, to 30 March 2003, the company made £157 million from a sale and leaseback of properties, and £52 million more from disposals of discontinued operations. But their use of financial engineering did not stop there, and warrants a far closer look.

The first three years of the Barclays' ownership of Littlewoods is a case study in how they used debt to buy businesses on the cheap, using the proceeds from future sales to pay off some of the debt – a type of transaction the private equity business would go on to dominate. The Barclays contributed just £100 million of their own equity capital, or cash, to the upfront fee for Little-woods, with £240 million coming mainly from those helpful people at HBOS, the new name for Halifax and Bank of Scotland after the merger in 2001.

The speed with which they not only repaid themselves but also doubled their bet is again notable. While keeping to his word of sticking to the principal businesses, Aidan disposed of some elements such as a small stake in Jacques Vert, which sold women's occasionwear. The company then reduced working capital by essentially selling off the debt owed by consumers to banks.

Littlewoods had offered loans to its typically low-income consumers, who used the 'never-never' to buy essentials and Christmas presents despite interest rates that could be as high as 39 per cent (or twice the standard rate for a credit card bill). The Barclays sold that debt on to a bank for a tiny fee, so that they got cash up front while the banks were happy to wait for the repayments. This process, known as 'securitizing receivables', is all about releasing cash for a company sooner rather than later. The extra cash flow from this, along with the disposals, allowed the Barclays to pay themselves a £52 million dividend within six months of buying Littlewoods, which meant they had stumped up just £48 million for a company worth £750 million.

The Barclays did not rest there. They next did a deal which was far more audacious, and they did it in even less time.

John Peace had made it clear, almost as soon as he had arrived as chief executive at Littlewoods' rival GUS, that he was keen to restructure the retail conglomerate, which included diverse brands ranging from Argos to Burberry as well as several ailing catalogue businesses including Kays, Abound and Choice. At the start of 2003, just a few months after the Barclays bought Littlewoods, Peace started meeting Aidan Barclay for coffee in the Ritz, which happened to be close to the GUS headquarters in Mayfair.

David and Frederick started to say that they had stepped back from the business by this point. This is true in the sense that they appointed senior and powerful managers for each division who reported in to them, but they were still heavily involved in plotting takeovers and ways to make money. They typically made the initial overtures, often via faxes from David, but then Aidan would take over.

Most of those who have worked with David's eldest son

describe him as shrewd, if somewhat inscrutable. Considered slightly less eccentric than his father and uncle, but just as ruthless, it was Aidan who had been sent to go through the books of Ellerman, and Aidan who was the brother sent to learn about tax in a blue-chip law firm in the early 1980s. At the end of their go-go decade, Aidan, then thirty-three, had given his Uncle Freddie a cigarette case engraved with their deals to date and the words: 'In recognition of and thanks for many years of much fun, laughter, aggravation and experience. To those that were caught and those that got away.'[26]

After the Ellerman deal made the Barclays seriously rich, Aidan had married Ferzana Aziz, known as Fizzy, who also came from a wealthy family. Their first child, Sofia, was born in August 1988, followed by another daughter and a son, Andrew, almost exactly three years later. Aidan's wife was sociable and lively, and there was understood to be little love lost between her and her father-in-law, who had met and married his second wife at the same time his eldest son married Fizzy.

Although he was said to have attended good schools, including a boarding school in Surrey paid for during the successful sixties by David and Zoe, his accent made him sound more like a London dealer than the privately educated son of the very wealthy man he was – a trait he shared with Philip Green. The pair became friendly during the Sears takeover and subsequent break-up. Always immaculately turned out, with neatly pressed suit and polished shoes like his father and uncle, Aidan was most often to be seen with a fat cigar and wearing red braces as he took on a more public role. In late 2003, only a year after the Littlewoods purchase, Aidan bought himself a 244-foot superyacht from one of the richest men in the world. Larry Ellison, founder and head of Oracle, had called her *Katana*, as her sleek, pointed exterior with unusual convex mirrored glass echoed the long, single-edged sword used by the Japanese samurai. Aidan renamed her *Enigma*. It isn't difficult to see this rechristening as a knowing nod to both his inscrutability and the family's reputation.

In May 2003, just a few months after first meeting the chairman for coffee, the Barclay brothers made a bid to buy the UK home shopping and distribution arms of GUS. The name of the special acquisition vehicle they set up suggests the family thought they could have bought it even sooner: March U.K. Ltd, which is itself a subsidiary of a Jersey-based parent company called March Corporation.

The offer of £590 million – made up of £450 million up front borrowed from the Royal Bank of Scotland, obviously keen to join its Scottish rival in corporate lending, and a loan note payable in 2008 – was accepted in an uncontested battle. The Barclays took control immediately, a surprise given the near certainty that the merger would be referred to the competition authorities.

The businesses of Littlewoods and GUS had a combined 30 per cent share of the home shopping market and some 70 per cent of the agency market – where customers pay an agent, or rep, an agreed sum in instalments over a period of time. Competition rules stated that any merger which controlled more than 25 per cent of a market had to be referred, which meant that, in the event of a rejection, the Barclays would be forced sellers of the business, a unique situation for them in a deal of this size. The City was surprised that they had eschewed the standard escape clause to give them a get-out if the takeover were blocked by regulators.[27]

By taking this risk, the deal was done quickly and there was no need for the publicly listed GUS to issue a circular to shareholders, since the home shopping and White Arrow delivery business represented less than 25 per cent of its assets.

As one banker told the *Telegraph* at the time: 'That's extremely helpful to the Barclay brothers. Now we don't really know what they have bought, and what buildings and stock they might have got for free. Perhaps all this explains why they were willing to take a bet on the competition authorities.'[28]

Another reason might have been that the Barclays had managed to mitigate the risk by securitizing another £472 million due from unpaid customer balances via an arrangement with the Royal Bank of Scotland.[29] Once again, they had made a fortune having risked very little of their own money. The financial engineering involved was impressive in many ways.

With tens of thousands of new staff and plenty of overlap, the Barclays argued that cost-cutting from the merger would add up to some £58 million – roughly equivalent to the amount made by Littlewoods in 2002 operating profits. Their argument that a forced sale of one part would lead to significant job cuts in a struggling market won the support of local MPs and the Union of Shop, Distributive and Allied Workers (USDAW). They also promised to bring back 250 call centre jobs to the UK from India.[30]

Their argument that a combined GUS-Littlewoods would account for less than 3 per cent of the entire UK non-food market also convinced the Competition Commission, which cleared the deal in January 2004. The decision, backed by Labour trade and industry secretary Patricia Hewitt, surprised City analysts given the fact that seven years earlier the previous Littlewoods management had been blocked from buying Freemans. The brothers, who hated all such bureaucratic reviews, must have been pleased. Their gamble had paid off.

By this time the Barclays had used just £48 million of their own cash and lots of bank debt to buy two retail businesses for a total of £1.34 billion. They had truly become the masters of leveraged finance.

Littlewoods and the GUS home shopping division, which included Kays, Additions and Choice, were merged into a holding company with the simple name of 'Catalogue Group'.

This was quite quickly turned into Littlewoods Shop Direct Group (LSDG), which is when the ownership structure becomes more complicated.

The merger was structured by LSDG issuing £327 million of ordinary shares to its Jersey-based parent company LW Corporation in payment for the Littlewoods business. At the same time, it paid £368 million in cash (financed by bank debt) for 100 per cent of March Corporation (the parent company of March UK, the vehicle used to buy GUS).[31]

So the Barclays had effectively paid themselves £368 million, which dwarfed the £48 million of their own money they had invested since the start of the shopping spree. The Barclay family ended up not only owning a large, if heavily indebted, retail group, but were also £320 million richer.

Not content with their bargain buy, the family's accountants – led by Michael Seal, one of the loyal family retainers known by some as 'apparatchiks', and prized for his accounting and tax expertise – worked out a way of reclaiming some more of the purchase price.

Soon after the Littlewoods purchase, Seal and his clever team of accountants spotted that the business had paid too much VAT to HMRC. The fact that this had been paid out between 1973 and 2004, before they bought the business from the Moores family, did not stop the Barclays claiming it back. This proved to be incredibly lucrative. By 2010, HMRC had paid them some £473 million, based on an overpayment of £205 million and an additional £268 million of simple interest. Not content, their lawyers went on to argue that they should have received compound interest on their overpayment, which added up to some £1.25 billion.[32] If successful, that argument would have set a precedent and created a lucrative loophole that could have seen the British taxpayer landed with an estimated £17 billion from companies claiming for compound interest.

Aidan Barclay said in a statement to the BBC: 'This represents tax taken incorrectly by HMRC and held incorrectly for many years, facts which HMRC publicly recognise and accept. Directors of companies have legal responsibilities and duties to recover and secure their companies' assets from the perspective of each company itself and its various stakeholders. It would be a dereliction of their duties not to pursue repayments which are properly due from HMRC.'[33]

Once Littlewoods and GUS became one company, the family could then set about achieving merger savings. Despite their successful careers as property developers, the Barclays decided to focus on home and online shopping, forsaking the bricks-and-mortar high street shops. Several of those who worked with the brothers cite this as one of the things that showed their genuinely forward-thinking business skills. David Barclay had always been interested in new developments and particularly technology, according to Jeff Randall. 'David was genuinely interested in ideas. He was a bit of a futurologist and liked to see business patterns. You know, what the *FT* calls the long wave. He was interested in the long wave . . . He also saw a business opportunity there that if he could work out what the long wave was going to bring, he could react to it in advance.'[34]

David was delighted that the *Sunday Business* hired Jason Pontin, editor of Silicon Valley magazine *Red Herring*, to write a weekly column. His views on new technologies helped convince the Barclays that the future of shopping was not in physical stores. Besides, something had to be done to pay down net debt levels, which added up to a giddying £541 million in early 2005.[35]

In April 2005, they sold thirty-three of the Index stores to Argos for £44 million and closed down the rest. In July the same year, they sold all 120 Littlewoods stores to ABF, the conglomerate owners of Primark, for £409 million.

The Barclays first used these proceeds to buy back the 5 per cent in LW Finance owned by HBOS; then, together with an equity injection of £152 million from another part of the empire,

LW Corp, they cut net debt from £541 million to £158 million during the financial year ending 30 April 2006.

Their timing seemed impeccable. Almost like a gambler walking away from the tables after making a killing, the Barclays pocketed £168 million – the difference between the £252 million they had put into the business and the £420 million they had taken out in dividends and cash payments sent upstairs. The shop sell-off also reduced both the risk and the presence on the high street at a good time for the coming credit crisis and shift to online shopping. If they had continued to do this for all the businesses they went on to buy, their fortunes post-crash might have been different.

At the same time as moving out of high street property, the family splurged on some prime properties in London. They bought the former home of the Spiritualist Association of Great Britain – one of the grandest mansions on Belgrave Square, home to several embassies – which had fallen on hard times. The membership of the charity, which once included the writer Sir Arthur Conan Doyle, had dwindled while property prices soared. A BVI-registered company called Rose Season Enterprises, ultimately controlled by David Barclay, bought the building at the end of 2010. When it was sold for a profit, the offshore ownership was thought to have avoided a potential capital gain of £5 million.[36]

In 2010, the family also bought Forbes House, an enormous nineteenth-century mansion that the Queen had reportedly said made the nearby Buckingham Palace 'look dull'. The house – one of the few London homes bigger than 50,000 square feet – was reportedly bought for Aidan for just over £40 million in 2010, using companies registered in Jersey and the British Virgin Islands.[37]

When the old Littlewoods headquarters in the centre of Liverpool was closed down, the Littlewoods name vanished from the high street. As of 2023, the only part of the company that retains the name is the retail website, littlewoods.com. A ghost of the historic name lives on in a form of corporate word-play evident in LW Corp and its offshoots. The corporate parent company name was changed from Littlewoods Shop Direct Group to simply Shop Direct in 2008, and then, in 2020, to the Very Group. One consequence of – if not inspiration for – the latter iteration is that the company became harder to track.

Although they had sold off a huge chunk of Littlewoods, removing its name altogether, the Barclays kept hold of GUS's parcel delivery business, which City analysts had expected them to have to sell. Given their bet on the growing strength of home delivery to support online shopping, it must have made sense – but in the years to come, the Barclays would have reason to wish they'd sold it after all.

The Barclays' path would eventually diverge quite sharply from that of Philip Green. They remained friendly until they fell out over journalism. When BHS, a chain store sold by Green in controversial circumstances after he and his wife had extracted £589 million from it, collapsed into administration in 2016 – with the loss of 11,000 jobs and a £571 million pension deficit – Green was dubbed 'the unacceptable face of capitalism' by members of parliament.

In 2018, the *Daily Telegraph*, a newspaper by then owned by the Barclays, was ready to run a story alleging that Green had tried to gag former employees from revealing any details of his allegedly physically and verbally abusive behaviour. Green called on the newspaper's editors and executives in an attempt to block publication, but any entreaties, including to the owners he had once considered friends and business partners, fell on deaf ears.

He then took out a temporary injunction blocking the *Daily Telegraph* from publishing allegations made by five employees, all of whom had received substantial payments and signed non-disclosure agreements after settling their claims.[38] He dropped the case once he had been named in parliament. After he lost the court case, Green called on the *Telegraph* and its owners to do the 'decent thing', which he believed to be respecting the non-disclosure orders and not publishing the story. Green and the board of his Arcadia Group said: 'The *Telegraph* has pursued a vendetta against Sir Philip Green and the employees and management of Arcadia Group for the past nine months, harassing many of its staff and their families at their homes, often at night and at weekends.'[39]

The court case cost Green an estimated £3 million, as he had to pay the *Telegraph*'s fees. He would never talk publicly about his former friends, the Barclays, again.

7.   'Why then do you want to own newspapers?'

The story of how the Barclay brothers came to own the *Daily Telegraph*, becoming the press barons of Brexit Britain in the process, is unlike any of their other takeovers. It was not just that their passion for privacy and liking for legal action – against journalists, among others – made them most unlikely newspaper owners, but that their determination to buy it, just a few short months after they merged two giant retail groups in 2004, marked their position as real power brokers as well as the beginning of the end.

Founded in 1855 by a British army colonel, the *Daily Telegraph*'s motto – 'Was, is, and will be' – reflected its place at the heart of post-war British conservatism. The broadsheet title had broken the news of the Second World War when Germany invaded Poland in 1939, and helped with the covert recruitment of Bletchley Park code-breakers during it. As redolent of a certain kind of Britishness as Earl Grey tea and umbrellas, the *Telegraph* was read by Conservatives with a small and a large 'C'. Its stereotypical reader was a former member of the armed forces who lived in the Shires and enjoyed hunting, shooting and fishing. Talking of money was grubby, but fierce debate about whether jam or cream should be added to scones first was entirely proper. Its loyalty to the Conservative Party earned it a nickname, the 'Torygraph', which it has never shaken off.

A year before its centenary year, in 1954, its proprietor Viscount Camrose died, leaving his younger son, Michael Berry, to take over. 'Young Berry', as the then forty-three-year-old was called, was a product of Eton and Oxford and had been a lieutenant colonel in the artillery in the Second World War.[1] He loved the newspaper and, as Lord Hartwell, was said to have worked six days a week for more than thirty years as both chairman and editor-in-chief.[2] Circulation increased under him to a market-leading 1.5 million readers and he launched a Sunday sister title.

But by the mid-1980s, a decade in which banks were lending millions to property developers, the septuagenarian newspaper proprietor, possibly always more journalist than businessman, could not find anyone to lend him the £105 million he needed to build necessary but expensive new printing works.

In stepped Conrad Moffat Black, an ebullient and erudite Canadian businessman and author. In 1986, Black asked for a 14 per cent stake in return for the loan, but inserted an ownership clause into the terms which allowed him to seize control not long after. A defeated Hartwell, who had not fully considered the consequences of the contract he signed, retired without ever moving into the sparkling new print plant in London Docklands he thought would guarantee his beloved newspaper's future.

Black was an unusual owner of the *Daily Telegraph,* being neither titled nor British. Nevertheless, the forty-one-year-old announced that he would never sell a paper he regarded as the 'passport to other people's drawing rooms'.[3] David Barclay was not to know this when Alistair McAlpine, the Conservative Party treasurer who had become close to David after the Ellerman deal, engineered a meeting between the two men by inviting them both to an annual dinner for party donors just before Christmas that year. Not long after, David made an unsolicited call to Black.

The Canadian remembered that first encounter with fondness in an interview via email thirty-five scandal-filled years later: 'I told David that I was not interested in flipping the *Telegraph* and mentioned that if I had taken the offer he had made me over the telephone when it first came to light that I was buying it, I would have been crazy. He agreed, and I said that the same reasoning still applied, that I was a career newspaper owner and not a chance entrant to this business.' He described the exchange as 'cordial'.[4] It did little to deter David Barclay from owning newspapers.

A few years after Black rejected David's first offer for the *Telegraph*, the Barclay brothers made the inaugural list of the UK's richest people published by the Rupert Murdoch-owned *Sunday Times* in 1989. Despite its publication in the final year of the 'loads-amoney' 1980s – a time when greed became good and fortunes were made in the City and property – the first *Sunday Times* Rich List was dominated by inherited wealth. Topped by the Queen, its 200 members included eleven dukes, six marquesses, fourteen earls and nine viscounts.

The Barclays were among just eighty-six self-made millionaires. At number 27, they were some way behind another self-made man, Robert Maxwell, the attention-grabbing, domineering owner of the *Daily Mirror* and the New York *Daily News*. The year after, in May 1990, Maxwell – a Nazi-surviving Jew born in rural Czechoslovakia – launched an English-language weekly called the *European*. A London-based paper sold across the continent, the title aimed to be Europe's first 'national newspaper' – its first front page trumpeted a future single currency. Eighteen months later, Maxwell was dead, having fallen from his yacht, *Lady Ghislaine*. When he was found to have illegally raided the company's pension funds, his empire was put up for sale.

The Barclays spotted an opportunity, not in Maxwell's established left-leaning titles but in the fledgling pan-European part. In some ways, The *European* seemed an odd target for men who hated the idea of governance by bureaucrats in Brussels. Jeff Randall, who worked for the Barclays for many years as both editor of *Sunday Business* and then the *Telegraph*'s editor-at-large, says, 'They were always against the EU, going back to the late 90s when a Brexit vote wasn't even on the table. They felt Britain was stifled by it and thought Britain should be an independent sovereign state.'[5]

After Maxwell fell from his yacht, the *European*'s 145 employees were made redundant. The then deputy editor Charles Garside – an entrepreneurial northerner who had once advertised his services in the industry trade magazine after he left another Fleet Street title – re-employed a skeleton staff of around thirty-five as freelancers, using his own company, to keep the paper coming out until a buyer was found by the court-appointed administrators. Money was tight; only key journalists and commercial staff were paid for hours worked and the lights went on only during a forty-eight-hour production window.

So it was that Garside was sitting alone in the dark in the Holborn offices of the *European* when the security guard put a call through and the man at the other end of the line introduced himself as Frederick Barclay, calling from a mountainside somewhere.

A short time later, Garside found himself on a plane to Monaco, where he met the brothers in the Hôtel de Paris in the principality's grand central square, next to the casino. On 6 January 1992, just two days after the meeting and almost exactly two months after Maxwell had fallen off his yacht, the Barclays snapped up their first newspaper with a purchase price of less than £5 million. The paper was selling around 225,000 copies but losing almost £200,000 a week.[6]

The choice of title might have been a surprise but the choice of industry was even more so. 'Ask anyone in the City what they know about the Barclay twins, Frederick and David, and the answer is likely to be that they are intensely secretive,' wrote Heather Connon, a journalist at the *Independent*. 'That makes their entry into the media, which is traditionally dominated by flamboyant press barons such as the late Robert Maxwell, look rather out of character.'[7]

The *European* was also effectively a start-up newspaper, not the unloved or under-managed asset typical of the brothers' best-known deals. Somewhat surprisingly, given the fact they had made him a director of Ellerman Lines, Victor Matthews told one reporter: 'I don't think they want to be press barons. They buy things cheap and work the oracle on them – I think that's what they want the *European* for.'[8]

Two factors made the paper an attractive proposition, however, as well as the fact that the brothers were avid newspaper readers. The first was that court-appointed administrators made for keen sellers; the second was that the newspaper industry was going through a revolution of its own in the wake of Rupert Murdoch's attack on the print unions in Wapping. The door was open to new owners looking to cut costs in an industry that had grown used to healthy sales and advertising revenues.

On his first day under Maxwell, Garside had been asked first what alcohol he wanted in his office, and second which newspapers and magazines from around the world he needed to do his job. 'Under the Barclay ownership, the control of cost became real, rather than what life was like under Maxwell, when it was like the last days of Rome.' The Barclays introduced proper cost control and said it would be 'run like a business'.[9] The skeleton staff they inherited was added to over the six years that the brothers owned the *European*, but to about 100 rather than the 145 of their predecessor.

Among the unusual features of the deal was the fact that a member of the Barclays' small executive team spoke at a press conference to announce the takeover. On 9 January 1992, Alan Chamberlain, the former Ellerman finance director appointed as the newspaper's managing director, uttered words unheard at a press conference by anyone before or since when he told reporters: 'There are four or five people close to the Barclays and I am one of them.'

Chamberlain also referred to the forthcoming formation of the European Union as a business opportunity. 'It's a question of timing. It's 1992 and this is an extremely exciting period for Europe and an exciting period for the *European*.'[10]

Just a month after the Barclays bought the newspaper, the Maastricht Treaty effectively created the European Union that still exists today, firing the starting gun for a single currency and closer cooperation between member states. One of the few associates ever to publicly speak of his relationship to the twins, Chamberlain stopped working for them two years later.

As proprietors of the *European*, the brothers' reputation was helped by the behaviour of the megalomaniac who had previously owned it. Maxwell had had a penchant for putting stories and pictures about himself in the paper. Garside has told of how his then editor, John Bryant, stopped Maxwell telling him what stories the paper should run by asking after his helicopter. When he was told with some pride that it was on the roof, Bryant asked: 'And do you tell the pilot how to fly it?'

In contrast, the Barclays proved helpful, according to Garside, using their contacts to help him get interviews, either with the then Lady Thatcher, who was living in David's former home on Chester Square, or with sponsorship at the Monte Carlo Grand Prix. Years later, Garside said: 'I have to say with my hand on heart, they were not interfering, they were bloody helpful, amazingly helpful.'[11]

Garside, who went on to become a long-serving executive at the pro-Brexit *Daily Mail*, denies that the *European* became 'anti EU', insisting that it aimed to report on the increasingly powerful institution at the heart of a 'democratic Europe where elected leaders held sway over unelected bureaucrats'.[12]

By 1997, Garside had been replaced. Andrew Neil, the Scottish former editor of Murdoch's *Sunday Times* who became an important intermediary for the brothers in 1996 (and still worked as chairman of the *Spectator* magazine in 2023), made a series of changes, including bringing back a journalist who had spent time working as an aide to Maxwell called Peter Millar, to become managing editor. Millar resigned a short while later and wrote about the increasingly hostile tone taken by the paper against the EU and its institutions. Helmut Schlesinger, ex-head of the Bundesbank, had told Millar that the paper was simply an 'anti-Europe' propaganda sheet.[13]

The *European*'s last executive editor, Gerry Malone, was overheard pleading with Tory plutocrats: 'This could be the intellectual vehicle of the anti-European movement.' Millar was horrified that Maxwell's dream of an internationalist newspaper for the 'new Europe', born after the fall of the Berlin Wall, had instead become 'a last refuge for a handful of xenophobic nationalists from the ruptured rump of the Tory party'.[14]

Faced with distribution hurdles in a pre-internet era, the *European* was perhaps ahead of its time. It eventually cost the Barclays some £70 million before it closed at the end of 1998, just a month before the launch of the single currency that its launch edition had trumpeted. This unlikely purchase was in some ways a harbinger of what came next.

The cost of closing the *European* did nothing to deter the Barclays from newspaper ownership. By the time the loss-making title closed, the brothers had launched *Sunday Business* as a rival to the *Financial Times*, and bought Scotsman Publications Ltd, which owned the *Scotsman*, the *Edinburgh Evening News* and *Scotland on Sunday*.

They both read a lot of daily newspapers, often testing associates on the stories covered. One early associate, who would learn to never go for a meeting without having a view on that day's papers, said: 'They had a fascination with [newspapers]. It felt . . . it felt like a boys' toys thing, the way some might buy cars.' Or as David had said: 'I owned the toy shop and got to play in it.'[15]

It was always David who liked to talk about journalism and to journalists. Focused on the bottom line, Frederick was the one who had to be convinced about the point of newspaper ownership, especially when they lost money.

When they bought the Edinburgh-based papers in November 1995, the brothers invited all three editors in Scotland for lunch at their newly purchased hotel, the Ritz. They also gave them an unusual gift: a book on privacy called *Freedom, the Individual and the Law*, by Geoffrey Robertson QC. Brian Groom, the then award-winning editor of *Scotland on Sunday*, remembers: 'They were generally very keen on the idea of privacy and the notion of privacy. And I was thinking, why then do you want to own newspapers?'[16]

At the time, the only published picture of the Barclays was a black-and-white one from twenty years earlier that showed them with slicked-back hair and menacing gazes. The *Observer*, the first newspaper to publish this picture, has had a 'do not use' sticker on it ever since.

The three editors enjoyed a stiff gin and tonic to gee themselves up for a meeting with men who they thought looked like gangsters. When 'two quite short, balding, greying old men in glasses' appeared, there was relief all round and they enjoyed a lunch that was less memorable than the farewell. For, at the end of lunch, as the twins got into the lift to return to their suites, one of them said, 'You may never see us again'.[17]

Groom never did. He left the newspaper two years later – at the start of what would become a veritable merry-go-round of editors under the Barclays – without clapping eyes on the brothers again. During those two years, he had regular contact with David Barclay, who continued to send him almost weekly faxes from Monaco. Always marked 'Confidential', the proprietor did not realize that there was only one fax machine at the newspaper, so his private missives would land in the middle of the newsroom before being carried over, with some fanfare, to the editor's office.

Direct instructions were rare but Groom remembers the faxes

as 'a mixture of comments, suggestions, recommendations and sometimes criticism'. The suggestions occasionally made for some unlikely story choices. One led to reports about the medical research into obesity that the brothers had sponsored; another detailed the family's challenge to primogeniture on Sark in the Channel Islands, a good but slightly odd story for a paper focused on Scotland some 500 miles away.

'The idea that the Barclay brothers are hands off with a newspaper is wrong, wide of the mark, in my experience,' recalls Groom, who later spent many years working for the *Financial Times*. 'They were more hands on.' While there were no overt orders to publish, or indeed to spike a story, 'they would definitely let me know if I published something with which they were unhappy'.[18]

The power and influence of newspaper proprietors, like so much involving the family itself, is a world of shadows and wisps, half-nods and suggestions. Owners rarely need to give direct orders to influence content, especially those like the Barclays who delegate the day-to-day running of their businesses to senior and powerful managers. A process of osmosis, in which the parameters are never set but are nonetheless left crystal clear, is not uncommon in newsrooms. The development of an understanding of which stories to ignore as well as promote is far from unusual.

Brian Groom was made aware of the owners' dislike of an interview with the then editor of the *Observer*, Andrew Jaspan, for the *Scotland on Sunday*'s media pages. 'There was no instruction. He [David] just told me they were very upset about it . . . They kind of came to regard Andrew and the *Observer* as an enemy, so the fact that I published an interview with him didn't go down very well.'[19]

Jaspan's *Observer* had run a story that was an early indication of the Barclay brothers' treatment of coverage they did not like. Back in 1995, when the brothers' decision to build an island fortress helped make them more newsworthy proprietors, BBC journalist John Sweeney landed on Brecqhou without an invite. Immediately apprehended, he used the experience in a piece for the *Observer* newspaper as well as for a short-lived late-night BBC Two programme on the media called *The Spin*. He also gave a three-minute interview to BBC Radio Guernsey that landed him in deeper water.

The Barclays launched several legal actions against both Sweeney and the BBC's director-general at the time, John Birt, in both the UK and – largely because of the local radio report – France. They also complained to the Broadcasting Complaints Commission about the invasion of privacy, which was upheld.

The legal complaints against Sweeney alleged invasion of privacy for landing on Brecqhou without an invite, and libel for the way he had talked about their involvement in the Crown Agents scandal. The complaint was not just focused on the abortive landing on Brecqhou but also alleged that, by naming the street on which they lived in Monte Carlo, the brothers had been put at risk of kidnappers. An accompanying picture also infringed their 'absolute right to their own image'.[20]

The *Observer* issued an apology while the case against the BBC was eventually settled out of court with the journalist and broadcaster apologizing for any distress and retracting the defamatory allegations. The BBC paid £11,000 damages to charity while Sweeney made a public apology and paid 20,000 francs (£2,200 at the time) to the Malcom Sargent Cancer Fund for children, a charity chosen by the brothers.

The multiple actions, using a foreign jurisdiction despite the small number of people who could hear the English-language report from the UK, not only sought to punish Sweeney but acted to deter all reporting ever after. Few journalists would ever write about the Barclays again without checking with their lawyers first.

★

The brothers could also defy expectations. When they bought the Scotsman group, the newspapers were proud of their political independence, having never backed a particular party in an election. Rival newspapers predicted a shift to the right now that Thatcherite billionaires were in charge. Instead, the opposite happened.

In 1997, the Edinburgh-based papers owned by the Barclays backed Tony Blair's New Labour Party in a landslide general election victory that all but destroyed the Conservatives north of the border.

Andrew Neil told a House of Lords inquiry into news ownership years later that he had simply told David Barclay which party the three Edinburgh-based editors wanted to support in 1997. After asking whether Neil agreed with the decision, David had said: 'Well, if that's what you think, Andrew, that's what we pay you to do, then go ahead.'

He compared their behaviour favourably to his former boss, Rupert Murdoch, a proprietor who had more or less unilaterally decided which party his papers should support, according to Neil. 'All proprietors interfere in some things at some stage,' he told the assembled peers in 2008. 'Like editors, they have bees in their bonnets and, every now and then, they want to see the paper reflect what they believe and what they would like to see happen.'

He added that there was 'no model . . . no template' for proprietorial involvement.[21] In a separate interview, he insisted that the guidelines signed by his editors which urged them to be supportive of a market economy and the Union between Scotland and England (all policies of the Conservative Party) were his, not his proprietors'.[22]

Groom's recollection of the landmark election coverage supports this. He recalls one of Aidan Barclay's visits to Edinburgh in 1997: 'I said I'm proposing to back Labour and . . . he said that's alright.'[23]

The timing of their ownership of their only newspapers to ever back the Labour Party was also fortuitous perhaps. In 2000, three years after the general election in which Labour wiped out rivals in Scotland and Wales as well as much of England, the Barclays were knighted by the relatively new Labour prime minister, Tony Blair.

The award was for services to charity, having donated some £40 million to causes close to their heart such as medical research. It still comes as a surprise to many that men who were so supportive of Margaret Thatcher were not knighted by the Conservative Party, which had been in power for most of their adult lives.

Two people close to Blair have hinted that the fact the right-wing media owners were knighted under his watch is a matter of some regret. Both suggested that the brothers' gongs were far more likely to be due to the fact that their names were 'going through the system and just happened to fall in Tony's watch'. Tony Blair's office declined to comment.

David used the first double dubbing in modern times to say their investiture was 'a great example of what can be achieved in this country from whatever background or education or humble beginnings'.[24]

He would go on to develop relationships of a sort with several journalists over his long life. Associates attest to the brothers' dislike for the *Guardian*, yet in 2004, when they bought the *Telegraph*, David granted David Leigh, then the investigations editor of the *Guardian*, an exclusive interview in which he appeared to suggest that the true blue newspaper might consider voting Labour.[25]

The comments forced the *Telegraph* to deny there would be any change in its editorial stance. Charles Garside, no longer at the *European*, wrote in the *Guardian*: 'What he actually had said was that the *Telegraph* titles should not be seen as the house organs of the Conservative party.'[26]

The report did not harm the unlikely relationship between

the two Davids. David Barclay had first contacted David Leigh after the *Guardian* journalist wrote a series of critical reports about tax dodging on Sark, the neighbouring island to Brecqhou and a bête noire of the Barclays. David invited Leigh to Brec-qhou, partly in recognition that 'my enemy's enemy is my friend'. Years later, Leigh remembered a pleasant if strange day trip that started with him 'hopping about on the rocks at the back of Sark, waiting for Dr No's launch to turn up and trans-port me to the rocky jetty on Brecqhou, with David coming down in his golf cart'.

The contact continued, with Leigh going on to receive an out-of-the-blue phone call, which started with David's assistant asking if the billionaire could be put through and an unmistakable voice greeting him with ''ello David'.[27]

As well as its unlikely political support, the Scotsman group was fairly unusual for their newspaper assets in that they made the Barclays money. Having paid £85 million for the group in 1995, they sold the newspaper's grand Edwardian headquarters in a separate deal to a hotel developer, who turned the old news-paper offices in a desirable location into a luxury boutique hotel (also called the Scotsman).[28] The Edinburgh-based titles then moved to a purpose-built modern office block called Barclay House, opened by the Queen in 1999, a year before she knighted the brothers.

In December 2005, the Barclays sold Scotsman Publications Ltd for £160 million[29] – almost twice what they had paid for it – to Johnston Press, an eighteenth-century newspaper group that was at the time one of the UK's largest local newspaper publishers. The deal marked the top of the market for UK newspapers and a triumph for the Barclays. Johnston Press collapsed in 2018 amid a disastrous decline in local newspaper revenues. The newspaper's former head office, Barclay House, is now home to the digital gaming giant behind *Grand Theft Auto*.

*

The money made by the *Scotsman* would be dwarfed by how much the brothers spent on buying the *Telegraph*, even though they had hoped to buy it for a song.

In 2003, almost seventeen years after he had first met David Barclay, the inimitable Conrad Black was in trouble. He owned the *Telegraph* via a private company that had a majority of voting shares in Hollinger International, the newspaper's immediate parent which was listed on the New York Stock Exchange. Black was under investigation by Hollinger's shareholders over fraudulent payments to his private companies. The brothers spotted an opportunity in the ensuing legal drama, in which Black faced not just a cash squeeze but criminal charges. David Barclay sent a fax on 23 May 2003 marked 'Private and Confidential' that said: 'I wish to register our interest should you contemplate any serious change in your UK interests.'[30]

Black, still fighting to retain control, fired back: 'Conditions are quite manageable. No assets are for sale.' He rebuffed a further approach from David a month later.

David kept asking. In November, a tetchy Black wrote:

Dear David,

You have made your desire to buy the Telegraph abundantly clear. You may recall that when we actually met we agreed that I would be mad to sell it. In the unlikely event that my views on this subject change, I will not forget your interest.

Please keep in mind how tiresome you would find it if every time I saw a negative article about you in the press I wrote of my unquenchable desire to buy an asset of yours that is not for sale. I'm happy to hear from you, but not on this subject again, please.[31]

David persisted: he would go on to describe owning the *Telegraph* as a 'once in a lifetime opportunity'.[32]

A week later, amid reports of a more serious investigation by the US Securities and Exchange Commission, Black changed his mind. When asked why thirty-five years later, Black replied via email: 'They were the most insistent party, and they had a refreshing informality, as they were so familiar with the asset. I changed my mind reluctantly but in response to the gravity of the circumstances generated by the corrupt American criminal justice system.'

Asked why such reclusive men would want to buy such a landmark newspaper, an approving Black wrote: 'It was a very influential and respected and profitable company, with widely admired titles. It was a perfectly natural ambition for very wealthy men who had been avid and approving *Telegraph* readers, (David told me) all their conscient lives.'[33]

On 3 November 2003, Black had decided to fax David about 'a 'thought worthy of discussion'.[34] In response, Aidan got straight on a flight to New York to meet him.[35] The communications had something of the cloak and dagger about them right from the start and not just because this seemed to be David's preferred mode of doing business. 'They had to be handled carefully because of the illegal telephone intercepts regularly applied by the FBI,' said Black. 'David sent a senior emissary to meet us in New York and Toronto and this moved things along.'

Apart from this meeting, and talking to 'Freddy twice when David was unavailable', Black dealt almost exclusively with David via telephone and faxes – in the latter case often on paper headed with a map of Brecqhou.[36]

Black's 'thought' was to sell his controlling stake of the *Telegraph* to the Barclays without going through a sales process run by the public shareholders and company directors. The subsequent court case heard how this would benefit him but not his fellow shareholders, who first heard about it when the Barclays announced their purchase of the *Telegraph* for US $346 million in January 2004, two months after Black's missive and the same month as their retail merger was cleared.[37] This $346 million deal, worth £260 million at the time, was below even the bottom end of the range of values Hollinger's bankers had come up with.[38]

The Hollinger International directors and shareholders were furious and filed a suit against Black, Hollinger Inc. and Press Holdings International Ltd, the Barclays' Jersey-based acquisition vehicle, over the secret negotiations. There would be a three-day trial in Delaware, where Hollinger was incorporated.

On 26 February 2004, Judge Leo Strine blocked the Barclay agreement and issued a 130-page verdict, which was scathing about Black, who went on to be found guilty of fraud and obstruction of justice and was sentenced to six and a half years in prison. A proper auction was likely to attract a far higher price for control of such a renowned newspaper from those willing 'to enjoy the prestige and access to the intelligentsia, the literary and social elite, and high government officials that comes with that control', the judge wrote.

Strine was also sharply critical of the Barclays. 'In this litigation, the Barclays have portrayed themselves as innocents, who have tried to do right by all . . . But this expression of interest was unaccompanied by the kind of candor necessary for me to draw the inference of highly honorable conduct that the Barclays desire', he wrote, accusing them of being 'less than fully candid'.[39]

David had failed to attend court to testify, citing a neurological complaint he had suffered from for 'many years', a fact the judge contrasted with 'his daily and vigorous pursuit of the *Telegraph* assets over many months'. The judge also found the evidence of Frederick and Aidan less than satisfactory. The latter 'admitted at many points that he did not know what his father had actually done or why'.[40]

David was so furious with this that he took legal advice and issued a rare and lengthy public statement criticizing Judge Strine's comments as 'damaging, unwarranted and uncalled-for'. He took particular umbrage at the judge's comments about his health, and insisted that Strine had since clarified that he had not intended to 'cast doubt on the sincerity of the representation that it was medically inadvisable for David Barclay to be deposed'.[41]

In their most public acquisition of a high-profile business, the Barclays had engaged in behind-closed-doors negotiations with a compromised and much-criticized seller. It was not perhaps the way they would have wanted to burst into public consciousness with their once-in-a-lifetime purchase.

The resulting public auction for Hollinger, which included other assets such as the Chicago newspaper groups as well as the Telegraph, attracted a huge number of bids, with 116 parties signing confidentiality agreements. Nine bidders were invited to continue to the second round, including the Barclays.

The sixty-nine-year-old twins left Aidan, with his by now trademark red braces and cigar, to lead the negotiations at the Ellerman offices in St James's, alongside his brother Howard and Rigel Mowatt, a South African executive who would become one of the small coterie of ultra-loyal 'apparatchiks'. They also hired a team of bankers from UBS, including Ken Costa, a veteran financier and future Conservative Party donor.[42]

In his dealings with them, Black had called the Barclays 'the most insistent party',[43] and few of those working with them on the subsequent bid were left in any doubt of their desire to win, even at a price elevated by competition from the owners of the Daily Mail, the German publishing giant Axel Springer, and several private equity groups.

Jeremy Deedes even spoke in favour of them in a call to the Hollinger directors handling the process.[44] The son of Bill, Lord Deedes, who had been the editor under Lord Hartwell and wrote his last column for the Telegraph in 2007, when he was ninety-four, Jeremy was a popular chief executive brought back from early retirement during the Hollinger imbroglio. But in the end, this support mattered far less than the fact that when the sealed bids were opened in the Manhattan boardroom of Hollinger

International on the afternoon of 22 June 2004, the Barclays had offered $18 million more than their nearest rival, 3i.[45]

Five months after Strine's verdict, the Telegraph Media Group, which included the *Daily Telegraph*, its Sunday sister and the *Spectator* magazine, was sold for £665 million to the Barclays. The price was £400 million more than their original backroom deal.

Their first attempt to buy Hollinger Inc., Black's controlling company, was made by a Barclays vehicle, Press Holdings, and came without the promise of 100 per cent control. After Judge Strine blocked the deal, the Barclays set up another UK holding company called Press Acquisitions to join the auction for the Telegraph Media Group.

On 16 January 2004 Frederick and David signed a personal guarantee to Bank of Scotland, making them personally liable for any failure to repay.[46] This document was witnessed by Siri Watson,[47] who would go on to have a senior if shadowy role on one of their newspapers.

For the larger amount, signed on 4 July, the new debt was guaranteed by the assets of a by-now fully owned Telegraph Media Group. The final £665 million purchase price was funded not only by raising £272 million of bank debt in Press Acquisitions (they had already agreed a stand-by credit facility of £285 million with Bank of Scotland to do so),[48] but also an extra £404 million from a Jersey-based parent company, May Corporation. In a year in which the Barclay family got the go-ahead to merge GUS and Littlewoods into a huge home shopping empire, it was never entirely clear where this extra money came from. In the absence of published accounts, the money was conjured from lands offshore but as subsequently became clear, increased bank debt smoothed the way. Both the size and nature of this debt – the price of wanting this 'passport to other people's drawing rooms' – would only grow in significance.

Newspapers were always about more than money though,

especially for David. According to Jeremy Deedes, the staff of the *Spectator* had offered 'a hell of a lot of money' for the influential but barely profitable magazine. 'David said absolutely no chance whatsoever. He regarded it [the *Spectator*] as the jewel at the top of the crown and that there was no price he would sell at.'[49]

As for Black, he remained appreciative of David Barclay to the end. 'I found him direct, courteous, straightforward, a man of his word. In any case, I have a policy of never saying anything uncomplimentary about people to whom we have sold assets.'[50]

The purchase of one of the best-known and -regarded newspapers in Britain did not just cost more money than the Barclays had hoped, it also led to an explosion in press interest.

Most articles sought to lift the lid on two men most often dubbed 'reclusive'. A long and detailed piece by Bloomberg prompted Aidan to issue a statement that said: 'We do not consider our financial, business or charitable affairs to be of public interest as we are not answerable to shareholders, or indeed members of the public. We would prefer it if you did not write about us at all.'[51]

The Times put a dedicated team of reporters onto the Barclays, quashing any hope the family might have had of a 'publishers' agreement' – in which all other British proprietors put a kibosh on articles about fellow owners – with a series of articles spread over several days.

In the end, it was a throwaway line in a 300-word sidebar – a short companion piece to the resulting three-day investigation – that caused the Barclays to launch legal action. Under an initial headline of 'The bargain hunters who stalk owners in distress', Dan Sabbagh, the then media editor, had written: 'The Barclays often take advantage of owners in distress to pick up assets on the cheap.' As evidence, he mentioned the abortive back room deal for the *Telegraph*.[52]

Again, the Barclays raised eyebrows by suing for criminal libel in France. The London-based newspaper shipped about 3,500 copies to France, a tiny fraction of its circulation. Their lawyers argued that the French courts offered speedier redress and insisted on a *droit de réponse*, or right of reply. Robert Thomson, the then editor of *The Times*, argued that his paper was defending 'press freedom in Europe'.[53] Members of Scotland Yard's extradition squad turned up in Wapping to issue Thomson and Sabbagh with a summons. They were filmed by employees at a newspaper that seemed to be enjoying the attention.

It took more than two years and expensive trips to the Palais de Justice in Paris for a settlement. Much of the hearing involved a discussion of the different meaning of 'distress' in both French and English. Two British newspapers squaring off along the Seine added a layer of farce to the proceedings.

Finally, on 9 February 2007, the Barclays withdrew their complaint after *The Times* agreed to publish a clarification on page 61 stating that the offending article had not meant to suggest, 'as some people may have understood it', that the brothers 'exploit vulnerable people in financial difficulty in an underhand and unfair way for commercial gain'.[54] No money was said to have changed hands.

Few journalists could square the Barclays' ownership of newspapers with their hatred for publicity and fierce control over their image and information, all patrolled by the country's most expensive lawyers. Even a journalist who was fond of them described their desire for privacy as 'almost loopy'.

John Sweeney, who had been pursued by the Barclays through courts in France as well as the UK, never grew fond. 'One of the things that gets my goat is their hypocrisy. If you own a newspaper you have ticked the publicity box. Rupert Murdoch understands that. He gets that he is in the public eye, it's part of the game. The Barclay twins own a newspaper, which is more and more partisan, and hide behind thickets of libel lawyers.'[55]

Dominic Lawson, one of their many former editors – but the

only one whose father was one of Margaret Thatcher's chancellors – told a House of Lords inquiry: 'I think the Barclay brothers want a quiet life, do not want any aggro, want it all to be nice and smooth, and that is all very well but you should not own a newspaper if you do not want any aggravation. It is the wrong line of business.'[56]

Legal action may have made rival newspapers more cautious but it did not stop them reporting on the brothers' stewardship, particularly after the once almost static *Telegraph* turned into a maelstrom of management upheaval.

Aidan, installed as chairman of the group, appointed *Daily Mail* executive Murdoch MacLennan as chief executive of the Telegraph Media Group. With his soft Scottish burr and frequent demands for more cost-cuts, MacLennan became known as the 'whispering assassin'. Within a year of the takeover, 300 jobs out of 1,500 had been lost. In the eighty-one years before the Barclays bought the *Telegraph*, there had been just six editors; there were another six in the next eleven years.[57] There were three editors in 2014 alone.

Despite the increasing use of non-disclosure agreements, there appeared to be no shortage of former editors and executives willing to talk about how the home of conservative thought was being traduced. Lawson, again, wrote: 'The management of the *Telegraph* reminds me of a chimpanzee that has captured a Swiss watch. In its clumsy attempts to try and understand what makes it tick, the brute completely destroys it.'[58]

The revered Bill Deedes was even quoted calling the owners a 'stinking mob' in conversations with his biographer. When the term was changed in a review for the Barclay-owned *Spectator* to make it seem as though he was talking about the staff, the writer Peregrine Worsthorne went public.

The family took no notice of such criticism and focused instead on trying to recoup the extra cost of buying the *Telegraph* in the first place. One of the first things Aidan did was sell off the paper's renowned wine cellar, marking a new era in editorial lunches. More significantly, in August 2007 they sold the Telegraph Media Group's headquarters on Victoria's Buckingham Palace Road to a Greek businessman called Achilleas Kallakis for a reported £224 million.[59] Kallakis, who lived between London and Monaco, was convicted of fraud against AIB bank seven years later,[60] but his contribution to the family coffers must have be helpful. By 2014, however, the bank debt held in Press Acquisitions had been reduced by just £78 million, which presumably left some £150 million for the family either to spend or use to pay off another debt.

At the same time, an ageing readership and a shift to cheaper online advertising was piling on the pressure across the whole industry. In the ten years after the Barclays bought the *Telegraph*, print circulations across the newspaper industry almost halved and the impact of declining revenues from both circulation and advertising was intense. Insiders shared a macabre joke that the *Telegraph* did not have long as, with every year, half its readers died.

Serious cost cutting of staff – and not just wine reserves – meant that operating profits almost doubled to £60 million a year in the first five years under Barclay ownership. There were, it has to be said, also editorial successes during this time. But cost cuts continued, ensuring profits stayed above £50 million for four years, until 2015, before falling to a low of £7.8 million in 2018, the year after Murdoch MacLennan stepped down as chief executive.

As the pressure to meet profit targets and therefore reassure lenders increased, journalists talked of more aggressive commercial demands from senior managers. Some of it was hardly unexpected: the largely pro-market *Telegraph* speaking up for the value of banks and the City to the British economy at the height of the financial crisis, for example. But complaints from within about the increasing influence of the commercial department intensified after 2014, an influence that ran counter to the church-and-state distinction in quality journalism.

There were several instances of important advertisers or busi-nesses with links to the family businesses being treated differently by the *Telegraph* compared with their rivals. The *Telegraph* was seen as less critical of China's treatment of Hong Kong, for exam-ple, after it started publishing a monthly English-language supplement paid for by the Central Propaganda Department of the Chinese Communist Party. The deal reportedly earned the group £750,000 a year.[61]

Matters came to a head with a series of scandals involving another international banking group (not Bank of Scotland) and a multi-award-winning journalist turned unlikely whistle-blower. The son of a brigadier, educated at Sherborne and Cambridge, Peter Oborne was appointed the *Telegraph*'s chief political commentator in 2010. A corduroy-wearing, church-attending, conservative cricket enthusiast, Oborne was a *Telegraph* man from central casting, the sort of one-nation Tory behind its nickname.

After one of his stories about HSBC bank was spiked on what he believed were dubious grounds, Oborne started to notice how often critical stories about the group were discouraged, even stor-ies widely covered by rivals. When, in 2015, an international investigation into wide-scale tax evasion at the bank prompted huge amounts of coverage in other papers, the *Telegraph*'s deci-sion to bury the news was the final straw.

On 17 February 2015, Oborne resigned and wrote an excoriat-ing piece for the openDemocracy website in which he accused the *Telegraph* of committing 'a fraud on its readers' by putting commercial demands over its duty to cover the news. The *Tele-graph* under the Barclay Brothers, he wrote, 'has been placing what it perceives to be the interests of a major international bank above its duty to bring the news to *Telegraph* readers'.[62]

His assertion about readers needing a 'microscope' to read about HSBC's alleged wrongdoing in the *Telegraph* was supported by a subsequent study by the Media Standards Trust, which found that there were significantly fewer articles about the global scandal than in any comparable UK newspaper. The articles that were published focused on the political or economic fallout from the story rather than any alleged wrongdoing at the bank.

Having noticed how negative articles about the bank had been discouraged since 2013, Oborne was told by one *Telegraph* executive that HSBC was 'the advertiser you literally cannot afford to offend'.

The relationship with the bank was not just based on advertising, however. In December 2012, Yodel, the Barclays' loss-making delivery arm that had been spun out of the retail business, had borrowed £250 million from HSBC.[63] In 2008, the bank was also involved in the huge securitization programme for Very, the name of the business known formerly as both Littlewoods and Shop Direct, to the tune of £200 million, a sum which was still outstanding in 2015.[64]

The Telegraph group rejected the allegations. In 2012, Aidan Barclay had testified to the Leveson Inquiry into the culture, practices and ethics of the British press – set up in the wake of the News International phone hacking scandal – that company policy was to set good governance standards and not to interfere in editorial content. The damage from the HSBC allegations would be difficult to shake however.

Meanwhile, the extent of the industry decline was there for all to see in the book value of the newspaper. The original value of Press Acquisitions' investment in the Telegraph Media Group was £736.8 million. This valuation was written down by £280.7 million in 2013, a further £180.8 million in 2015, and a further £135 million in the following two years. By 2018, when the family was facing a cash squeeze in other parts of the business, some £569.9 million of the original valuation of more than £700 million had been wiped out. The Telegraph Media Group was last valued at just £164.9 million,[65] a fraction of the £665 million the Barclays paid for it. The debt to pay for it had not shrunk in the same way.

8. The Neighbours from Hell

When David Barclay wanted to express an opinion to his editors, he tended to fire off a fax – a habit he continued with officials on Sark, the island next to Brecqhou. In twenty-five years, he never once attended the parliamentary meetings that were his right as a landowner, restricting himself to a blizzard of faxes and law-suits instead. After buying the *Telegraph*, he also used newspapers in his campaign against the island and its denizens, a campaign which most often dealt with taxation and control.

The Barclays have often been described as 'eccentric' in news-paper profiles,[1] but it was their fight with a tiny island in the British Channel that always seemed the most peculiar.

After the Barclays unexpectedly dropped their bid for Brec-qhou's independence at the start of the new millennium, Sark's lawmakers voted to abolish primogeniture and set up a review committee to consider constitutional reform. The last feudal state in Europe had been encouraged to look at changing its centuries-old system of governance on the island – and to move, with the rest of the Western world, to a democratic system despite the tiny size of its electorate. As part of this review, parliamentarians had to change a system of taxation that effectively upheld the archaic system of feudalism. The review considered a tax based on the size of each property as well as a personal charge for any resident who failed to declare their worldwide assets. The brothers con-sidered this a direct attack on extremely wealthy men living in enormous castles, of which there were just two locally.

Any islanders who might have hoped that the new neighbours would stop objecting to Sark were quickly disabused of the notion. 'We are more than willing to make our contribution to the community of Sark, but not to be discriminated against as far as tax is concerned,' David wrote to the chair of the financial review committee, Jonathan Brannam, in September 2002 in a fax addressed from the Montaigne apartment building, on the Avenue de Grande Bretagne in Monte Carlo. 'We are unlikely to receive a proper and equitable hearing on a debate of such nature in an unelected feudal Parliament, whose members have a vested interest in maintaining the status quo and some of whom have a history of financial opportunism. Imposing a tax on Brecqhou and its residence is tantamount to subsidising their existence.'

Sark's parliamentarians, perhaps conscious that the Barclays were already paying about £50,000 a year in property tax, agreed a concession to exclude the inhabitants of any island separated from Sark by a clear stretch of water from this annual personal capital tax. Although this concession did not refer to the brothers, the only other inhabitants of nearby islands were the puffins found on a rock called L'Etac.

Following this concession, David's fax sent in May 2003 was far warmer. 'Common sense' had prevailed. 'Our relationship with Sark will be very much enhanced and indeed Sark will benefit much more as a whole, by the recommendation by your committee that only property tax should apply to the island of Brecqhou,' he wrote, before promising to support the island's transport lifeline, Sark Shipping, and the proposed school and island hall building project.

Sark's children had been taught separately until then – the boys in the small stone building used as the island's parliament and girls near the two-person jail. An area with plentiful space for playing fields as well as a community centre and hall had been identified in the middle of the island, just off the main road to the Seigneurie. A generous inheritance from a long-term resident had kick-started the campaign to build a new school and island hall, but the project was running out of cash.

Determined to show his support, David went to Sark with

Frederick, his wife Reyna, and the twins' younger brother Douglas to visit the proposed site in September 2003, despite being too poorly to go inside.[2] He rested on a stone outside the unfinished island hall while Frederick went inside with the chair of trustees, John Carré, who told him about the funding shortfall. Afterwards, during coffee with Carré, David agreed to double the £100,000 they had already donated to the hall, there and then.

David had previously mentioned, in another letter to a member of Chief Pleas, 'in passing' the offer of a £250,000 loan to the Sark school project 'free of interest and without security, which shows a willingness to be good neighbours and make a serious contribution to the community'.

This use of both carrot and stick would prove a common tactic, but the attempt at conciliation did not last.

As time went on, members of Chief Pleas would 'get threatening letters about once a month from the Barclay lawyers' concerning its decisions, according to the Seigneur Michael Beaumont,[3] who sat at the head of parliament but without voting rights, a little like the King.

Although the early lawsuits were often brought on behalf of both brothers, it was David who took the lead in writing strongly worded articles for newspapers, including the *Guardian*, about the evils of feudalism.

Between 20 October 2005 and the end of July 2007, before the launch of the Barclays' own newspaper on Sark, David Barclay signed his name to nine articles attacking feudalism and Sark's governance in the *Guernsey Press*.[4] Most took up a whole page; some were edged with a thick black line as though for a death notice. Headlines included 'My Hopes for the Future of Sark' and 'The Unacceptable Face of Feudalism'.

Any attempt to prove the pen was mightier than the sword did not ignore the power of the law however. It would take an entire book to detail all the legal actions launched on Sark and its inhabitants, especially by David, for whom the island soon began to seem like an obsession. The legal onslaught against his island neighbours, which started in 1996 with the bid for independence, did not really stop until he died twenty-five years later. As Christopher Beaumont, the current Seigneur of Sark, put it years later, the Barclays 'weaponised the law – they use the law like a cat burglar uses a cosh'.[5]

An impressive array of London-based lawyers launched ground-breaking battles on matters of constitutional importance, some of which involved the House of Lords and the UK's Supreme Court, as well as the European Court of Human Rights. Then there were pages of sternly worded warnings from lawyers, often threatening serious consequences for seemingly petty misdemeanours. Jennifer Cochrane, the then seventy-two-year-old who produced the parish newsletter from her living room, received a letter from local solicitor Gordon Dawes – who cites his work for David Barclay prominently on his website[6] – after using a picture of the Barclays chatting in a public lane. One local bar manager was accused of slander after displaying a satirical poem about Dawes and two senior local Barclay employees in the pub. Yet another letter accused the postmistress of wrongdoing after she refused to stock the Barclays' newspaper. When Stephen Henry, a septuagenarian seriously ill with lung cancer, arrived home from hospital, he found a letter from Dawes demanding to know if he had written an online attack on the brothers.[7] (Dawes subsequently apologized for this last incident.)

Because they had lost the battle to prove that Sark had no jurisdiction over Brecqhou, the brothers realized that even a democratically elected parliament could increase their tax bill. They petitioned the Queen in 2005 because they did not like the way the island's democracy was being planned.

Dawes drafted a memorandum of understanding, asking the Sark legislature to promise not to 'impose or seek to impose any other or any new taxes, charges, licence fees or fiscal measures of whatsoever kind upon Brecqhou'. He told the *Guardian* that this was due to fears 'that Sark would seek to turn Brecqhou into a cash cow in the crudest of ways'.[8] The memorandum also asked that all 'existing and future Sark legislation relating to the govern-ance of day-to-day life on Sark shall not have force and effect in the Island of Brecqhou' – a sort of blanket ban on any govern-ance whatsoever.

It wasn't long before the islanders started to see signs of a con-spiracy. How else to explain why such wealthy, powerful men would be so vexed about an anomalous island of 500 souls in the middle of the Channel? The memorandum, which was rejected, only served to increase the suspicion that the Barclays wanted their own sovereign realm. They wanted to rule over their own domain, a step above the 'latter day earls' of Rivett's biography.

Paul Armorgie, former conseiller (or parliamentarian) and manager of Sark's Stocks Hotel, said just before David died: 'I believe they genuinely felt . . . that they could be in full control of Sark, and masters of their own destiny, responsible only to them-selves. They could make their own rules and so, effectively they could have their own mini-state. My theory is that this is all about their own domain. Like a mini-Monaco with privacy, secrecy, tax benefits and to be in control of all of those things.'[9] Sark, with its tiny population, handful of parliamentarians and a seeming pen-chant for tax avoidance (given the Sark Lark), must have seemed like an easy target if this were the case.

Such theories flourished on Sark. 'Their ultimate goal was to control Sark,' said one long-time resident. 'They could have got control of Chief Pleas, passed all sorts of legislation allowing helicopters and big houses on long leases, imported other people with a similar interest in tax avoidance. The only thing that could have stopped them would have been the need for Royal Assent but they could use the media to control the privy council. That's what the *Telegraph* is for.'

'What they want here is . . . a mini Monaco,' said another.[10]

Almost every opponent of the Barclays on Sark believed they

wanted to create a sort of 'mini Monaco', except with no prince to rule over them. According to this theory, Sark – an island that is 2.5 times bigger than Monaco but just a forty-five-minute helicopter ride from London – could fly under the radar of international authorities trying to clamp down on offshore jurisdictions. Guernsey, after all, had a financial services commission to keep an eye on offshore transactions,[11] regulation more belatedly applied to Sark, which also has only two police officers.

A less conspiratorial view is that the brothers saw Sark as a genuine investment opportunity. 'My guess is it was a commercial venture for David. They could buy properties on the island, change the Constitution for the better, build better infrastructure, encourage tourism, and therefore the value of these properties would go up,' said one old associate, who themselves had never been to Sark.[12] Attempts at making sense of an interest that often bordered on the obsessive would continue for years.

The view that the brothers saw Sark as a way of making money was bolstered in January 2007, when they started buying land there. By this time, Sark's first-ever democratic elections were all but assured after a vote to end feudalism. The first properties they bought were along Sark's west coast, which overlooked Brecqhou. They included a large, unfinished gabled house built by Jess Hester, whose stepson Carl would go on to win three Olympic medals for Great Britain riding horses, and his wife, Claire, who also owned the island estate agency and building company. The Hesters eventually sold their house, their building company and their estate agency to the Barclays.

In 2008, Frederick testified in a local court case that David was the main driver of all the purchases on Sark. Whoever was ultimately responsible, the Barclays made several other purchases along what passes for a main road in Sark: a wide dirt track running from the harbour to the Avenue, home to shops and a post office. They bought four of the island's six hotels. By the end of the year, they owned 27 per cent of the freeholds on the island, including Brecqhou. One islander called it a 'financial blitzkrieg'.

As well as government by landowners, the feudal system insisted that land was owned by individuals. The consent (or congé) of the Seigneur for property sales dated back to Helier de Carteret's approval for his forty garrison members. Papers relating to their sales show that all eight of the main tenements and properties bought by the Barclays in 2007 and 2008 were owned by individuals, usually David alone – though one, the Jaspellerie, was bought by both David and Frederick. Other 'owners' of the properties included David's son Duncan and two of their longest-serving local employees, Kevin Delaney and Mark Harrisson.

The brothers were renowned for having a nose for a bargain, but the prices listed for their purchases on Sark looked like a real steal. To give one example, they bought the Aval du Creux – a huge tenement including the hotel and several houses – for £25,000 in early 2007. The same property had been bought by Duncan Spence, who had made a fortune from greeting cards, for £950,000 back in 2001. This was less likely due to some gravity-defying real estate deflation on Sark than to the fact that the Barclays had agreed far more expensive long leases on the same properties. By doing so, they avoided paying the feudal tax known as a treizieme to the Sark Seigneur, as leases were exempt from such a charge in a feudal system based on land ownership, not lease. The Barclays bought seven tenements (essentially Sark freeholds), previously valued at more than £4 million in total, for less than £200,000 over a two-year period.

By paying less than £50,000 for each property, the Barclays also fell below the limit that had been set by Chief Pleas in order to encourage young families to build their own homes. There was no such limit on the value of a leasehold, which in any other market would be less valuable than the freehold. In this way, the Barclays simply exploited a loophole in the system, while the new constitutional reforms – which would have taxed leases as well – were snarled up by their legal challenges, among other things. Using leaseholds in this way also denied the Seigneur what would be his last year of claiming a treizieme ahead of the elections set for 2008.

It confirmed the fears of some islanders, who had now changed the system so that the property taxes went to the local Exchequer rather than the Seigneur, that the Barclays simply did not want to pay any tax. Jennifer Cochrane told *Private Eye* in 2007: 'Sark is being cheated of income.' Richard Axton, the academic and Sark enthusiast who had been instrumental in setting up the historical society, the island's first observatory and even a dairy business, said: 'The structure of the sales of the tenement was changed so that the island got peanuts.'[13]

After exploiting a taxation loophole in the last year of feudalism, all Barclay properties were subsequently transferred from individual ownership to a company, Sark Estate Ltd, which had a registered office in Tortola in the British Virgin Islands, an offshore jurisdiction with a PO Box number. Several signed and witnessed documents show that, by 2014, all the properties owned by the brothers or individuals connected to them on Sark had been transferred to this offshore body.[14]

Under feudal laws, only individuals could buy tenements, but it was not the Barclays who first broke this ancient compact. Another company had been listed as the owner of a relatively small freehold property, Clos de Camps, before the Barclays started to buy property on the island, due to what has been described as an administrative error. Although the Sark authorities insisted that the Clos de Camps owner agreed to some personal obligations in order to make amends, the precedent had been set. It did not take long for the Barclays to work out that it was now perfectly acceptable for offshore companies to own property on the island which had once insisted on individual responsibility.

*

Cunning tax wheezes on their own were unlikely to have ruined the Barclays' relations with all the neighbours, given the island's history. What really ended any chance of détente was their decision to launch a newspaper.

One of the first properties the Barclays bought, at the beginning of 2007, was called La Friponnerie, which roughly translates as 'cheating' or 'joke' in English. In this property they installed Kevin Delaney, the man who had so impressed them at the Ritz that they brought him to Brecqhou. He has lived on Sark ever since.

Born Patrick Delaney on 9 April 1957 at Oldchurch Hospital in Romford, Essex, he was the eldest of five boys in an Irish Catholic family. Once employed at the car factory, he soon went into property refurbishment, working for Adams and Palmer, which specialized in 'classical interiors'.[15]

A lean, dark-haired man with darting eyes, Delaney was admired by the brothers, particularly David. By 2007, he was running the building company the brothers bought from Jess Hester as well as Sark Estate Management. His subsequent career shift to newspaper editor, publisher and 'proprietor' is less than clear.

Sark News, which launched in September 2007, was owned by Brecqhou Developments, a Barclay company set up in 1994 and registered in Guernsey. Its first editor was identified only as Mrs S. Oliver, who from 2007 wrote several letters to the *Guernsey Press* arguing with anyone who opposed the Barclays. Letters in reply from islanders asked who S. Oliver was, as no one on the island had met her – unusual on such a tiny island. She became a 'mystery' and never introduced herself by a first name. Later, it was rumoured to be Siri, perhaps coincidentally the first name of the woman who had countersigned a personal guarantee for the brothers in 2004, and also the wife of the Barclays' yacht captain.

The newspaper launch coincided with the Barclays inviting seventy Sarkees and guests of their hotels over to Brecqhou for tours of their by then extensive gardens, while David Barclay wrote a campaign leaflet of sorts: 'I am sure you have heard a number of malicious rumours and gossip regarding our intentions, which are completely unfounded . . . our long term policy is to improve the future prosperity and preserve the independence of both Brecqhou and Sark.' Duncan, David's third son, who played a greater role on Sark than he ever did in the business – occasionally attending Chief Pleas on his father's behalf – argued that his father's motives were altruistic.

To this day, there are people on the island who are supportive of the Barclays – not just those who worked for them or sold property to them, but also those who welcomed inward investment and employment. While most of the island's landowners tended to be wealthy, either from inheritance or a previous career, the majority of its residents were working class, earning a living from tourism or fishing while enjoying the lifestyle on a beautiful island just five kilometres long. They were not all huge fans of the old ways – particularly its complicated land tenure – and had a nickname for their landowning elite, calling them 'the Raj'.

Yet the excesses of the paper, which campaigned against both the 'deeply undemocratic, self-interested and self-serving regime' and islanders on an individual level, united many Sarkees, whether rich or poor.[16] Few islanders spoke warmly of a paper which was delivered free through their doors despite its cover price. Any resident who asked not to receive it could expect a negative story in the next week's edition, alongside the usual victims: parliamentarians and Lieutenant Colonel Reg Guille, the island's chief law enforcer and speaker.

But it was the Seigneur who really came in for the worst press. Michael Beaumont was accused of having Nazi sympathies and of being cruel to his wife by the Sark newspaper, which in its tumultuous history had at least three names – including the *Sark Newsletter* and *Sark News* – as did so many of their businesses. After he criticized the Barclays in Chief Pleas, three subsequent entire editions of the paper were devoted to criticizing him.

His supporters were accused of involvement in the Sark Lark, their every personal indiscretion fair game.

The newspaper would go on to compare several islanders, many of whom still remembered the occupation during the Second World War, to Nazis. The irony of such a newspaper being owned by men who fiercely upheld their own right to a private life with the full weight of the most expensive lawyers in London was not lost on many.

Aware of his anachronistic position in the upcoming democracy and exhausted by the attacks, Beaumont revealed in his unpublished autobiography that he tried to 'resign' from his position in November 2007, ahead of the first-ever elections, writing to the Queen and the then Lord Chancellor Jack Straw via Guernsey's Lieutenant Governor. 'Rightly or wrongly I still have a feeling of responsibility which I am unable to fulfill and at 80+ it is time to retire. I wished to avoid the Barclays getting full control of the island which I believe to be their aim. My only defence would be to return my lease to the Crown.' After a meeting with Straw in January 2008 Beaumont decided to stay as the titular head of state, with a stipend of £28,000 replacing his treizieme.

A few months ahead of the historic election scheduled for 10 December 2008, the brothers decided to sue to return the £200,000 given years earlier to replace the decrepit island hall and improve the local school facilities. David argued that he had not realized there would be a bar on site, which made the island hall a 'commercial enterprise' and was therefore unacceptable. The brothers insisted that they had always kept their business and charity as 'separate issues'. Islanders said the bar had been in the plans all along.

A judge from the mainland was brought over to try the case in October 2008, hearing evidence on Sark for two days and on Brecqhou for two because of David's health. This legal battle held eight past and present trustees of the Sark school and community hall trust personally liable for the return of money already spent building the huge community centre. Among them was a refuse manager and someone who was terminally ill and feared penury if they lost the case. As a way of winning hearts and minds, it was not optimal.

Sark News ramped up its electioneering during this time, endorsing nine candidates for the twenty-eight seats in one edition while criticizing twelve others. On 21 November 2008, the twins even signed an eight-page manifesto for Sark with glossy pictures and a plea not to vote for any candidate who disagreed with its suggestions. It is an astonishing document that, among other things, suggests a funicular railway for the tiny island and also a Brecqhou appointment to committees after the democratic election.

So the stage was set for a historic election heralding the end of feudalism in Sark and the whole of Europe. The vote attracted journalists from around the world. Delaney, one of the nine Barclay-backed candidates, told *The Times* in 2008 that his employers were 'two good, old fashioned gentlemen in their conduct and business dealings, who have the island's welfare at heart'.[17] To others, including a Spanish television crew, he said that the brothers were ready to invest £5 million a year if things went well. 'We've come, not to ring on the doorbell of feudalism and ask to be let in, we've come to smash that door down.'[18]

The Barclay camp planned a big election night party with champagne and lobster at the Aval du Creux, the big hotel at the top of the harbour hill. The newspaper attacks accelerated and tension mounted. Amanda de Carteret, who had married a descendant of Sark's first Seigneur, told the *New York Times* that the mood was 'vicious': 'Everyone's falling out with each other.'[19]

With turnout at 87.3 per cent, not one of the Barclay-backed candidates was elected. The party was cancelled; the lobster went to waste.

In what was meant to be a conciliatory letter to David Barclay on January 2009, Michael Beaumont told the billionaire that his newspapers on the island had hurt his chances. In his autobiography, he called the promotion of some candidates a tactical error for the Barclays and a 'Godsend' for their opponents as their identities were made clear.

Reg Guille, the island's chief judge and speaker of the house – and a man who had earned an MBE for his services in the Falklands War – referred back to the Nazi occupation of the island when he said: 'The last time the people of Sark were told how to vote was in 1940. We got our independence back in 1945 at the point of a bayonet. The people have voted. They've chosen their government.'[20]

The day after the election, all 140 people working in the Barclay-owned hotels, shops, estate agency, building firm and restaurants were sacked.

A huge number of journalists, there to bear witness to the fall of the last remaining feudal state, were all due to leave on a specially chartered boat from the harbour when a member of a Spanish film crew staying at the Aval du Creux told them the shocking news. Kevin Delaney said that by voting against reformers Sark had 'written the longest commercial suicide note in human history'.[21] These words are understood to have echoed the blind fury felt by David Barclay, who had simply not believed those he called 'reformers' would not win.

The shock was widespread. Residents of the neighbouring islands of Guernsey and Jersey offered to help the workers sacked just before Christmas, sending cash donations and food parcels for the festive period.

After a few days of relentlessly negative publicity, the Barclays offered to re-employ all their workers, which also helped with the fact that they could not operate any of their businesses without them. But the damage had already been done. This one action on 11 December 2008 served to confirm the fears of Sarkees that what the Barclays were capable of giving they were even more capable of taking away.

In early 2009, the judge in the island hall and school case also found against the Barclays and they had to pay costs.

Sark historian Richard Axton went to his grave baffled by the Barclays' behaviour. 'Their aims were totally contradictory and opaque. They had positioned themselves as wreckers of "feudalism" and champions of democracy and reform, but when Sark didn't elect any of their candidates they claimed that they had no representation.'[22] The idea of making others suffer when they didn't do your bidding seemed like a parody of bad feudalism.

The Seigneur was delighted, later writing in his autobiography: 'The whole atmosphere in Sark changed with the election as though a great dark cloud had been lifted.' Fewer islanders reported stress and anxiety to the doctor, he said.

The Barclays' fit of pique led to the closure of *Sark News*, but it was reopened less than a year later, by which time it had changed its name. By November 2009, relations between Sark and Brecqhou had taken a particularly nasty turn, Siri Oliver had left, and at the end of every edition of the newspaper was printed: 'The *Sark Newsletter* is edited and published on Sark by its proprietor Sark resident Kevin Delaney.' He was still the managing director of the Barclay-owned Sark Estate Management.

The war between the islands intensified. One senior conseiller, Charles Maitland, was quoted as saying that an older neighbour preferred being in Sark under the German occupation, as at least she knew who the enemy was. A blog by someone with the pen name Ebenezer Le Page dropped all honorifics and took to calling the brothers 'Monaco Dave' and 'Swiss Freddie'.

The Barclays did not buy very much on Sark after 2008, but then the financial crisis of that year put a stop to many of their big purchases anyway. It did not stop David pursuing one property he appeared to have set his heart on, however.

*

In January 2010, after democratic elections thwarted his desire to stuff its parliament with his own supporters, David Barclay offered to buy Sark instead. He wrote to Michael Beaumont from Monaco offering £1 million for the fief, the lease and title, and a further £1 million as compensation for loss of office. He outlined a seven-point plan and promised to drop his current complaint to the European Court of Human Rights. 'I am not interested in the Seigneurie, nor any feudal rights, not having any influence in Chief Pleas. My concern is only for the economic future of Sark.'[23]

Beaumont doubted this, writing, 'If it wasn't for control it is difficult to imagine any other genuine reason.'[24]

Beaumont declined an invitation to Brecqhou to discuss terms for a possible truce 'until the *Sark Newsletter* desists from its weekly vitriolic attacks which go way beyond acceptable criticism'.

In response, the owner of the *Daily Telegraph* wrote in support of his Sark paper, 'The freedom of the press is the guardian of democracy and the most effective opposition to those who abuse the trust of those who elected them and governs the lives of ordinary people and the economic welfare of their future.'

The Seigneur told the Sark parliament, and their correspondence – which Beaumont had believed to be confidential – was published in the *Sark* newspaper. In March the following year, the Barclay lawyer Gordon Dawes wrote to the *Guernsey Press* that David's desire to purchase Sark was entirely philanthropic. 'The only purpose of buying Sark was to de-feudalise the island and make it a true democracy.' Which must be the first time someone has tried to buy a state for the sake of universal suffrage.

Throughout the final section of his autobiography, which deals with what he felt was decades of bullying by the Barclays, Beaumont is constantly disappointed by the lack of support from the authorities in either Guernsey or Whitehall. He came under pressure from the Ministry of Justice to meet with David Barclay despite the fact that he had long lost faith in his offers of financial aid or a legal ceasefire. 'It would appear that money buys every-thing if you are ruthless enough and certainly influences Prime Ministers if they are also Newspaper Barons and skews any sense of justice.'

While not part of the UK, Sark belongs to the Crown, and the then Queen had to give her permission for the fief of Sark to be sold. Yet there were signs that this might not be so easy to obtain even with the support of the *Telegraph*. In 2010, the Commons justice select committee on Crown dependencies noted that there could be problems with the 'considerable economic and political power exercised' by 'individuals' on Sark. The report said: 'In a very small jurisdiction, there must always be the possibility that individuals wielding very significant economic, legal and political power may skew the operation of democratic government there.'[25]

David Barclay had long raged against feudalism, but even after the Sark system of governance had been overturned, the feud between the two sides continued. At times it became surreal. In the glossy brochure produced ahead of the elections – in which they proposed a sort of railway from the harbour – the Barclays again returned to the idea of a helipad, which could be used for 'medical emergencies'. Their newspaper promoted such a heli-pad, and a circular lawn on one of the Barclay hotels was laid, despite the flight ban, with lights displayed in the shape of an 'H'.

Sark residents were almost universally opposed to the idea, arguing that their sea ambulance was better equipped for medical emergencies, especially in bad weather, while a true emergency helicopter could use any available field nearest to the casualty. When the helipad plans were rejected, Gordon Dawes wrote another threatening letter warning that the conseillers would be held responsible for any 'lives lost because of the stance taken in respect of their offer to build a state of the art helipad at no expense to the Island'.[26]

Battle lines were thus drawn when, on the evening of 5 January 2012, Diana Beaumont, the Seigneur's wife, suffered a stroke at home and was taken by lifeboat to the nearest hospital in Guernsey. The *Sark Newsletter* went ballistic. Under the headline 'The emergency medical evacuation of Mrs. Beaumont: wilful negligence', the paper accused the island's only doctor, Peter Counsell, of 'wilful neglect' and 'unethical behaviour' for not calling on the Barclay helicopter. Even those relatively close to him wondered why David, always the brother most interested in Sark and its newspaper, allowed such attacks on the doctor. Delaney, like all other Barclay editors, has always said the proprietors had no involvement in the running of the Sark newspaper. In evidence given during the island hall case, David Barclay had even said: 'On this island we don't read the local Sark newspaper, whatever they call themselves.'[27] Yet David, who loved writing – as his many faxes and occasional newspaper articles attest – took a close personal interest in Sark's newspaper. As well as writing several by-lined articles himself, he directed many more. Frederick, whose name was occasionally added to these attacks, was said to be growing increasingly unhappy about the, by now very public, battle with Sark.

When parliamentarians spoke out against the details of a woman's medical emergency being described in the paper, Kevin Delaney penned an article which asked, 'Do they mean invasion of privacy or the invasion of secrecy?'[28]

Peter Counsell, the thirty-something doctor who had moved to Sark from London to bring up his young family, quit. In an eight-page resignation letter he wrote of the 'attacks upon my professional reputation and competence of the most defamatory kind' in 'a dangerous propaganda sheet'.[29] His departure prompted a protest march down the Avenue to the newspaper offices, the first on Sark in living memory.

In the ensuing furore, the fact that Diana Beaumont had arrived at the hospital within the hour and survived somehow became less important than the row.

The *Sark Newsletter* continued to write about the decision not to use the helicopter with a total of fifty-three critical pieces before 7 June 2013, according to Michael Beaumont. By the end of that month he had had enough and, along with two other island-ers, he brought a case of criminal harassment against the newspaper. One of the complainants, Edric Baker, sat on the Chief Pleas committee whose members had been called the 'feudal Taliban' for refusing permission for a helipad. With no harassment laws as such in Sark, the court in Guernsey found no case to answer. Beaumont called it 'a waste of time and money'.[30]

Outraged supporters decided not to let it go, and in 2014 a class action lawsuit claiming harassment was brought by fifty-four resi-dents, about 10 per cent of the island. Without a press complaints body or the means to take on libel lawyers, the complainants felt they had no other option. 'You can only be accused of being a criminal, part of 1930s Germany and other such filth, so often,' said one of the fifty-four.

In an increasingly febrile atmosphere, those working for the Barclays on the island also felt under attack, and none more than Kevin Delaney. Back in 2010, posters had started to appear around the island with 'Kelvin Delooney – The Great Dictator' and the Barclay man's face – sporting a toothbrush moustache and Hitler hair style – superimposed onto the face of Charlie Chaplin in the classic movie.

Delaney launched civil proceedings against what he called 'a poster harassment campaign', telling the justice minister that he was a 'target of abuse'. He called on Guernsey Police to arrest a local man and called for a local woman to be investigated for attempting to 'steal his fingerprints in order to plant them at some crime scene at a time of her own choosing'.[31]

His lawyers also accused opponents of vandalism, threats of vio-lence and the detonation of an explosive device outside Delaney's offices. Even though locals described this as a bird-scarer, Delaney stopped travelling around the island on his own, preferring the company of a man with the same name and a fondness for martial arts whom the locals nicknamed 'Kickbox Kevin'.

Gordon Dawes told the *Guardian* that his client, this time Kevin Delaney, had needed witnesses to ensure he was 'not deliberately placed in a difficult position by those hostile to him'. Delaney himself described the atmosphere on the island as '*Lord of the Flies* meets *Animal Farm*'.[32]

Supporters of the Barclays argued that the newspaper was simply fulfilling a vital democratic function in an unequal small society. Delaney issued a statement through his lawyers claiming that he was championing free speech and describing his role as 'being in the best traditions of pamphleteers of the 18th and 19th centuries, holding up a mirror to the actions of those who seek to control Sark'.[33]

The extent of the warfare had attracted the attention of the Ministry of Justice, which implied that the island's fledgling democracy was not working. By 2012, Lord McNally, the British government minister with responsibility for the Crown dependencies, criticized the newspaper's tone in the *Guardian*, admitting that 'the sustained nature of attacks in the *Sark Newsletter*' had made several islanders 'withdraw from public life'.[34]

By 2015, Professor David Lowenthal, a distinguished historian and geographer, described the Barclays' 'assault' on Sark as 'the most savage and sordid I have seen in sixty years of studying islands'. In 'The Scourging of Sark,' the academic blamed the brothers for eroding the 'general sense of mutual trust and accord' he remembered from his first visit to Sark in 1995.[35]

When Michael Beaumont died in July 2016, the Sark newspaper published an obituary which compared the eighty-eight-year-old to Hitler. The front page described his 'abuse of power, abuses of human rights and crimes against humanity – all of which has been unseen in the western world since the days of Nazi Germany of the 1930s'.[36]

A day after Michael's death, his son and heir Christopher received a letter on Brecqhou-headed notepaper from David Barclay offering to buy the Seigneurship again, this time for a total of £3 million. 'The thing that struck me is that he forgot to mention that my father [had died] or to offer any condolences,' said the younger Beaumont.

Nonetheless, the man who had just become the 23rd Seigneur sought advice from the Queen's then private secretary and the Ministry of Justice, pointing out, 'I'd only been in the job for two days.'

It was clear that the special status of a Crown dependency could not survive such a takeover. Sark would most likely have to be governed by the nearby islands of Guernsey or Alderney. 'The whole rigmarole of fief goes into obeisance,' said Beaumont, who did not accept the offer.[37]

The next edition of the Sark newspaper called Christopher Beaumont the 'unaccountable ruler of a lawless island hallmarked by the mob rule of unelected people' and accused a man about to launch a music festival on Sark of holding 'dictatorial powers not seen in Europe since the rise of Hitler's Germany in the 1930s'.[38]

Much of what happened between Brecqhou and Sark remains baffling. Why spend so much time and money fighting for a tax haven when the twins already enjoyed tax-free status? Why fight so hard for democracy and then never even bother to register on the electoral roll?

They denied anything but the loftiest intentions. In a Manifesto for Sark, they wrote, 'We have not invested in Sark to make money . . . Our motivation is the common interest of Sark and Brecqhou, as well as a genuine love for the Bailiwick, where our family has spent a considerable amount of time for decades past, long pre-dating our purchase of Brecqhou.'

It is hard not to conclude that the brothers had attempted full control of their own destiny and that of others, but had failed. In the years after 2012, the family decided that it was better to close down most of the hotels and the restaurant rather than pay for their upkeep. By the summer of 2019, only one hotel and one restaurant had been partially reopened following the post-election hissy fit. More than 200,000 vines, planted in a failed viticulture experiment, had been pulled up, and the land returned to beef farming.

There were already signs that Sark's fledgling democracy was struggling by the time David died in 2021. The number of conseillors had been reduced from twenty-eight to eighteen, and there would be eight uncontested elections by 2022. Kevin Delaney, who remained managing director of Sark Estate Management, was finally appointed as one of them. By then, Sark's newspaper was more like any other local gazette, full of news about openings and problems with the boat times.

This would have surprised Michael Beaumont. He ended his unpublished manuscript by saying that he almost wished the Barclays had not lost their very first battle for independence. While the Barclays cannot have had much love for the inhabitants of the island next door, Beaumont's final words in print were: 'The Barclays are our neighbours from hell. Q.E.D.'

Christopher Beaumont, an amiable ex-army captain who would go on to develop a far better relationship with David's youngest son, Alistair, than his father did with any Barclay, remains baffled by the years of antagonism. 'Why Sark? Perhaps because it's something money can't buy?'[39]

9. *Power to the People*

In 2009, the *Daily Telegraph* published details of expense claims submitted by British parliamentarians in an award-winning exposé that would rock the UK's political system to its core. Members of parliament had claimed money from the public purse for moat cleaning, for ornate houses for ducks, and even for phantom mortgages. The revelations ended the careers of some, but more critically diminished trust in the whole demo-cratic process.

Aidan Barclay used the story to disprove Dominic Lawson's claim that the *Telegraph*'s owners wanted a quiet life, telling the Leveson Inquiry in 2012, 'The newspaper's created plenty of trouble'.[1]

Such trouble did not prevent a series of political leaders from enjoying cordial relations with the chairman of the Telegraph Media Group. Aidan's submission to the inquiry listed more than thirty meals or meetings with senior politicians, often followed up by messages and asides on the geopolitical situation or book reviews. There were dinners, meetings and texts with Labour leaders Tony Blair and Gordon Brown, as well as Conservative Chancellor of the Exchequer George Osborne. Meetings were most frequent with David Cameron. In 2010, the year the Conser-vative Party leader became prime minister, Aidan met Cameron four times, with breakfast at the Ritz in March followed by a meeting and drinks at Number 10 in July and a private dinner there with his wife, Fizzy, in November. There had been at least five breakfasts or dinners since 2005, the year Cameron became leader of the Conservative Party.[2]

Aidan's notes and emails make his dislike of regulation clear.

He sent articles about Europe and tax, the gist of the latter being that taxing high earners was not good for the economy, but rather counterproductive.[3]

The *Telegraph*'s chief executive seemed to echo Aidan's affection. A handwritten letter from Murdoch MacLennan in February 2010 thanked David Cameron for dinner, and said, 'We desperately want there to be a Conservative government and you to be our next Prime Minister. We'll do all we can to bring that about and to give you great support in the gruelling months ahead. And as we are no fair-weathered friend, we'll be there with you too when you're in Downing Street.'[4] Asked by legal counsel, Aidan agreed that this position 'encapsulates the political standpoint of the *Telegraph*'.[5]

The 'Torygraph' was hardly going to object wholeheartedly to a Tory prime minister, of course, but its political power would go on to be transformed by the man who eventually replaced David Cameron as both leader of the Conservative Party and the UK prime minister.

Boris Johnson, with his mop of unbrushed hair, untucked shirts and dishevelled appearance – matched by an even messier private life – was everything that the Barclay brothers and David's eldest son were not. Johnson threw his arms up and twirled in the glare of publicity and attention, while the always neat-as-a-pin Barclays shrank from it. Yet their symbiotic relationship would do more than anything else they did to reshape Britain.

It did not start well. When the Barclays bought the Telegraph Media Group in June 2004, Johnson was editor of the *Spectator*, a favourite of the Conservative chattering classes and the home of some of David Barclay's favourite columnists. Under Johnson, it had gained a reputation as the 'Sextator', and not just for its lively parties, full of writers, roués and respectable young women. Johnson was sacked as shadow arts minister in November 2004 after lying about an affair with a *Spectator* colleague. Although subsequently proven to be true, the verbose Johnson had delighted in denouncing the rumours as 'an inverted pyramid of piffle'. Meanwhile, one of the magazine's columnists had left his wife for a colleague who was half his age, and the publisher Kimberly Quinn was having an affair with the UK Home Secretary at the time, David Blunkett.[6]

Such shenanigans made the Barclay brothers queasy. When Cameron brought his Old Etonian school friend Johnson back into the shadow cabinet at the end of 2005, Andrew Neil, as chairman of the Spectator group, insisted that Johnson resign as editor of the magazine.

But while their views may have differed over publicity and what went on in the bedroom, the Barclay brothers and Johnson had always agreed on a far bigger landscape: Europe.

Johnson's Euroscepticism – and indeed, that of parts of the *Telegraph* – pre-dated the ownership of the Barclays. Johnson's journalistic career had really taken off in 1989 with his appointment as the paper's Brussels correspondent, where his often-exaggerated stories about bendy bananas and out-of-date vibrators helped turn the serious job of reporting the EU into a bad joke. Jeremy Deedes, managing editor of the *Telegraph* at the time, said the perception that the EU was run by highly paid civil servants for the benefit of the people at the top was held by the paper long before the Barclays bought it. 'You could say it's another reason that they bought it – they were in tune with it already. The *Telegraph* had already written the music to a tune that they approved of.'[7]

Johnson continued to write a popular and increasingly well-paid column for the *Daily Telegraph* – earning an editorial salary of £275,000 a year, which dwarfed his parliamentary earnings – right up to his appointment as prime minister.[8] While his political career was often bumpy, his occasionally bumptious and humorous columns were nearly always popular with *Telegraph* readers. David and Aidan Barclay in particular were convinced that Johnson had a bright political future.

By 2016, Boris Johnson was a staunch if opportunistic Brexit-eer, going on to become elected leader of the Conservative Party, and prime minister, in 2019. Dominic Cummings, a close aide to Johnson before falling out with him, said that Johnson, always cash-strapped, referred to the *Telegraph* as his 'real boss'.[9]

Aidan and the twins were delighted with Johnson's elevation. Finally, a prime minister committed to Britain leaving the European Union was in Downing Street. Even better, he was one of theirs.

There is no doubt about the Barclays' own Brexit-backing views. In their later years, the twins were almost open about it. At one point, David had decided not to pursue a plan to commission Tim Walker, a former *Telegraph* writer, to ghost his autobiography on the basis that he was too pro-EU. Before this, he had told Walker: 'We gave our sovereignty to unelected bureaucrats in Brussels, who now make more laws and regulations than our own parliament does. We are a country of people who have lost their way and the will to govern ourselves . . . we have had years of relying on the state for our welfare and on promises no government can keep.'[10]

David was friendly with two consecutive long-lasting editors-in-chief of the Daily Mail newspaper group, David English and Paul Dacre. The latter's newspaper was stridently pro-Brexit both in the run-up to and aftermath of the referendum to leave. The twins were also friendly with Nigel Farage, a prominent campaigner for Britain to leave the EU and head of the UK Independence Party, or UKIP.[11]

In the run-up to the vote, Brexit campaign groups started to resemble the Monty Python sketch about the People's Front of Judea: with Farage's Leave.EU set up as a rival to the Vote Leave group around Boris Johnson. They united over the common cause of course, and Farage credits Johnson for helping to turn Euroscepticism into a popular pursuit in the UK through his early reports in the *Telegraph*.[12] With the Conservative Party divided by the vote, the *Telegraph*'s support for Brexit was full-throated and became even more so after 2016.

Frederick's support was personal as much as political, according to Farage. While he met David several times, the politician-turned-broadcaster calls Frederick 'a great friend' and 'very, very supportive'.

Farage describes his first meeting with the Barclays as 'complete chance'. They happened to find themselves in the same place, 'somewhere in the Med' (but not Monaco) when he contacted the older man, who invited him for coffee.[13] The men shared a liking for cigars and a dislike for the EU, and within a relatively short time Farage was spotted on Sark. He denies that the family paid for an expensive back operation necessitated by his plane crash in 2010, but Frederick was a great fan and hosted several parties for Farage, not at the *Telegraph* but at the Ritz. Frederick, after a lifetime eschewing such public soirées, not only attended, but allowed himself to be photographed at some of them.

There was a particularly memorable gathering in the early hours of the morning after the referendum vote to leave the European Union, 24 June 2016. Having watched the results come in, Farage made a speech just after 4 a.m. from his campaign headquarters in which he said: 'I now dare to dream that the dawn is breaking on an independent United Kingdom.' Brexit, he said, was 'a victory for real people, a victory for ordinary people, a victory for decent people' and a victory against 'multinationals' and 'big merchant banks'.[14]

Frederick, awake and overjoyed in his suite at the Ritz, called his friend Nigel as soon as he saw these early results come in, and invited Farage and his campaign team to celebrate in style. After stopping to take a picture of the sun rising over the River Thames and talking to the broadcast media in front of the Houses of Parliament, Farage headed to the Ritz.[15]

Ahead of their arrival, Frederick had been seen hurrying along the hotel's famous long gallery, happily bedecked with fluttering Union flags, to greet his guests. The octogenarian – small, dapper and grey-haired, a man who still took regular ballroom dancing lessons – was 'skipping' with joy, according to one eyewitness.

Dressed in full suit and tie and immaculately polished shoes as usual, despite the early hour, Frederick – ever the stickler for detail – was particularly pleased with the decor. The Union flags put up to celebrate the Queen's ninetieth birthday just two weeks before now seemed a perfect backdrop to celebrate Britain's exit from the European Union.

When they arrived, a member of staff told the Leave.EU team that Frederick was waiting for them in a private room, with hotel staff primed to serve a breakfast of champagne and kippers, the smoked and salted fish which was not only a favourite of the pre-war working classes but also an homage to the UKIP faithful (known as 'Kippers').

In a small room with a large circular table, Frederick thanked his friend for his success in the campaign. Inside the main room were Farage's main supporters including financier Arron Banks, the former Belizean diplomat Andy Wigmore, director of communications Gawain Towler, and strategist Chris Bruni-Lowe. The dozen staff members of the group – mainly young besuited men – mingled in a larger overflow room next door.

The Barclays could look upon Brexit as one of their greatest achievements, a matter perhaps for personal as well as professional pride. There were so many parties held at the five-star hotel that members of the subsequent Brexit party were known as 'Ritz rebels'.

On the evening of 23 November 2016 there was another gathering at the Ritz, attended by 120 guests,[16] to thank Farage for his role in the referendum campaign. Farage stood, champagne flute in hand, on the gilded staircase of the Ritz Hotel's Grand Hall and said 2016 would be known as 'one of those great historic years'. Attendees included Richard Desmond, owner of the

Brexit-supporting Express group, and Wigmore, who had taken a picture of Farage with Donald Trump in a golden elevator soon after Trump was elected US president.

Before the party proper, Frederick posed for a photo alongside his wife, Hiroko,[17] and Farage, while presenting him with a large copy of the photograph.[18] Wearing the red and gold decorative sash and medal of his papal knighthood, Frederick smiled broadly in his first photograph to be made public for decades – not only a rare photograph, but the first to emerge of Frederick without his twin.

In October 2017, Farage was filmed for a fly-on-the-wall documentary about the controversial former White House strategist Steve Bannon, discussing a plan to head a proposed global alliance of populist and far-right causes. In a clip that did not make the final cut of the subsequent show, *The Brink*, Farage suggests a meeting with Frederick at the Ritz to raise funds for the alliance. It would be a 'very very private way of doing things' says Farage, who tells Bannon to use a special side entrance at the hotel.

The way he describes the meeting could be used to describe so many of the Barclays' meetings. 'This is proper wealth,' he says. 'And you'll literally be in, have a meeting, and be out without anyone even knowing you've been there.'[19]

Given their desire for privacy, it is perhaps no surprise that the Barclay brothers never appeared on a list of donors. Indeed, Aidan had testified in 2012 that neither he personally nor any of the family businesses had donated money to a political party in the previous twenty-five years, which would have made 1987 – at the height of the Thatcher years – the last time the family had donated to a party.

Only a tiny handful of the perhaps more peripheral members of the family ever allowed their support for Brexit to be publicly acknowledged. Frederick's property developer stepson, Ko Asada Barclay, a small boy when his mother moved in with Frederick, was identified as one of UKIP's biggest donors after giving £80,000 in cash in the run-up to the referendum. His support for Brexit also led him to do a very non-Barclay thing by telling Buzzfeed News that he was an 'economic libertarian' and 'anti-EU'.[20] Describing himself as 'an advocate of laissez-fair capitalism, anti-statist and anti-socialist' on social media sites,[21] he wrote for the right-wing website Breitbart and appeared on BBC radio.

Aidan's wife, Fizzy, was also thanked for hosting an event for Farage and his Brexiteers. On 9 April 2019, in a public post on Facebook, a man called John Mappin wrote a tribute to 'Nigel Farage and the Ritz Rebels' which began: 'This afternoon we were welcomed at the Ritz by Fizzy Barclay for a gathering of the Ritz Rebels.'[22]

Mappin, subsequently described as a 'pro-Kremlin cheerleader' and anti-vax conspiracist,[23] continued: 'These freedom fighters and campaigners for personal familial and national sovereignty are going to change the Face [sic] of this country for ever. History tells of small dedicated groups that have shaped the past and the future. In a thousand years some poor school boy will almost certainly be studying all about this afternoons [sic] meeting.'

The only other member of the family to express any view on politics was Aidan and Fizzy's son Andrew. A keen user of social media, unlike the older generation of Barclays, on 31 January 2020 the young man wished his Instagram followers a Happy Brexit Day, though the post was subsequently taken down.

Whatever parties or posts were made in support of Brexit, the *Telegraph* was not uncritical of Farage, particularly ahead of the referendum, with many staff writers regarding him as a threat to the Conservative Party as well as to the cause.

Gawain Towler, the former UKIP director of communications, says the Barclays, particularly Frederick, were hugely helpful as 'door openers' rather than direct influencers via the newspaper. At the very least, he suggests, the pro-Brexit views of the owners meant that Eurosceptic voices at the newspaper were given greater support. 'Broadly and deeply, the support from the Barclays allowed more Eurosceptic journalists on the *Telegraph* to be more positive about us than they would hitherto have been . . . The [Barclays' position] allowed their people to be more Brexiteer, because it was going to be hard to get bollocked by your boss when your boss knows that their boss is onside.'[24]

After Brexit, a bust of Farage was seen at the family HQ in St James's, only the second politician to be awarded such an honour in one of their main buildings, the other being Margaret Thatcher.

On 31 January 2020, dubbed Brexit Day by supportive newspapers, with a former employee in Number 10, the *Daily Telegraph* celebrated with a special edition, hailing its part in Britain's departure from the European Union with a front page that trumpeted: 'How the *Telegraph* stood up to the establishment elite to reflect and push forward the views of the silent majority.' Just as in 1992, when Rupert Murdoch's tabloid claimed to have held off Labour and secured John Major's Conservative Party an unlikely win in the general election – 'It's the *Sun* wot won it'[25] – the newspaper boasted: 'It's Telegraph readers wot won it!'[26]

When David died less than a year later, Boris Johnson, then British prime minister, tweeted: 'Farewell with respect and admiration to Sir David Barclay who rescued a great newspaper, created many thousands of jobs across the UK and who believed passionately in the independence of this country and what it could achieve.'[27]

Owning the *Telegraph* and the Ritz represented the pinnacle of power and influence for two brothers born with neither. Brexit Day, at the start of a new decade, was their finest hour – yet behind the scenes, all was not well.

10. *The Midas Touch*

One of the key turning points in this story can be traced back to the moment Derek Quinlan, a former tax inspector, bought some of London's best-known luxury hotels in 2004 and found himself feted by those he described as 'the richest people on the planet'.[1] Amid the invites from oil-rich sheikhs and Russian bankers, one stood out: in November 2005, the Barclay brothers invited Quinlan and his wife, Siobhán, to visit Brecqhou.[2]

The timing of the invite to a wintry Channel Island might have seemed odd, but the brothers' interest in the newest recruit to the world of luxury hotel ownership was not.[3] In bringing together a group of investors to buy the Savoy, the Berkeley, the Connaught and Claridge's hotels, Quinlan had landed a golden share over any future sale of some of London's finest hotels. He was a very useful man to know.

The cachet and history of Claridge's at least matched, if not surpassed, that of the Ritz. Queen Elizabeth II loved to take lunch at Claridge's – she even celebrated her ruby wedding anniversary to Prince Philip there – and its art deco rooms had long attracted rock stars and celebrities as well as royalty.

'I do not know how many times over the years we have looked over Claridge's, but it is a great many,' Frederick admitted sometime later.[4] The Barclay brothers had considered bidding against Quinlan in the early part of the millennium, but had been kept busier than usual that year with the unexpected six-month auction for the *Telegraph* and the giant merger of their retail empire. Besides, one competitive auction was more than enough for the brothers.

A tall man with a large girth and healthy appetite that earned him the nickname 'Two Dinners', the red-haired Derek Quinlan seemed a strange bedfellow for the small, slim abstemious twins obsessed with their health. He once wept in recounting stories of his humble beginnings to a journalist from *Vanity Fair*.[5] Some thirteen years younger than the twins, he shared their appetite for buying property, and he was married to a woman who was twenty years his junior, as Reyna was to David.

Some six months after their trip to Brecqhou, Derek and Siobhán invited David and Reyna to dinner at their Villa La Carriere on Saint-Jean-Cap-Ferrat, some 10,000 square feet of the most expensive real estate in the world – a short walk from the beach and a short limousine ride from Monaco.

Quinlan already had a reputation for paying over the odds – his consortium had paid £750 million for the hotels. Like the Barclay brothers, however, Quinlan had built a fortune borrowing money to buy properties, making money for the banks when they sold and even more for himself. Banks fell over themselves to help, causing such a growth spurt that Ireland became known as the Celtic Tiger, and Quinlan was its poster boy. He was dubbed the 'Irish Midas' for his relatively sudden success and for his control over Coroin, the hotel-buying consortium in which he had a golden share.

Then, in September 2008, Lehman Brothers failed, provoking a chain reaction that affected both Derek Quinlan and the Barclays, along with the whole of the financial system. The resulting collapse revealed that, once again, supposedly cautious financial institutions had lavished loans on anyone who wanted the money to take advantage of tumescent prices. Reckless lending to property speculators was endemic, but remained largely hidden until the subsequent financial collapse increased the cost of borrowing.

Among the many banks that ignored warnings on excessive risks, and found themselves overloaded by bad debt by the time the banking crisis hit, were two of the most venerable institutions in Scotland and Ireland. HBOS, the bank behind so many of the Barclay deals, had trebled the amount of money it lent to customers from £35 billion in 2001 to £109 billion in 2007.[6] Across the Irish Sea, Anglo Irish Bank, one of the main backers of Quinlan's Coroin consortium, had also overindulged in the risky lending that led to a boom in property speculation. Both crashed along with the national economies in 2008.

As with the earlier Crown Agents scandal involving a once venerable financial institution turned loadasmoney gambler, it was left to taxpayers to foot the bill. The subsequent government bailout of Scotland's oldest bank and others cost the British taxpayer a total of £137 billion,[7] with £33.2 billion still not paid back in March 2023.[8]

The Irish government spent €64 billion bailing out the country's insolvent banks. Anglo Irish was effectively nationalized, while HBOS was forced into a merger with rival Lloyds TSB. Peter Cummings, the man who had helped finance so many of the Barclays deals – and had listened to Andrea Bocelli along with Frederick at Brandon Green's £4 million bar mitzvah – took a heavy share of the blame for the woes of the bank he had joined as a teenager; he paid a £500,000 fine and was handed a lifetime ban from banking.

Despite their debts, the Barclay family were believed to have been in better shape than most to weather the banking collapse and subsequent economic crash, which was the worst in over eighty years. The diversity of their assets afforded some protection – guests at the Ritz and readers of the *Telegraph* were less exposed to the vagaries of an economic decline than the poorer customers of the old Littlewoods catalogue business, for example. Their finances were complicated but they had paid off some of the debts from their over-burdened new acquisitions in 2006, just ahead of the crisis, leaving them exposed but not desperately so. After almost forty years in which almost everything they touched turned to gold, they were expected to snap up bargains as prices fell.

The same did not apply to the Irish Midas. Crippled by debt he had no means to pay back, Derek Quinlan found himself in severe financial difficulties after 2008. Despite his golden share, he started to go under, like a moneyed Augustus Gloop. The once proud tiger had turned prey.

The Barclay brothers pounced.

The battle for Claridge's lasted for five years and could make a book in its own right. Set among the luxury villas, yachts, ski chalets, five-star hotels and courtrooms of the French Riviera, Gstaad and London, it featured billionaire investors, oil-rich sheikhs, a former British prime minister, a controversial confidant to a US president, and Bono – the rock star. It started, as so many classic Barclays deals had, with a desperate seller, secret meetings and an ambush, which ironically is also the collective noun for a group of tigers.

But Claridge's in particular was neither unloved nor undervalued by at least one of its owners. The Barclays had not properly accounted for another Irishman who owned a stake in Claridge's – one who was as passionate about keeping the luxury London hotels as the brothers were about buying them.

Paddy Gerard McKillen had grown up Catholic in a working-class suburb of west Belfast. He had left school at sixteen and, like the Dublin-born Quinlan and indeed the Barclay brothers, grown rich largely by borrowing money to buy and sell property. By the time he joined the Coroin consortium, the silver-haired, softly spoken McKillen counted rock stars, artists and celebrities among his friends, but he had been brought up amid the Troubles in Northern Ireland and, as the Barclays were to find out, he was no stranger to street fighting.

Quinlan had first approached McKillen to join his consortium when he wanted to raise the money to buy Claridge's and the other hotels. Both men borrowed heavily to buy about a third each of Coroin Limited. The rest of the investors – assembled like a get-rich-quick avengers squad – included the two creators of theatrical entertainment *Riverdance*, an Irish stockbroker, and the one non-Celtic partner, Manchester-born but Bermuda-based billionaire Peter Green, who eventually held a 24.78 per cent stake and – in a twist which would become important in the subsequent battle – placed it in a trust in offshore Cyprus.

As leader of the consortium, Quinlan had a 'golden share', which meant nothing could be sold without his approval. Other details of the lengthy shareholder agreement included a clause offering first refusal for the other partners if one sold their shares or went bankrupt, a clause that would also prove key to the ensuing battle.[9]

The consortium had seen off competition from one of the richest men in the world, Prince Alwaleed bin Talal of Saudi Arabia, by borrowing hundreds of millions of pounds, largely from domestic banks such as Anglo Irish. 'Here was a group of Irish people buying the bastion of the British establishment,' Quinlan's adviser Gerry Murphy crowed to *Vanity Fair*. 'It was a spectacular, unbelievable dream.'[10]

After Coroin secured Claridge's, the jewel of jewels, the investors literally flew the tricolour Irish flag on top of the Queen's hotel, the heart of the British establishment.

The original idea had been to sell all but Claridge's to pay off the heavy debt burden, but in the end only the Savoy – which needed some £250 million of repair work – was sold to Prince Alwaleed, in a joint venture with HBOS.[11] The deal was struck after a meeting on his 282-foot yacht, moored off Cannes, and attendees included Bono, the U2 frontman who was also an old friend of McKillen's (they owned Dublin's Clarence Hotel together).

After this sale in January 2005, the consortium kept the three other hotels, along with its heavy debt burden, even embarking on a further £70 million refurbishment of the Connaught. When the banking sector crashed in 2008, the Irish government set up the National Asset Management Agency (NAMA) in an attempt to recover its €64 billion in (by now toxic) loans. Coroin's debts were transferred to the new agency with a due date of the end of 2010. By 2009, the investors realized they were short of between £150 million and £200 million to repay the £660 million loan. There followed a desperate race to either refinance or find a buyer for some or all of the business.

Only Paddy McKillen, still with huge debts outstanding but having diversified some assets out of Ireland before the crash, wanted to retain his stake in the company and therefore the hotels. He sought an extension on the NAMA repayment.

Derek Quinlan's finances, meanwhile, echoed the calamitous state of Ireland's. Having missed an interest payment on his Cap Ferrat mortgage in early 2009, he had his debts seized by NAMA in October 2009. He moved his wife and young family to Switzerland for financial as well as personal reasons; while his yacht, homes and extensive art collection, which included a Warhol of a big dollar sign, went under the hammer.[12]

The news was disastrous for his fellow investors, as under an 'associated debtor' clause, the asset management agency could sell on any assets held by an investor with more than 25 per cent of a company. They mostly feared a scenario in which NAMA sold to a vulture investor, who could then use the debt to seize the whole company in the same way a bank can foreclose on a home mortgage.

By the end of 2010, relations on the Coroin board were as toxic as its debts. After Quinlan's NAMA bombshell, McKillen and the others had asked him to both sell his shares and resign. When he refused, they sued him for unpaid hotel bills run up at Claridge's of $237,000, a spat that was leaked to the newspapers in a further embarrassment to the now-tarnished Midas.

As none of the investors could sell their shares without first offering them to the others under the pre-emption clauses, there followed a round of talks with possible buyers acceptable to all.

McKillen accused Quinlan of rejecting a sale to US private equity funds because they would not pay an additional 'facilitator fee' into his own bank account.[13] Quinlan has said in the past that he held out on this deal because he believed the hotels were worth more than the offer. Both Quinlan and McKillen, at different times over the next five years, also met a handful of powerful and ultra-wealthy men known in the ensuing court ruling as 'the Qataris'.[14]

In the summer of 2010, Quinlan had several meetings – in Doha, in a villa in the French town of Mougins, and in a hotel in Sardinia's Cala di Volpe – with the former emir of Qatar, Sheikh Hamad bin Khalifa Al Thani, sometimes known as HBK, along with his son Sheikh Jassim bin Hamad Al Thani.

While meeting in Cala di Volpe, Quinlan bumped into David Barclay, who occasionally travelled to the resort on the twins' yacht, *Lady Beatrice*. Over six weeks that summer, while negotiating a sale with the Qataris, Quinlan met the Barclay brothers quite a lot. Seven times he drove over to their favourite Monégasque meeting place, the Café de Paris, where they would 'shoot the breeze over a cup of coffee or a cigar'.[15] They also spoke regularly on the telephone.

By August 2010, talks with Sheikh Hamad had failed amid accusations that he wanted to pay Quinlan less than his consortium partners. The Irishman asked his friend and adviser, Gerry Murphy, to take the Coroin shareholder agreement to the Barclays. He did so by meeting Alistair, David's youngest son, who by now was twenty-one years old. David was keen for him to join the family firm.

The twins had reached their late seventies by the time they started manoeuvring for Coroin. Frederick was to say in a witness statement that he had 'effectively retired' with 'no work diary and no business secretary' and did not use email or text messages. He spoke on behalf of David, too unwell to make a statement as he was suffering with angina. Soon after, David made a statement in which he said: 'We have not attended office, management or board meetings in the UK since leaving the country . . . My brother and I have no editorial, political or economic power in the UK.'[16]

Still based in Monte Carlo in 2011, whenever the twins spent any time apart – for example, with their wives and children on the yacht – they would say to regulars in their Monaco haunts to 'look after this one'. Frederick was in London more with his daughter and two grandchildren, while David was on Brecqhou or in Switzerland, but they were still using Monaco's Avenue de Grande Bretagne as their main address at this time. The family also owned a sort of complex with several chalets in Gstaad, a ski resort believed to be the world's most expensive.

The Quinlans, now living in Switzerland, became 'good friends' with David and Reyna, according to Derek. Such good friends that, as his financial woes deepened during the battle for his company, the brothers lent the Quinlans €500,000 in 2010 followed by more than £2 million in 2011.[17] Later, when asked about the timing of this generosity as he looked for buyers of his golden share, Quinlan told the court: 'The Barclay brothers would not seek to profit from a friend's distress . . . Sir David has never made his support for myself or . . . [my wife] Siobhán conditional on anything in return.'[18]

Either way, the friendship stood in marked contrast to the brothers' relationship with Paddy McKillen. Although there is some disagreement about the first meeting between McKillen and the Barclays, both sides agree that the meeting – which would go on to be known as 'tie-gate' – took place in the Ritz towards the end of 2010.

McKillen turned up at the hotel in Piccadilly to meet Frederick: 'He met me and said: "You wouldn't be allowed in here unless you were meeting me." And I thought it was a joke so I gave a sort of nervous chuckle.' When a hotel butler pointed out that ties were mandatory at the Ritz, the tie-less McKillen realized he was serious and thought about leaving. 'I thought, shall I get the hell out of here? Otherwise, just be cordial and just sit down. Grit my teeth. And I sat down. And then he started on the Irish vote for enlarging Europe . . .'

According to McKillen, Frederick was furious about the Irish referendum of 2009 to ratify the Lisbon Treaty, which among other things allowed more of Europe's poorer countries to join the European Union. After what he describes as a twenty-minute rant against the Irish, McKillen left. 'I said, "You know Frederick, you sound really busy. It's really nice to meet you." And I head to the door as quick as I could before he could say another word . . . He'd asked me to meet, to say we're in the same business, that we should meet and compare notes. No agenda . . . And then he insulted me for not wearing a tie.'[19]

Frederick tells a similar story in which McKillen not only breached the hotel's jacket-and-tie-only policy but 'his shirt was hanging out'. 'I made a joke about it being fortunate that I was there to meet him, because otherwise he would not have got past security. Mr McKillen took umbrage, and the encounter turned distinctly frosty.' He admitted that the meeting ended soon after. There had been no coffee.[20]

There was to be no meeting of minds over what to do with the Coroin hotels either. Sears had been one of the few occasions where the Barclays had willingly shared ownership of something, even for a short time; McKillen wanted to stay as both shareholder and manager of a huge planned transformation project for Claridge's.

The Barclays then hatched a cunning plan to outmanoeuvre McKillen. In early January 2011, with McKillen flying to Doha to negotiate a sale and contract with the Qataris, and Quinlan meeting David Barclay in Gstaad, Peter Green's family grew both sick of the board infighting and concerned about possible intervention by the state agency NAMA. They wanted out. Richard Faber, an Old Etonian investment banker and the first husband of

Frederick's daughter Amanda, was sent to meet their representative in Ireland. Frederick and Aidan were both on the call when the £70 million purchase of Green's 24.78 per cent stake in Coroin – or rather the sale of the Cyprus-based trust called Misland Investments – was agreed. By selling the trust rather than the shares to B Overseas, a company controlled by the Barclays, the deal avoided triggering the pre-emption rights as the shareholder had not officially changed.

The news, delivered via text on 18 January 2011, was a bombshell to McKillen, who had invested six years of his life and finances in the hotels. Although it was the Green family who had sold the trust, McKillen turned his ire on Quinlan, who still had the golden share. He called Frederick, who later described the call as 'a barrage of what I can only describe as foul-mouthed abuse about Mr Quinlan, calling him a fat so-and-so and using a stream of four-letter words about him. It was very unpleasant and threatening . . . I do not like or tolerate swearing. I was not going to listen to Mr McKillen's rantings and I cut off the call.'[21]

Unlike those held by the Greens, Quinlan's shares were not in a separate trust and so any sale would have to be offered to his remaining investors under the pre-emption rights. In May 2011, Quinlan gave Richard Faber power of attorney over his shares for a year after the Barclays bought one of his several outstanding debts from Bank of Scotland (Ireland).[22] McKillen, still fighting to keep his stake in Coroin, accused his former partner of 'throwing him under a bus'. The Barclays then settled another of Quinlan's debts, which had been bought by Jho Low, a controversial Malaysian investor also circling the wounded finances of the Irish Tiger. Later in the same year, they paid NAMA for some of the company's debts.[23]

Frederick and Aidan, with David largely dealing with his 'good friend' Quinlan, looked to have managed to outmanoeuvre McKillen and the complicated Coroin shareholders' agreement in an entirely legal and cost-effective way. First, they had bought the Green family's offshore trust, Misland, for £70 million; then, after giving personal guarantees of £260 million, they had raised enough money to buy up not only the main shareholders' debts but some of the company's too, held by NAMA.[24] Although they could not buy Quinlan's shares outright without sparking the pre-emption rights protected in the shareholders' agreement, he had given a Barclay executive power of attorney over his shares. The Barclays had effectively gained control of almost 64 per cent of Coroin by paying a fraction of the estimated value of the hotels, put at between £900 million and £1 billion excluding debt in the subsequent court case.[25] What's more, they had done so in their typically speedy fashion and without doing any official due diligence, allowing them to outflank their Qatari rivals.

As well as Richard Faber, the Barclays appointed two other 'apparatchiks' to the Coroin board: specialist tax and pension accountant Michael Seal and management accountant Rigel Mowatt.[26] Alongside general consigliere Philip Peters, these men had worked for the Barclays for years. With majority control and dominance on the board, it should have been game, set and match to the Barclays in the battle for Coroin's hotels.

It was a David *v* Goliath battle from the start. The brothers had an estimated fortune of £2.3 billion, while McKillen had only appeared once in the *Sunday Times* Rich List, the year after the crash, with £66 million. He also had a huge debt still outstanding with NAMA, set up as Ireland's 'bad debt bank'. But McKillen, outmanoeuvred and cash-strapped and by this point the last man standing against the Barclays, decided to use one of their favourite devices against them. He took them to court.

Patrick Gerard McKillen accused a total of thirteen people and companies – from Derek Quinlan to the trustees of the family settlement at the heart of the Barclay empire – of unlawfully breaching the shareholders' agreement, and the Barclay-appointed directors of failing in their duties.

When the two cases came to the Chancery Division of the High Court in London's Fetter Lane in March 2012, the list of those involved and the lawyers representing them took up two sides of A4. There were so many people – eighteen senior barristers dealing with fifty-four files, nearly 20,000 pages, and a lot of journalists, as well as the defendants – that the only room big enough in the Rolls Building of the Royal Courts of Justice was courtroom 26. Just a few months before, the same room had been used for the biggest private litigation battle in British legal history (between Russian billionaires Roman Abramovich and Boris Berezovsky). *Guardian* journalist Simon Bowers described looking out across a 'sea of wigs', some of whom – such as Lord Grabiner, acting for the Barclay side – were said to charge fees of up to £3,000 an hour.[27]

Neither David, Frederick nor Aidan gave evidence in person, but the directors they had appointed, as well as the two Irishmen at the centre of the case, did. Both sides attempted to stop reporting of the case, but failed. Hundreds of pages of documents lifted the lid on how the two sides worked.

Then the battle turned nasty.

When McKillen was photographed coming out of a club with his fellow Irish wheeler-and-dealer Denis O'Brien, he grew suspicious. He told the court that he had started to delete text messages as he believed his phone was being hacked, but admitted he had no evidence to support this allegation. He said he had been advised to check whether his phone had been hacked with one company, who had told him they were conflicted as they worked for the Barclays. Lawyers for the Barclays denied such allegations.

Companies owned by the Barclays had employed private investigators before. In 2011, the *New York Times* discovered that the Telegraph Media Group had appointed Kroll, a global security firm, to find out how a story had been leaked to a rival – focusing on former editor William Lewis after he left the paper in May 2010.[28]

Employees in other parts of the business grew uncomfortable at the use of photographers to follow McKillen's every move from the anonymity of a black cab. 'There was a team totally following him 24/7,' said one. Rather than using Kroll this time, the Barclays turned to Quest Global, a London investigative group run by a former head of the Metropolitan Police turned peer. McKillen was advised not to stay at any of his hotels while his battle with the Barclays was in full swing. 'I was warned . . . It's very easy to send in a technician or something during the day to fix your phone alarm or something.'[29]

For his part, McKillen employed a former member of the fraud squad at Ireland's police service, the Garda. Denis O'Sullivan was hired on a two-year contract in 2013 to 'do research in relation to the dispute with the Barclays', according to subsequent court proceedings.[30] Both McKillen and O'Sullivan had visited Sark, in an attempt to understand the bitter dispute brewing between the Barclays and Sarkees.

The Barclays argued that they alone had been able to save the hotels – paying off the debts, while McKillen blocked their efforts to help. After two months of argument, the judge, Mr Justice David Richards, dismissed McKillen's case, finding that the Barclays had used legal means to gain control of Coroin. Ordered to pay the brothers' costs, McKillen was left with a €25.5 million bill.[31] So many companies and interests were involved in the court case that the judge explained that he would simplify his reference to two groups throughout his 158-page ruling: the 'Barclay interests', which referred to the web of companies involved, and the 'Qataris', which referred to several members of the ruling family of the oil-rich state who had played a significant role from start to finish.

The Qataris had been interested in buying the hotels as soon as Coroin's financial troubles became obvious, and had kept in touch with both sides throughout these proceedings. McKillen had first been introduced to Sheikh Hamad by Tony Blair, who had set up a consulting business in December 2008 after leaving Number 10. The Irishman was a huge admirer of Blair for his part in the Good Friday agreement that had brought peace to Northern Ireland.

Between 2010 and 2015, Qatar's sovereign wealth fund bought up a chunk of London's best-known real estate, including Harrods and the Shard.[32] At one point, Aidan took the surprise step of signing a tentative joint venture with Sheikh Jassim, but McKillen refused the mooted offer of a one-year management fee. He had plans for a grand renovation at Claridge's and wanted several more years to see it through. While the argument was dragged through court, the Barclays were unable to sell off any of the hotels, blocked as they were by McKillen and his by now 36 per cent stake. In court, the Irishman's lawyers submitted that the Barclays had lined up international buyers for two hotels, which could have delivered the family a £300 million profit.[33]

In total, there would be eleven court hearings brought against the Barclays over the next three years. Paddy McKillen lost every one.

The running battle with McKillen was not the only problem facing the Barclay brothers at the time. In the same year the brothers had invited Derek Quinlan to Brecqhou, they had made a decision that marked a departure from their usual way of breaking up companies. In 2005, when they sold the 120 high street stores belonging to Littlewoods and GUS, they were expected to sell the merged group's loss-making online delivery arm. They decided to expand it instead. The business that became Yodel ended up costing the family hundreds of millions of pounds.

Money worries tend to exacerbate underlying disagreements and tensions in most families, and the Barclays were no exception, even if the amounts involved were on a different scale. While success has many fathers, failure is an orphan – a proverb that had not really applied to the Barclays since the collapse of

Candy Corner. Not, that is, until the online delivery company turned into a disaster, and sparked a row over the future shape of the Barclay empire.

This isn't to say that their vision in 2005 – to sell off the physical stores and focus on online shopping – did not make complete sense; the problem was that others had the same idea. Online delivery was a madly competitive business, with heavy fixed costs. And with the extra upheaval caused by merging two large retail groups employing more than 20,000 people, the online delivery business became a managerial as well as a financial headache.

As ever with the Barclays, the number of companies, subsidiaries and names involved in even one division of the business were about as as simple as a spider's web, or a maze with different threads throughout. Repeated name changes can make it hard to follow where each thread leads.

Yodel started life in 2004 as a company called Parcel Delivery Network Ltd, a subsidiary of March U.K. Ltd, which itself was a subsidiary of Littlewoods Shop Direct Group. In 2005 it changed its name to Home Delivery Network Ltd (HDN).

No amount of name changing helped the company make any money, however. In the first three years after 2004, the online delivery arm lost at least £10 million a year, or £47 million in total. The Barclays spent £81 million not only stemming these losses in the run-up to 2008 but also buying several more, smaller, businesses in an attempt to compete in a rapidly consolidating market. They eventually split the loss-making delivery arm from its retail parent, which gave banks more confidence to lend money to the cash-generating Littlewoods without worrying that it was all being sucked up by the loss-making delivery division.

In May 2008, the Home Delivery Network (HDN) was spun off into a standalone company when March U.K. Ltd 'sold' the delivery business to its parent company March U.K. Ltd. The book valuation or price given was £250 million.[34] This intra-company valuation was all completely above board, and signed off by the accountants despite the operating losses of some £20 million a year.

Continued losses did not prevent the Barclays from doubling down on their online delivery bet. On 1 March 2010, Parcelpoint, another subsidiary of HDN, bought DHL Express, the loss-making UK arm of Deutsche Post, the German mail and logistics group, for just £1. This apparent bargain doubled HDN's work-force and added seventy-one service centres. With a market share of 17 per cent, the merged delivery business was second only to a troubled former monopoly, Royal Mail.

The new business was eventually renamed Yodel, which stood for 'Your delivery' rather than any desire to sing about its success. Jonathan Smith, who came from DHL to run Yodel, told the *Mail on Sunday* that the merger had 'a clear logic . . . it meant econo-mies of scale and the ability to offer a wide range of delivery services to create sustainable long-term profit'.[35]

The group introduced new flexible delivery slots, which con-sumers could organize with the newly self-employed drivers. A joint venture with retail payment network PayPoint, Collect+, allowed customers to collect and return packets at thousands of corner stores, and in the first quarter of 2011 the number of pack-ets quadrupled largely because of the increased demand for online fashion. Yet the DHL purchase failed to make the Barclays any money. In fact, the losses got far worse. In 2011, a year after the purchase, Yodel was haemorrhaging much more than £1 mil-lion of cash a week, with net losses of £150 million.[36]

The introduction of radical new employment practices and cost cuts – including closing warehouses and slashing 1,500 jobs – hurt customer service, which was all important in a competitive market. Online forums and social media sites filled with com-plaints about the number of missing, misdirected or damaged Yodel parcels. YouTube featured videos of parcels being lobbed over customers' gates.[37] The company lawyers, Weil, Gotshal and Manges – who had advised the Barclays over the purchase in the first place – threatened to sue Twitter over 'malicious' statements that claimed Yodel was 'incompetent and negligent'.[38] Some of the tweets were deleted but the complaints remained. BBC's *Watchdog* programme featured the complaints in 2012, when there was even a dedicated website called SayNoToYodel. Meanwhile, by 2021 Yodel had been voted one of the UK's worst parcel delivery firms every year but two since 2013, when the poll by consumer website MoneySavingExpert started.[39]

Others in a highly competitive field also suffered – Amtrak closed its UK parcels arm, and Rentokil's City Link lost money every year before collapsing into administration – but Yodel kept slipping down the rankings and lost contracts from major retailers John Lewis and Currys. Losses ballooned to more than £100 million a year after the purchase of DHL Express from Deutsche Post.[40] Yodel was becoming a case study in how mergers fail.

By 2011, something really significant was happening. Money, which had nearly always flowed from the Barclays' profitable UK-based businesses to their offshore concerns by way of intercompany loans, started to flow the other way. By 2012, Littlewood's Jersey-based parent company, LW Corporation, had paid £409 million into its failing online delivery business via March U.K. Ltd. Having turned Yodel into a standalone business already, the family decided to further protect Littlewoods from its losses. The profitable retail business was loaded with debt.

In June 2012, just before the first Coroin verdict, part of the empire still called Home Delivery Network was demerged into a specially created company called Yodel Distribution Holdings. What was highly unusual about this was that it was structured as a dividend *in specie* (in kind) worth £500 million to offshore parent company LW Corporation. LW Corp then immediately sold it to a newly formed UK subsidiary, which in turn 'sold' it to its own subsidiary Yodel Logistics Ltd for £500 million. The acquisition was funded by a £500 million inter-company loan, settled by the issuance of 500 million shares in Yodel Logistics Ltd.

What matters less than this game of corporate pass the parcel was the net effect: a company valued at £250 million in 2008 had essentially doubled in value in four years, despite losing hundreds of millions of pounds.

The inter-company sales process boosted the perceived value of the loss-making business, but it is not entirely clear why such a convoluted set of transactions was used. One possible reason is to insulate the retail arm and maintain its ability to borrow money. Another motive might have been to confuse, but it is difficult to say who the target was. Both journalists and bankers?

A clear distinction between the delivery and retail arms was also helpful in the long-running and audacious legal claim for VAT overpayments launched by the Barclays against HMRC in 2007.[41] Any potential payout – and the payout in this case was set to be huge – would need to be ring-fenced from a business losing some £100 million a year.

While Yodel continued to haemorrhage cash and HMRC fought the VAT claim, Paddy McKillen was still blocking the Barclays' bid to sell the London hotels. By early 2014, he faced a further headache. The huge debt he had secured against his shareholding in Coroin was about to be sold off by its owner, the Irish Bank Resolution Corporation (IBRC), forged from the embers of Anglo Irish Bank to recover as much outstanding debt as possible. The Barclays spotted an opportunity to get rid of their nemesis by attempting to buy this debt. They could then have demanded instant repayment, forcing McKillen to finally give up his shareholding after years of courtroom battles.

McKillen accused the Barclays of using 'every Wall Street hostile takeover tactic in the book'.[42] McKillen sued NAMA first (using former Nobel Prize-winning economist Joseph Stiglitz to support his case), and expanded his search for a white knight who would buy the debt from IBRC but not call it in. He found Tom Barrack, a Lebanese-American investor and one of the private equity investors who had sold the hotels to Coroin in 2004. Now, ten years later, he was running his own US property investment company, Colony Capital, through which he had done several headline-grabbing deals, including buying the Hollywood studio Miramax and football club Paris Saint-Germain, in association with the Qataris. Barrack, who was already known for deals involving the rich and famous, and would go on to become a controversial fundraiser for Donald Trump, lent McKillen the money to refinance the loan held by IBRC, saving him from the clutches of the Barclays. By March 2014, McKillen was telling the *Belfast Telegraph* that he would 'never sell' the hotels.[43]

Having reached deadlock with an opponent who now seemed to be backed by at least one wealthy investor, if not an even wealthier state fund, the Barclays started to look for other buyers.

Previously known as pretty secretive himself, McKillen decided to talk about his even more privacy-conscious rivals. He referred to the Barclays as 'gypsies' in *Vanity Fair* and then invited a journalist from the *Guardian* out to his art-drenched estate in Provence – which he had opened to the public – describing them as: 'Traders. Out to turn a quick buck. Highly aggressive. And philistines. I've told them: these hotels are jewels, to be cherished. Nearly 200 years of history. Not assets to be sold down to the highest bidder.' Somewhat ruefully, he added: 'My father gave me two pieces of advice: stay out of court and out of the newspapers. I've let him down, on both counts.'[44]

While McKillen spoke publicly about his battle, the Barclays did not. However, the two newspapers they owned launched a timely and extraordinary attack on the Qataris. The Sark newspaper accused them of indirectly funding state-sponsored criminality on the island, via their links to Paddy McKillen.[45] The Barclays insisted they had nothing to do with editorial policy in the newspaper, whose tiny island readership must have been bemused at the possible connection to a High Court case involving London hotels. Meanwhile, over a two-month period in the autumn of 2014, the *Telegraph* ran a series of articles – including eight front-page stories and four editorials – in which it accused the Gulf state of funding terrorist groups including al-Qaeda and the Islamic State. These allegations of funding terrorist groups in the Middle East have always been denied by Qatar. Articles called for shoppers at the Qatari-owned Harrods department store to stop 'buying into terror', and for the UK 'to cut business ties' with Qatar.[46] This connection was first made by the *Middle East Eye*,[47] which in turn has alleged links to Qatari backers.

Perhaps even more astonishing was David Barclay's decision at around this time to get in touch with the journalist who compiled the *Sunday Times* Rich List. Sometime later, he admitted that the contact, in which he said positive things about his privately owned business, was initially driven by his desire to 'show we had the resources to finance the [Claridge's] deal to the opposition'.[48] Showing off his assets in this way, like a despot might parade a country's firepower to warn off potential aggressors, could surely deter McKillen as well as cheer any lenders who might otherwise have started to fret about the falling profits.

Philip Beresford, a business journalist with an eye for a story and a less-than-typical way with statistics, had first started to think about publishing a list of the wealthiest people in Britain in the early 1980s. He was inspired by efforts in the US media, where business reporting was more advanced, but also by cultural changes in a decade of deregulation and rising property prices which had spawned a new breed of self-made men such as the Barclay brothers. For Beresford's first attempt, while working at the *Sunday Telegraph* in the early 1980s, a duke who was one of the richest landowners in Britain was so shocked at being asked to comment on the extent of his wealth that he rang the newspaper's then proprietor, Lord Hartwell, while another target complained to the

police. The *Telegraph*, whose readers were still somewhat suspicious of anything nouveau riche, aborted the attempt. Beresford
moved to the *Sunday Times*, owned by a far more buccaneering
proprietor with no problem celebrating wealth, Rupert Murdoch.

By the time Beresford received an email out of the blue from
Jennifer O'Neill, David Barclay's secretary, in 2014, he had spent
the past twenty-five years compiling the Rich List for the *Sunday
Times*. The list had proved so successful after its first edition in
1989 that he worked on it more or less full-time, scouring public
records and daily newspapers in the pre-internet days to add
information to a huge database of thousands of companies. After
a decade or so, his archives took up most of the top floor of his
house. He would typically seek clarification or comment from
some of those mentioned. Highly complex private companies,
particularly those held by offshore entities, had long proved the
most challenging to assess.

So David Barclay's intervention was appreciated, if highly
unusual. Press officers, or at a push the corporate accountant,
would usually be the ones to comment. With privately held companies without the same need to give frequent updates to
shareholders, information from the horse's mouth, as it were,
was particularly helpful. David Barclay's intervention also led directly to an immediate stratospheric rise in the family's estimated
wealth. In 2014, the valuation of the twins' assets more than doubled, with a £3.65 billion jump to £6 billion, putting them back in
the top twenty. In his email, David Barclay made a point of men-
tioning the £1.2 billion tax rebate due on the VAT repayments.

No one outside the family was to know, least of all Beresford,
that this first surprise intervention came just after the brothers
had agreed a private 'informal valuation' of the underlying assets
of £2.6 billion, significantly below the Rich List valuation. Frederick had felt 'overwhelmed by his brother's pressure' to divide
their wealth in a way that saw his 25 per cent share valued at £650
million.[49] Either the valuation effectively cheated Frederick, or

David had other reasons to influence the Rich List. He continued to offer his 'thoughts on world affairs and the economy', and particularly how they affected the performance of his businesses, every year from 2014 until not long before he died.

Despite the nastiness of their battle, the end when it came was just as sudden as most of the Barclays' business decisions and took Paddy McKillen by surprise. One Sunday, as he was greeting guests, he was surprised to see a familiar figure walking with his hands behind his back across the Claridge's lobby. He had only met Frederick that one time before. This is how he tells the story:

> I go over and say, 'David?' And he says, 'Frederick.' And I say, 'Do you know who I am?' And he says, 'I do.' And I say, 'I've lost all these cases but I'm just starting this. Just to let you know, this is not a threat, but I'm not just gonna go away. This is my life's blood.'
>
> And he says, 'We don't know how you're surviving. We don't know how you've got the resources. I tell you what, you'll hear from my nephew shortly.'
>
> And within a week, Aidan contacted me and said: 'Our time's up . . . We know now we can't get 100 per cent of the hotel so we're gonna leave you alone and go our own way. So we want to sell our shares . . .'[50]

On 22 April 2015, just a few short weeks after this meeting, the Barclays agreed to sell their 64 per cent interest in the hotel company to Constellation Hotels, owned by Qatar's ruling Al Thani family. Constellation also bought McKillen's stake, after which McKillen was left nearly debt-free and with a potentially lucrative seven-year management contract due to run until the end of 2022, which is what he had fought for all along.

Accounts for the vehicle behind the purchase, Selene (a Luxembourg-based company initially used by Tom Barrack to provide the loan), suggest a sale price of €941 million (£673 million) excluding debt. This would have given the Barclays a £429 million payday for their 64 per cent stake, or a profit of about £140 million after the five-year battle.

As well as marking a significant turning point for the Barclays, the fight for Claridge's marked a sort of crossroads in Britain: a point where British-born Thatcherite property developers made way for global wealth in the shape of oil-rich sheikhs and Russian oligarchs in its high-end property market.

Richard Faber called Claridge's 'a very successful investment for us'.[51] The profit was enough to plug the Yodel losses for less than two years.

McKillen went on to transform Claridge's into the hotel he had dreamed of, with a £100,000-a-night penthouse suite and five-storey basement extension. He also went on to open other luxury hotels around the world. Yet by 2022, as his contract came to an end, he found himself in dispute again, this time with the Qataris over the terms of their agreement. Even more surprisingly, the brothers he had fought against for years and who had always presented a united front – the Barclays – were back in court, fighting each other.

When friends asked if he enjoyed a sense of *Schadenfreude*, McKillen was horrified: 'Families ripping each other apart? Suing each other? Spying on each other? No. But I do think our win was a catalyst. It was definitely the start of the end.'[52]

11. *Bugged*

For almost eighty years, Frederick and David had appeared as two halves of one phenomenally successful whole. From a shared womb, born with little but their natural talents, the twins had built one of the biggest fortunes in Britain. They had ridden the post-war property boom to create a financial empire that encompassed luxury hotels, newspapers and their own private island. They were early adopters of the use of offshore trusts and companies to hide their identity and also avoid 'tax liabilities arising either in life or on death'.[1] Incredibly close throughout their lives – they would speak for each other and finish each other's sentences – they enjoyed large and frequent family gatherings.

Publicly, these mirror twins could rarely be told apart, yet privately they were far from identical. That is, apart from an agreement, which could almost seem like the code of *omertà*, to live intensely private lives, away from the public gaze their wealth attracted.

The brothers had started to think about succession and what should be done with their fortune, as so many people do, in their fifties, a decade in which they pulled off some of their most deeply held ambitions – buying the Ritz Hotel, a super yacht that they named after their mother, and an island on which they could hide, safe from prying eyes. It was also the decade when David started to have health concerns.

Ten minutes older and always the more dominant twin, David had convinced his brother that he would not live long, that they needed to start handing over control to the next generation. In turn magnetic and menacing, he also insisted that his four sons inherit more of the joint fortune than Frederick's one child, the only female and born two decades after her older cousins. It was not an easy decision and they fought – Frederick's wife, Hiroko, witnessed them 'punching each other'[2] – but eventually Frederick agreed to hand over half of his share in the business to his nephews. Much later, he said he had felt 'forced' to deny his daughter her full share of the fortune he had helped build. He would call it the greatest mistake of his life.[3]

Under these original plans, the underlying family fortune was split, with David's sons sharing 75 per cent while Amanda was left with 25 per cent. At the time, and in most of the intervening decades, it must have made sense given the nature of the next generation. Aidan, David's eldest son, had been seriously involved in the business from the Ellerman takeover, the deal that changed everything. He went on to be instrumental in creating a retail empire and was the first to hop on a plane to buy the *Telegraph*, before helping the twins manage an ever-growing empire. Shrewd and more than twenty years older than his cousin Amanda, Aidan was the first among equals even though he spent almost as much time with his closest brother, Howard, as his father and uncle spent with each other.

Neither David's third son nor Frederick's daughter appeared to have inherited much of their fathers' business nous or interests. Although close to his two older brothers, Duncan was described as 'softer' than either of them. He never had as much to do with the business outside Brecqhou, where he occasionally took his father's seat on the island parliament before the 2008 elections. In his forties, without real involvement in the Ellerman headquarters in St James's, he had invested in a loss-making desalination plant called Subsea Infrastructure[4] and a video platform called WinkBall,[5] which was dissolved, according to company registers, at the end of 2016. David's youngest son by his first wife, Zoe, he appeared to be more interested in theology and mysticism than business. He became a trustee of the evangelical Christian mission Now Believe,[6] and a few years later a director of the Live

Free Foundation, a Christian foundation that offers events and courses. Its website states: 'If you would like to break free from the past, connect deeply with God, and discover your destiny, then this is for you.'[7] Their shared faith possibly bonded Duncan to his father even when he was removed as a main beneficiary of the main underlying trusts that owned the family empire. Although he lost his rights to a share of the underlying capital, Duncan continued to receive a 'salary' according to his eldest brother's subsequent evidence, along with other members of the family.[8]

Duncan had effectively made way for Alistair, David's youngest son, born thirty years after his stepbrothers and the child of Reyna, David's second wife. Taller than his father and brothers, and with his mother's dark skin, the good-looking Alistair has been described as a bit of a 'tearaway' by those who knew him as a young man. His parents had sent him to one of the best schools in the country, where he occasionally got into trouble. He enjoyed frequenting private members' clubs like Jalouse in Mayfair, with its crystal ceiling and art interior, and loved fast cars like MacLarens, flirting with a career as a racing driver.[9] In his twenties, he received a six-month ban after driving his £168,000 Bentley Continental too fast through a 30-mph zone in a Hampshire village. He was fined £3,000 for charges that included failing to identity himself and driving with an expired licence.[10]

Alistair soon showed a desire to get involved in the family business, a desire that did not always turn out well. In 2011, as a consultant at an offshoot of one of the family firms, Hillgate Property Investments, he sued Lady Nina Bracewell-Smith, heir to the Ritz family fortune and a significant stake in Arsenal football club, after she failed to pay him the £1 million he claimed she owed for his introductions in Monaco. In defence documents lodged at the High Court by her lawyers Mishcon de Reya, Bracewell-Smith said she would not have appointed a young acquaintance who 'was obviously not qualified or able' but who

nevertheless 'would from time-to-time press' her to look at business deals. The row was eventually settled out of court, in
private.

Alistair was close to Aidan's eldest son, Andrew, who was similar in age and looks and shared an enthusiasm for the new world
of online start-ups. Aidan and Fizzy's children were regarded as
well brought up and adjusted by many. Both Andrew and his
actress sister Sofia used social media, as other successful twenty-
somethings did. More opinionated than his father or grandfather
ever were in public, Andrew also posted about his wedding to
Australian model Nadine Leopold in 2022. A few years earlier, he
joined his uncle Alistair when he set up several companies that
invested in property and other real estate, including Hillgate and
Yopa, an online estate agent. Fifty-five when his youngest son
was born, David was said to be both a strict and doting father to
Alistair. In his later years, David's WhatsApp would show a picture of just the two of them.

David's older sons had spent a lot of time with their cousin
Amanda growing up, as well as with her stepbrother Ko. Living
in close proximity through the year, the families would spend
Christmases together on Brecqhou. The son of a Japanese businessman, Kenji Asada, Ko was far closer in age to his cousins,
having been born in 1967, six years before his mother met Frederick on a beach in Cannes. Although he took the family name, Ko
Barclay was never regarded as a fully paid-up member of the clan
and took no part in the family business, although he did launch
his own property company.

Half-Japanese and the only woman, Amanda had long stood
apart from her cousins. Artistic and beautiful, she developed a
talent for photography and – like her father – ballroom dancing.
She married Richard Faber when they were quite young and had
a wedding reception at the Ritz. Her second marriage, to Andrew
Lubin, ended after she had had two children. The elder, a girl, was
born with special needs. Even though he lived abroad for most of

her childhood, Frederick and Amanda were exceptionally close. While he was also 'very close' to his nephews,[11] particularly the older two, his only daughter gave every impression of wanting to live a very different life.

Amanda also had a limited involvement in the family business. Her eleven known directorships offer a window into her status in the family firm, especially compared with her older cousins. Unlike them, she was not a director of any of the main companies that controlled either the Ritz or the *Telegraph*. Amanda did run Ritz Fine Jewellery for a while and joined some family-owned development companies – including 202 Clarges Estate in 2014 alongside her younger cousin Alistair, Aidan's son Andrew, and the company apparatchik Michael Seal.[12]

Like most families, there was some underlying tension. Hiroko, who was friendly with Zoe, David's first wife, and had helped look after the boys when they were young, did not get on with Reyna, David's younger second wife. Neither did Frederick, it emerged in court. 'He didn't like her,' Hiroko said. 'I don't like her either.'[13]

Women, with the exception of the twins' long-dead mother, rarely seem to have been driving forces in the Barclay family, but there appears to have been an extra thread of dislike for Reyna, sometimes connected to her status as the much younger second wife and sometimes to her Latin American heritage. Some of her in-laws were said to call her 'Taco Bell' behind her back.

A lot of families fall out over money, even extremely wealthy ones. In the case of the Barclays, the tensions would eventually lead to a complete breakdown in the relationship between the brothers, and between husband and wife, and would eventually help detonate the whole carapace of secrecy they had built around themselves, their family and their business affairs.

Tension mounted after 2008, when banks that had once flocked to lend money to men with long and successful careers became more cautious after the credit crisis. HBOS, saddled with Bank of Scotland's bad debts and more, ran into major financial problems and was merged with Lloyds Bank. Peter Cummings, a man who had agreed so many loans to the Barclays and others, departed. By January 2009, Lloyds itself had to be rescued by the UK government, which paid £20.3 billion for 43 per cent of the share capital. A new chief executive was appointed in 2011, charged with sorting out its toxic loans.

The Barclays carried on buying properties but the abortive bid for the landmark London hotels including Claridge's would be their last big deal.

To those who could read the signs, the brothers also started to seem interested in different things. David – always bossy, some said paranoid, and long worried about his health – became more and more fixated on becoming Seigneur of Sark. As early as 2008, Frederick made it clear in a court hearing that it was David who led their campaigns. By the end, he was overheard calling it the 'Sark nonsense'. Frederick, meanwhile, increasingly pushed for hotel deals, a reminder of the brothers' earliest successes.

At no point until now had Frederick seemed to consider the weak position his only child could be in, with her minority share in the trusts fed by the underlying businesses, if those businesses struggled or if her cousins turned against her. He would later be rebuked by a High Court judge for not recognizing that 'the potential for the nephews ganging up together, outvoting and side-lining Amanda should have been obvious'.[14] Frederick would later describe her as 'at the mercy of the other side of the family'.[15] Of course, until now, there had only been one side.

Frederick found himself increasingly aggrieved about the succession plans he had agreed decades before, and was worried about the future for Amanda and his grandchildren when he was no longer there. Matters were said to have come to a head in 2013, after David tried to give a bigger share of the underlying trusts to Alistair, something Frederick is understood not to have agreed with.

The 75 per cent made over to David's three children was not divided equally. Aidan, who had effectively been the chief executive of the family firm for some time, held 'by far' the biggest share. Together with the brother he was closest to, Howard, they shared day-to-day responsibility for the business empire and control of the offshore trusts where most of the money went. Together the two eldest sons had a controlling stake. After Amanda's quarter-share, Howard and Alistair held less than 25 per cent each. The twins had settled each other's main trusts, which meant that when David tried to increase the share for Alistair, possibly by diluting Aidan's, Frederick refused. At around the same time there was a 'significant deterioration' in the relationship between the twins.[16]

By December 2013, Frederick was concerned enough by the changing family dynamic to draw up an 'informal valuation' of the family fortune, which would put an actual figure on the money he could access, along with his daughter. Amanda's share was put at £650 million, suggesting a total value of the Barclay family business of £2.6 billion.[17]

In 2014, in his eightieth year, Frederick moved to live entirely separately from his twin for the first time ever. He moved to London and organized his affairs in a way that meant he would give up his non-domicile status but remain living the tax-free life he had grown used to. 'He wanted to return to the UK but not to pay any tax,' his wife Hiroko would later say.[18] The complicated system he put in place to do this depended on his daughter's trust continuing to receive income from the underlying businesses. Among Frederick's growing concerns, along with his loss of control, was what happened if these businesses started to lose a lot of money.

As 2013 came to a close, Frederick went to Brecqhou with Hiroko in what was to be his final visit to the island. David told him that because he had stepped back from the running of the island – not just by failing to pay as much for its upkeep but perhaps by failing to keep fighting the locals – he would no longer be welcome there. The breakdown of the relationship with his brother made Frederick ill, prompting medical treatment for a stress-related skin complaint, according to his wife. It was 'a big shock', she said, suggesting he had needed to be hospitalized.[19]

Although the Barclays had long organized their affairs in such a way that it was hard for anyone to follow the money, there had been signs that all was not well for years before the feud broke into the open. On the surface, they insisted that all was going swimmingly.

Having started writing to Philip Beresford – the journalist behind the *Sunday Times* Rich List – during the battle for Claridge's, David Barclay did not stop. 'It is not normally my style to talk about ourselves but having started I can see we have to continue,' he wrote in 2016.[20]

His annual missives gave guidance on how well his privately held conglomerate was doing, as well as his 'thoughts on the world at large'.

Entrepreneurs are rarely known to undersell their businesses, but the valuations afforded to the Barclay empire by David in the years before he died were eye-popping. In March 2016, after Japan's Nikkei bought the *Financial Times* for some £840 million, he suggested his own more profitable Telegraph Media Group was worth 'more than double'. As 'the most luxurious hotel amongst the leading hotels in the world', the Ritz was worth £1 billion, he said, while seriously loss-making Yodel was 'in the region of £700m'. In the same year reports suggest the group had rejected a bid of just over £2 billion for Littlewoods, he valued the entire family fortune at almost £10 billion before 'substantial personal assets'. Although always clear that the final valuation was up to the compilers of the list, David ended by saying he would be 'happy with £7bn if you agree'.

These notes – an odd mixture of *de haut en bas* philosophies and corporate promotion – grew shorter over the years, but always emphasized that the final decision regarding his net wealth was up to the journalists involved. Given the opacity and complexity of the Barclays' private businesses, it would have been hard for the *Sunday Times* team to explain any dramatic devaluation after the big jump in 2014; so the family's estimated fortune continued at or above £7 billion until after David died in 2021.

In 2016, before the British referendum that led to the UK's departure from the European Union, and the last Rich List before Philip Beresford himself retired, David wrote: 'My concern for the UK going forward is – the increasing powers of the State and as a result a less free market economy; banks' lending is governed by government regulation . . . each piece of regulation means less freedom.' His belief in the value of the British market economy was clear: 'No country in Europe can offer the same democracy and the rule of law.' Such a situation made UK businesses such as his highly prized by 'foreign investors'.

The sale of Claridge's and the other hotels had introduced the family to foreign investors with cash to spend. The Barclays would go on to sell more assets to the ruling family of Qatar over the coming years. One which was likely to have made them an attractive return was Forbes House, the grand mansion that the Queen had said made the nearby Buckingham Palace 'look dull.' In 2016, the Barclays were reported to have sold it to Sheikh Hamad, the former head of the Qatari sovereign wealth fund and a key player in the Claridge's battle, for an estimated £150 million.[21] Land Registry records suggest that the lease was sold to a BVI-registered company for just under £34 million in 2013, which suggests the owners had made a tidy profit, even after gaining planning consent. By 2022, after extensive renovations to the twenty-five-bedroom property in the heart of an area now known as 'Little Doha', Forbes House was reported to be the UK's most expensive private residence, worth £300 million.

The 'rise in buyers for UK assets from the Far East' much mentioned by David was not the reason for the initial spike in the value of the family assets in the Rich List, which more than doubled in 2014; it was the promise, mentioned explicitly by David, of a huge payout from Her Majesty's Revenue and Customs.

Since 2007, Littlewoods had been pursuing its claim for a VAT overpayment plus compound interest worth as much as £1.25 billion.[22] The company had already won its case, arguing that HMRC was acting contrary to the law in the High Court, the European Court of Justice and the Court of Appeal; David, as well as most analysts, was confident of a windfall from the British taxpayer. Instead, in 2017, the Supreme Court ruled in favour of the Revenue,[23] a decision which saved the British taxpayer an estimated £17 billion from other companies that had been encouraged by the Barclays to lodge similar claims. Not only did the British revenue save billions, the Barclays also had to repay the £318 million that HMRC had already given them.

The timing was not optimal for the Barclays. There were increasing signs that the family businesses were facing a cash squeeze, despite David's protestations to the Rich List.

The old Littlewoods business had churned out cash for years by selling everything from fast fashion to homeware, to consumers typically too poor to shop without some kind of consumer financing. After it first emerged that many of these in-house financing options not only charged relatively high interest rates but had mis-sold payment protection insurance schemes to often-vulnerable consumers, Littlewoods was among several companies forced to pay compensation. After the first payment for this PPI mis-selling scandal in 2015, Littlewoods would pay out more than half a billion pounds (£583 million) by the time David died in 2021. Very / Shop Direct's auditors, Deloitte, raised a red flag with a note about 'material uncertainty' in the accounts for the year.[24]

The online delivery business Yodel had been losing money for years. Accounts for Logistics Group Holdings showed that Yodel had lost a total of £620 million since 2012 by this point.

After defying the headwinds hitting the newspaper industry, operating profits at the Telegraph Media Group also started to fall in 2015. Three years later they were at a low of £7.8 million. Even as early as 2018, there were visible signs that banks were getting nervous when parent companies owned by the Barclays effectively paid off £100 million in bank debts owed by Press Acquisitions.

Options for dealing with the cash crunch were limited, with a sometimes-mooted trade sale of Littlewoods now off the cards and the twins in particular opposed to any idea of a public flotation on the stock exchange, which would have raised money but led to a loss of control and more public scrutiny. In the eighteen months after the Supreme Court decision on the VAT tax refund, some £340 million was taken from the family's offshore assets and injected into its onshore businesses.

The pressure appeared to end the decades-long system of collective responsibility when Aidan made a surprise personal intervention. In 2016, even as his uncle Frederick was marking his own separation from his twin by buying his first solo yacht, *Leander*, Aidan sold his own superyacht, *Enigma*, to John Christodoulou, the British billionaire founder of property group Yianis, for €48.5 million.

There also seemed to have been a shift in Aidan's role in a business still generally referred to as 'the Barclay Brothers'. When the family bought the five-star Beaumont Hotel in 2018 it was via a Guernsey-based company, Beaumont Hotel Holdings, of which Aidan was the sole family member listed as a beneficial owner. The funding – which according to the accounts submitted to Companies House involved the payment of £116 million for the leasehold from the Grosvenor Estate – came from Wafic Saïd, the Syrian-born billionaire who had helped broker a controversial arms deal between Britain and Saudi Arabia.[25] Saïd's son had gone to Eton with Richard Faber. Both Faber and Saïd became directors of Beaumont Hotel (Midco) Ltd, the intermediate holding company between the UK limited company owning the hotel and the Guernsey one, and remained as directors even after Aidan sold out to Summit Trust Holdings for an undisclosed sum in 2021.

In the same year as the Beaumont purchase, ending June 2018, Aidan also personally lent the old Littlewoods retail business, now called Shop Direct, £125 million. Such a significant personal loan suggested not only that the usual offshore flow of funds had dried up but also that external lenders, nervous of negative cash flows and with other debts coming due, were making it more expensive for the family businesses to borrow more. There was more evidence to come of this.

The value of Littlewoods was partly its usefulness in raising debt from external sources such as banks. Although the possible trophy price of an asset like the Ritz, or even the *Telegraph* in its money-making heyday, meant banks were happy to lend their owners' money, catalogues turned online retailers were assumed to have access to other sources of debt financing.

One of the most common ways for a consumer-facing business to raise cash is to use a method of financing with the ugly name of securitized receivables. Essentially, every time a customer buys something, say a sofa, the full amount is booked as a sale on the retailer's balance sheet even though only a small down payment has been paid. This allows consumers to pay in instalments while the company has guaranteed income. Rather than wait for the full amount to come in, companies sell off this credit to corporate lenders in order to get the cash up front, typically to buy more goods from suppliers.

Former British prime minister David Cameron, the man who called for a British referendum and text buddy of Aidan Barclay, called this supply-chain financing 'win-win', as companies improved their cash flows and suppliers got paid faster.[26] Given the more or less guaranteed nature of the money, financial institutions did not charge much at all to take on this debt, so the arrangement offered a cheap way of improving cash flow. In 2017, Shop Direct had debts of almost £2 billion – the majority made up of a £1.3 billion loan raised on the back of customer sales.

In the same year, one in which Aidan also lent the company £125 million, Shop Direct had also raised a further £550 million via a high-yield bond,[27] a more expensive way of raising funds by corporate borrowers. Both this junk bond and Shop Direct's securitized debt facility were due to expire before the end of 2022 so had to be renegotiated. Typically, such debts simply get rolled over, unless lenders become nervous about the state of the company's finances. In the two years after 2017, Shop Direct announced worse-than-expected profits, largely due to the far worse-than-expected PPI compensation payout. A sure sign of investor concern that the company might struggle to repay its debts came as early as May 2018 when the yield on Shop Direct's bond more than doubled, to nearly 20 per cent.

Corporate lenders were not the only ones showing signs of concern about the group's finances. Frederick and Amanda also started to ask more questions, and in particular exactly how much debt there actually was and where. Then, in 2018–19, two companies owned by the family borrowed a total of £222 million from a corporate lender whose subsequent collapse led to a public inquiry as well as criticism for its well-paid adviser, David Cameron.[28]

Greensill Capital started life as a supply-chain financial services group, offering investors supposedly low-risk investment returns. It became a company that used investor funds to make far riskier loans, some of which were far from Cameron's 'win-win' scenario. In November 2019, Shop Direct Holdings Ltd took out a £150 million loan facility from Greensill for vague 'general corporate purposes' – that is, nothing to do with supply chain finance. This loan was relatively expensive, with an estimated interest rate of 5.75 per cent above LIBOR – the basic rate of inter-bank lending. It also required a personal guarantee of

£150 million from Aidan and Howard.[29] Greensill had already lent another Barclay firm money, having agreed a £72 million commercial mortgage for a subsidiary of Shop Direct Holdings called Primevere, to help fund the construction of a warehouse called Skygate in the East Midlands. Again, this loan to a company with sales of just £4 million a year had a relatively high interest rate of LIBOR + 5.75 per cent, and a short maturity.

Borrowing money from Greensill was unusual for a company with access to other kinds of cheaper bank debt. Stephen Clapham, the forensic accountant behind the popular website Behind the Balance Sheet, thought the presence of Shop Direct striking when he was investigating the collapse of Greensill, given the fact that the Barclays owned both retail businesses and trophy assets such as the Ritz. 'This is not the characteristic of an entity that's part of a cash-rich group,' he said. 'This is the characteristic of an entity which is living from hand to mouth.'[30] He assumed that other valuable assets owned by the family, such as the Ritz, were already overloaded with debt. In 2018 the Ritz took out a bank loan of £265 million with a 3.8 per cent per annum interest rate.[31] Then there was the position of the retail business. 'You would only be doing that if perhaps you'd already securitised as many receivables as you could. It's hard to know because the accounting rules don't require you to disclose this shit.'

A lack of transparency is an issue with most offshore accounts. The bigger question is why the Barclays' offshore concerns did not at this point simply repay just a fraction of the very generous, interest-free loans they owed to the cash-strapped parts of the group. LW Corporation could have just repaid its inter-company loan to Shop Direct Holdings, for example, rather than the latter company borrowing from Aidan and lenders like Greensill, loans that were expensive and required personal guarantees on top. After all, the parent company LW Corporation had managed to effectively borrow a total of £792 million by June 2020 from its UK subsidiary Shop Direct Holdings, without having to pay any interest at all. In 2008, Ellerman Investments Ltd 'sold' the Ritz, plus the hotel's casino and fine jewellery subsidiaries, along with the Cavendish Hotel, to the Jersey-based Ellerman Holdings for a consideration of £730 million – funded by an interest-free loan, some £709 million of which was still outstanding by the time Greensill was lending to family-owned businesses at a high interest rate.

UK-based businesses borrow money from banks and other corporate lenders which they then lend to offshore parents all the time in an entirely legitimate process – typically to reduce UK corporation tax. The interest payments due on the Ritz bank debt of £265 million lowered the profits on which tax was levied in such a way that the hotel had little incentive to call in the £224.5 million it was owed from its offshore parent company, for example. But to borrow hundreds of millions of pounds from expensive providers suggested that LW Corporation, the Jersey-based holding company, was suffering severe cash flow difficulties by 2018, following all the equity funding it had provided to Yodel and the repayment of interest to HMRC.

The big difference with the Barclays was the amount of offshore debt outstanding and the fact that it never seemed to be repaid. By this point, the family finances were so opaque and complicated even key family members seemed unsure where exactly the money was. There were fears, whether unfounded or not, that the trusts meant to provide Frederick and Amanda with their agreed share were in fact empty of cash.

The Greensill loans were repaid in the summer of 2021, by which time Skygate had been sold and Greensill had collapsed into administration. This, and signs of marginal improvement in the underlying business, came far too late to calm Frederick and Amanda's rising concerns over the way the group was financed, concerns which would culminate in a hideous legal battle with Frederick's own nephews.

*

As Frederick and Amanda's questions over the state of the business intensified, his nephews grew concerned – especially when the man who was meant to have retired decades ago started to come up with his own plans to safeguard his share of the business for the benefit of his now nuclear family. The distrust became mutual.

Several years after his major bust-up with his twin brother over their inheritance, Frederick started to worry that the nephews he had supported all these years were not telling him everything he needed to know. He would later say that there were no difficulties between him and his nephews until he started 'ferreting around to ascertain the true debts of the businesses'. When he found out from 'bank and senior employees that . . . the debts were very much less than he had been told' he began to fear that 'his nephews were not telling him the truth'.[32]

They in turn started to worry that the usually super-sharp Frederick, talking out of turn and acting out of character, was suffering from a condition subsequently described in court as 'cognitive dysfunction'. They would later argue that they behaved as they did because of these concerns, and to protect the interests of the whole family.

As the relationships broke down, the main protagonists tried to come up with a plan, a sort of Barclay 2.0. This was meant to ensure that each side of the family would continue to live a life of plenty, long after the twins had gone. One way out was for Amanda to swap her stake in the entire retail business, shopping and delivery, for David's sons' stake in the Ritz. Frederick must have begun to feel more sharply that the less profitable parts of the business, from the *Telegraph* to Yodel, had been driven by David and Aidan while his beloved Ritz was a trophy that continued to shine bright. He began to think that a swap might be a fair trade given that the retail arm Very was valued at a much higher price.

The alternative plan – one favoured by his nephews – was to

sell the Ritz itself. The hotel's history, cachet and Mayfair loca-tion made it attractive to the wealthy overseas buyers touted by David's annual missives to the *Sunday Times*. Frederick, however, talked about the hotel on Piccadilly, the one he had wanted to own for ever and the one he had bought in a heartbeat, as his life-time legacy.

There were more and more signs of estrangement during this time. While plans for Barclay 2.0 were unfolding, there were changes to a series of discretionary trusts with control over the family fortune, changes that suggested that Frederick started to worry that his interests were no longer aligned with those of his brother. The twins acted as settlors to each other's trusts, yet Frederick appointed his own trustees separate from the family office in Monaco and Guernsey.

Loyal staff, who had long believed that the brothers, sons and nephews spoke as one, started to hear raised voices for the first time. They fretted about divided loyalties. One marked the change by saying: 'If one said yes, they all said yes . . . Then eve-ryone sort of became awkward with each other.' Whose orders should they obey? Frederick, still hugely popular at the Ritz, for example, with his old-school manners and the perfectionist eye he turned on everything from the coffee cups to the square of Axminster carpet showing signs of wear; or Aidan, increasingly seen as the boss?

Ever the dealmaker, Frederick also started to consider an even more dramatic exit, by selling his 25 per cent stake in all the busi-nesses to an outside bidder. There were said to be overtures made to billionaire media and technology barons, including Rupert Murdoch and Jeff Bezos, about buying the *Telegraph*. The Amazon boss was also said to be considering a bid for the Ritz, with rumours swirling of him creating an entirely new floor at the top of the hotel.

A huge sticking point remained, however. How could any potential investor safeguard their holdings in a hugely complex private business majority owned by someone else's family – especially when that family was about to implode?

The Conservatory used by the members of the Barclay family as a private meeting room has never appeared on the Ritz Hotel's floorplans. Instead, there is a small, oblong gap in the publicly available layout of William Kent House. Close to grand public rooms that can be hired out for a fee – such as the William Kent room, with its crimson and gold decor of the imperial age – the Conservatory can only be reached via another private room, which in turn can only be accessed from the Grand Hall of the annexe by two single doors marked 'Private' in gold letters and a mirror that does not look like a door at all.

Once inside this private sanctum, family members could relax in a glass-covered space decorated like a posh lounge from the nineties, with chintz-covered two-seater sofas and fake trellises on the walls. A handful of photos were propped up on the sideboard and the sofa.

In happier times, Frederick, David, Aidan and Howard would sit there shooting the breeze in a fog of cigar smoke. Said to be fanatical about security, concerned that their phones could be traced whether on or off, they would sometimes leave their mobiles outside, in the private room next door, so convinced were they that their devices could be used for surveillance by rivals and other enemies. The entire hotel operated a no-camera policy, with an exception only made for those taking afternoon tea in its famous Palm Court.

Despite all these safeguards, in 2019 the Conservatory became a place of surveillance and sabotage, rather than safety and security. And the threat came from within. The bomb that blew the lid off the lives of these identical twins – men who had worked their way up from nothing to become two of Britain's most successful, if secretive, businessmen – blew up in their own private Conservatory.

Increasingly anxious to safeguard his daughter's share of the madly complicated conglomerate he had created, as well as that of his grandchildren, Frederick made sure that Amanda and her closest associate, Fardokht Aghevli, were installed on the main board of the Ritz in June 2019, replacing Aidan, Howard and Philip Peters, whose long-serving role as a director of B.UK Ltd in Bermuda had earned him a place on the Offshore Leaks Database. The move suggested that Frederick's only daughter was being groomed for a bigger role in the family business – or in the Ritz, at least.

Just a year older than Amanda, Aghevli had joined the fine jewellery arm of the Ritz in 2002. It was Amanda's only directorship at the time and she grew close to Fardokht, who went on to work for the charity behind Amanda's daughter's special-needs school in Chelsea. Apart from a picture of this attractive young woman in the pages of glossy magazine *Tatler* in the early noughties,[33] she had played a very behind-the-scenes role until appointed to the board alongside Amanda in the summer of 2019. In total, the two women replaced Aidan, Howard and Philip Peters on a total of six Ritz companies, making Aghevli – whose career had mainly been spent at the hotel by this point – the most senior non-Barclay director there.

Three months later, as the fractures in the relationship between the two sides widened, a report in *The Times* revealed that the Barclays were considering a sale of either the *Telegraph* or the Ritz.[34] The story effectively put a for-sale sign on the business at a time when debts were falling due and cash was running out. But what neither Aidan nor any of his brothers wanted was for their uncle to ruin any potential takeover talks with his own separate plans. After being ousted from the Ritz boards, Aidan and Howard became 'seriously concerned' about some of the things their uncle was both saying and doing.

What they did about this caused serious concerns of its own. The fallout between David and Frederick in 2014 had meant significant changes for Alistair as well as Amanda. Now in his mid-twenties, Alistair had launched his online estate agency businesses and become much more involved with Brecqhou and the properties on Sark, but he had far less to do with the family's main businesses. Despite this, he decided to try to help his side of the family find out what Frederick and Amanda were plotting between them and, having discussed it with Andrew, decided on a radical course of action. He went into a spyware shop in central London and bought a bugging device fitted into what looked like an ordinary plug socket, according to subsequent court documents.[35] Similar devices are available for less than £200 online,[36] but presumably this son of a billionaire did not want to leave digital traces.

In early November 2019, Alistair Barclay went into the Conservatory, waving away Ritz staff who wanted to know if he needed anything, and planted a listening device disguised as a plug adaptor in the room where his uncle and cousin sat and discussed business.

On 14 November, a week or so after it was fitted, one of his elder brothers, Howard, hired Quest Global – a private investigations company headed by Lord Stevens, the former head of the Metropolitan Police – to help listen to and transcribe the material. Quest also supplied a separate Wi-Fi bug. Over the next two months, over ninety-four hours of meetings between Frederick and his bankers, lawyers, trustees and daughter were recorded by the bugs in the Conservatory. A man so publicity-shy he was rarely seen in public had some 1,000 private conversations recorded.

It was the lawyers working for Frederick and Amanda who first suggested that the Conservatory be swept. The idea horrified Frederick, who refused to believe that he could be bugged in his own private room in his own hotel. Two cameras were installed; the one fitted by the hotel's own security staff failed to work, while the camera fitted by Frederick's lawyers caught Alistair on film.

It had taken Quest employees 405 hours, or more than two and a half weeks working twenty-four hours a day, to sift through all the material illegally recorded on the hidden bugs, producing some 2,800 pages of transcripts. As well as using his special access to fit the bugs, Alistair would help Quest by annotating the transcripts – correcting names or highlighting the most significant information – while Philip Peters, who had worked for Frederick since the early 1990s, highlighted 'banking and finance matters'.[37]

Frederick called the invasion of privacy 'commercial espionage on a vast scale'.[38]

The case caused outrage among privacy and data protection campaigners. Clive Mackintosh, a data protection lawyer at Harper James Solicitors, said: 'Your right to privacy doesn't just rest at home, but extends to wherever you are. So if you are being secretly recorded for a commercial purpose, there is no lawful basis for that.'[39]

Alistair, his elder brothers Aidan and Howard, his nephew Andrew, and Philip Peters referred to at least ninety-four hours of taped conversations as 'podcasts' in their WhatsApp group chat. There was mention of a potential purchaser or partner then called 'Squirrel'. Frederick grew suspicious that his nephews knew when he was talking to potential purchasers. There was an unnamed Russian businessman with whom Frederick had held 'extensive' talks. The transcripts showed that Alistair had messaged Aidan, who had replied: 'Good. Now I've got something to shoot at and an opportunity.'[40] After another discussion, lawyers for Frederick's nephews intervened, which made him even more suspicious.

Private investigators from Kroll were appointed to help find out what was happening and counter-surveillance cameras were also fitted. When Frederick and Amanda found what they were looking for, the surveillance team took it to Fardokht Aghevli, who then led the subsequent inquiry. On 13 January 2020, Amanda and Frederick saw incontrovertible evidence that Alistair had been recording their private conversations. CCTV video from the Conservatory showed David's youngest son, wearing a preppy uniform of loose-fitting but expensive-looking beige tracksuit pants and a maroon Harvard hoodie, walking suspiciously about the room, putting the plug adapter in the back pocket of his trousers. Rather than go to the police, Amanda and Aghevli went to the other family members with their complaint.

It was at this point they realized the significance of another shift in the boardroom bingo being played out. At the end of December 2019, Aidan and Howard had been made 'persons with significant control' of Ellerman Holdings, the main Jersey-based group responsible for the Ritz Hotel. In this position, they were able to force Amanda and Fardokht Aghevli to resign from the main board a little over a week after they reported the bugging.

Subsequent court documents call Frederick 'a man who is now left to contemplate his nephews' betrayal, and a father who has witnessed the prejudicial treatment of his daughter by her cousins'.[41] At the time, he went ballistic, calling his nephews greedy and crooked. There was talk of a fight to the death.

It was inevitable perhaps that a family that had so often used the law to deter their enemies and get their own way now turned the law on each other. Frederick hired Brown Rudnick, an international law firm founded in 1940s Boston which prided itself on services that were 'practical and business-driven' rather than 'abstract or opaque'.

On 30 January 2020, the same day the *Telegraph* claimed victory in the battle for Brexit, Frederick and his daughter issued a claim against Alistair in the High Court. A few days later, early in the morning, Alistair opened the front door of his London home on Chester Square only to find a court order thrust at him – a result of the Kroll investigation. He had just a week to hand over everything he had gained from what the court described as an 'elaborate covert recording system'. This doorstep delivery order, or DDO, was a costly but effective device to find out exactly what had been going on. Alistair, prevented from 'tipping off' his accomplices, hired Weil, Gotshal and Manges, the law firm whose private practice head, Marco Compagnoni, had been appointed as the brothers' agent when they signed a personal guarantee for the *Telegraph* back in 2004, before going on to help them with the Claridge's deal.

Frederick and Amanda sued Aidan, Howard, Alistair, Aidan's son Andrew and the long-time family aide Philip Peters for breach of confidence, misuse of private information and a breach of data protection rights, in proceedings that were eventually heard in the Queens' Bench Division (QBD), another division of the High Court. The judge later said there was 'ample evidence' that the covert surveillance had yielded 'a wealth of confidential business information', with three months of voice memos, transcripts and WhatsApp messages discovered. When the case appeared in court, Desmond Browne QC represented Frederick and Amanda. 'We all remember Tolstoy saying "each unhappy family is unhappy in its own way",' he said. 'Here, the children of Sir Frederick and Sir David have been at odds . . . concerning the family trusts, and cousin, sadly, has been pitched against cousin.'[42]

Feuds between families, particularly over succession, are far from unusual. However, the public fallout between David and Frederick was entirely unexpected. The highly public feud shocked and saddened many of those who had worked for and admired the Barclay brothers. 'It is such a tragedy because, to be honest, I've never seen two people so in tune with each other,' said one. 'It wasn't just the fact that obviously they were twins. They were twins who were different, with different aspects to their life and both had fantastic sense of humour.' Another said: 'I never saw them as a fractured family. I believe that Aidan and Howard reflected precisely the views of David and Freddie. And then this was the worst kind of washing your dirty linen in public. You could have blown me over with a hairdryer.'

'I was amazed that there was some acrimony between David and Frederick because they were as one when I worked with them,' said one long-term associate. 'And I found that terribly sad. I still do find it terribly sad.'

There were two notable features of the subsequent legal battle of Barclay v Barclay. One was the decision of an octogenarian newspaper owner to make public statements against his own family after a lifetime of avoiding the press; the other was the plea for the proceedings to remain private by defendants who had illegally recorded the private conversations of their own relatives.

Frederick, no stranger to lawfare, charged. When the judge, Mr Justice Warby, ruled that he had the right to release the candid camera clip of his nephew fiddling with a bug if he so desired, he did just that. In a statement that was unique for this supremely private man, Frederick said: 'The decision to release this video of this deliberate and premeditated invasion of my privacy is in the public interest. I do not want anyone else to go through the awful experience of having their personal and private conversations listened to by scores of strangers.'

He then turned his fire directly at Aidan and his role at the Telegraph Media Group. 'I believe it is very much in the public interest for people – and in particular readers of the *Daily Telegraph* – to understand that a newspaper proprietor is not abiding by the strict rules of the editors' code.' The code, which is meant to regulate the ethical standards among journalists, says that the press 'must not seek to obtain or publish material acquired by using hidden cameras or clandestine listening devices' and 'misrepresentation or subterfuge, including by agents or intermediaries, can generally be justified only in the public interest'.

Frederick went further: 'Newspaper proprietors hold positions of great responsibility and influence. For the editors' code to have any effect on journalists' conduct, it should be upheld by those at the very top of an organisation.'

A huge bone of contention still remained over the actual price of the Ritz. In March, just over a month after Frederick started legal proceedings against them, his nephews sold the Ritz Hotel to Abdulhadi Mana Al-Hajri, for a widely reported sum of £800 million. The sale both confirmed the Qatari ruling family as bigger owners of London property than the Queen, and infuriated Frederick, who smelled a rat. Believing that his nephews had sent him on a fool's errand to sell the Ritz while they were busy with a separate deal, he went public with claims that the Ritz had been sold for 'half the market price'. He went so far as to issue a press release, having hired his own press adviser, in which he said he had received 'a number of competing offers . . . in excess of £1 billion'. He then threatened further litigation. There were reports of offers as high as £1.3 billion from the Saudi Arabia-based Sidra Capital.[43] Others mentioned included French luxury-goods conglomerate LVMH.

Such comments seemed to particularly irk his nephews.

The reported price, which worked out at £6 million per key, or hotel room, was considered quite high at the time. Later public filings for Green Park (No. 1) Ltd showed that the company whose ultimate beneficial owner is Abdulhadi Mana Al-Hajri paid £267 million in cash and then paid off net debts of £313 million. So the total enterprise value of the sale was just £580 million, not £800 million. After deducting the £30 million to cover the cost of closing the Ritz casino, repaid in full soon after the sale of the hotel, the net proceeds to B.UK from the sale of the Ritz were £237 million. In another court case three years later, Aidan Barclay suggested that, largely as a result of the debts involved, the proceeds from the sale were somewhere between £100 million and £150 million.[44]

A spokesman for the nephews simply denied that Frederick or Amanda had 'any relevant legal interest which would allow them to disrupt the sale process of The Ritz hotel.'[45]

By June, the five defendants admitted liability for the covert surveillance – the evidence had no doubt made any other course of action difficult in the circumstances – but argued that their aged uncle's behaviour had made their actions 'necessary and reasonable'. His behaviour had caused them 'serious concerns'. The defence papers said the operation was instigated by Alistair, who was 'very troubled about what seemed to him to be a remarkable change' in his uncle's behaviour, while Aidan and Peter were 'the least involved'.

When they criticized Frederick's comments to the media, their lawyer, Heather Rogers QC, argued that their publication had breached the nephews' Article 8 rights to respect for private and family life; her argument was met with snorts from the press bench. In his subsequent judgment, Justice Warby said, with barely a hint of a raised eyebrow, that such rights must be diminished by 'someone caught out interfering with someone else's privacy by surreptitious recording'.[46]

The defendants offered to pay damages.

David stayed on the sidelines during this public spat, but there had already been some public signs of a fallout, albeit relatively petty. In 2016, a new black marble headstone had been placed on their father's grave in Mortlake Cemetery. The gold inscription read: 'Long gone but not forgotten, Nor the memories in the passing years.' The names of just two of his eight children were etched on the stone: Sir David R. Barclay first, and then his older brother Andrew Roy. Frederick's name was missing.

Just a few years after this, while his twin was facing a titanic struggle with three of his sons, David was in court too, suing a little-known French playwright for violation of privacy and defamation. Hedi Tillette de Clermont-Tonnerre had written an absurdist farce about two weird billionaire brothers who pretend to be feminists wanting a daughter to inherit their fortune. The play *Les Deux Frères et les Lions* (The Two Brothers and the Lions), was performed at the 150-seat Théâtre de Poche-Montparnasse in

Paris, and did not mention the brothers by name. The defence documents accuse David of having 'excessive sensitivity' and an 'exacerbated taste for secrecy'.

After the first hearing, Clermont-Tonnerre said: 'In France, there is complete freedom to talk about public figures. We are in the country of Voltaire, it is a case of freedom of expression.'[47]

David lost and was ordered to pay damages and costs of €56,000.

Just after the Ritz was sold in March 2020, the UK went into lockdown. Frederick did not see his twin brother again, hearing about his death along with the rest of the world in January 2021.

12. *There's No Money, Your Honour*

It was a searingly hot Monday morning eighteen months later at the end of July 2022, and the press photographers standing outside the Gothic arches of the Royal Courts of Justice on London's Strand wore T-shirts and looked longingly at patches of shade across the street. They were waiting for the appeal court decision, then dominating the news, about whether to turn off the life support for a twelve-year-old boy.

When a small, white-haired man arrived at the gates, his outfit – a bright blue jacket and polka-dot pocket square, with matching silk tie tucked into his sharply creased trousers – caught their attention. A photographer from the Press Association had been told to expect the billionaire owner of the *Daily Telegraph* but still had to double-check this was the right man. He took a picture.

Until that day, almost the only published photograph of Frederick Barclay showed him alongside his twin brother, David, on the day they were knighted, in a historic double dubbing, more than two decades before. Frederick's appointment this time, inside courtroom 40, was far less joyful.

Forced to attend court in person because of the severity of the charges, a year that had started with the death of his twin brother ended with Frederick contemplating a possible prison sentence for failing to pay his ex-wife any of a £100 million divorce settlement in May 2021. Several months and hearings later, Frederick faced four days in front of a High Court judge facing contempt charges for non-payment. At eighty-seven, Frederick's mirror twin had gone and the woman he had lived with for almost fifty years had left him. If his decision to take his nephews to court had offered a peek behind the curtains of this secretive family, this case threatened to kick the door open on the whole house.

By the end of the week, a photograph of him alone, dressed in scarlet trousers outside the court, would be splashed across the front page of the *Financial Times* beneath the headline: 'Seeing red: Tycoon Barclay risks prison time after divorce case ruling'.[1]

The picture and the entire case shocked old associates. One remembered David Barclay's riposte when asked to talk more to journalists in the early days: 'Do you put the balance in your bank account on the front page of the *Financial Times*? No? Well, neither do I.'

Although family proceedings are usually held in private, Frederick's refusal to pay the money owed to his wife, claiming he had none to give her, turned the case into a quasi-criminal one. If found guilty, a man considered one of the UK's richest faced a spell in prison.

The stress of it, he told the court, was keeping him awake at night. It was no way to end such a long and successful career or marriage. Or a life spent avoiding publicity.

Over four days, the court would hear of the Barclay brothers' lifelong tax avoidance, a family now at loggerheads over succession, and finances so complex that even the beneficiaries claimed not to fully understand them. A family once so close they did everything together – live, work and holiday – was now riven with division, with no love lost between husband and wife, but also between brothers, mother and daughter, uncles and nephews and cousins. The case would test whether a man's inability to pay a court order was a private affair or matter of public interest. And whether the very rich were now above the law.

Although Lady Hiroko Barclay, the woman he had shared more than half his life with, was unlike any of his previous adversaries, the case of Barclay v Barclay shared several hallmarks of the many other courtroom battles that had marked the Barclay brothers' careers: an insistence on privacy above all else, complex financial structures obscured by a veil of secrecy, and a seeming disregard for the law.

The presiding judge would have to decide whether there was genuinely no money left, as Frederick told a court-appointed expert, or whether he was simply lying about his wealth in order to avoid paying his wife. Hiroko accused Frederick and his family of conducting a conspiracy against her, effectively hiding the money in offshore trusts, where it could not even be reached by the highest court in the land.

In court, Frederick's lawyer, Charles Howard QC, blamed the family feud for the default, saying, 'All this coincides with the war between the two sides of the family and this was the reason for the drying up.' Before this, Frederick had argued that he was short of funds because the underlying businesses, hit by economic headwinds and saddled with too much debt, had started to run out of money.

Even people who knew Frederick struggled to understand how it had come to this. If he were still worth a fraction of the multibillion-pound fortune the newspapers said he was, £100 million would surely be worth paying, if only to avoid the publicity. And if he really had no money, where had it gone?

In awarding one of the UK's biggest divorce settlements, in March 2021, the judge Sir Jonathan Cohen had already made it clear that £100 million was nowhere near the 50/50 split such a long relationship should warrant.[2] In settling for a figure he estimated was about 18 per cent of the money available, his lordship had favoured speed over size, ordering the £100 million to be paid in just over a year[3] – partly because neither of these ageing litigants was getting any younger, and partly to prevent the sort of proceedings now dragging on in the courts.

Since then, every deadline had passed without Frederick paying a penny of the lump sum, nor any of his wife's costs. After a few months, he had unilaterally decided to halve her agreed monthly maintenance to £30,000. She had filed three summonses to recover the rest, plus the £100 million. Meanwhile, her legal fees were mounting. Her lawyers had not been paid.

Frederick argued that he was in a bind – that his minority share in an empire he had jointly built with his brother left him at the mercy of his nephews, who controlled underlying family businesses that had started to run out of money. The taps had been 'turned off' six months after his wife left him, he said, either because the money wasn't there or because of the feud. The court heard that Frederick believed the judge did not understand how the trusts worked: 'There is no money now,' he said.[4]

The Barclay family's use of offshore trusts made it hard for the court to force Frederick to pay. His emissaries insisted there was nothing he could do against the power of discretionary trustees and complicated ownership structures. Professional trust protectors in Liechtenstein – one of the most secretive jurisdictions in the world – declined to reveal all the details of the money held and, unlike in cases involving poorer men with UK assets that could be more readily seized, the British legal system could do little about it.

Frederick was not the first supremely wealthy man to fail to comply with this kind of judgment. Divorces involving the super-rich from around the world had become increasingly common in London, where laws that favoured equality were often more attractive for ex-wives who lived in British properties with children at British schools. None of which meant that their husbands, and it had to date always been men, felt the need to abide by the High Court judgments. In recent years some of the wealthiest men had simply ignored the court orders. One, an Azerbaijani billionaire called Farkhad Akhmedov – ordered to pay almost half a billion pounds to his ex-wife Tatiana – had compared the order with 'toilet paper in the sea'.[5]

What all these high-profile divorce cases shared was the use of offshore trusts in places ranging from Liechtenstein to the

British Virgin Islands, shadowy trustees, and a drawn-out saga involving super yachts and luxury mansions. And the relative impotence of the British court system to do much about them.

But unlike Akhmedova v Akhmedov, Barclay v Barclay involved a British-born knight of the realm, a man feted for his skill in business, a Thatcherite billionaire who had made most of his money in Britain. A man who had celebrated with Brexiteers on the day the UK voted to leave the European Union, and who owned the most British of newspapers.

By 11 a.m. on Monday 25 July, the courtroom in the somewhat brutalist Queen's Court building at the back of the Royal Courts was packed. There were three times the usual number of court reporters, with six news organizations represented on the wooden press benches to the right of the judge. But the number of law-yers in the room dwarfed the number of journalists. Alongside at least six solicitors there were no fewer than eight barristers, each earning between £500 and several thousand pounds for each hour of their time. Directly in front of the judge, at either end of the front row, were two people whose thirty-four-year marriage would now be discussed in open court, and whose only compan-ions in court were their own lawyers.

Courtroom 40 was so stifling in the midsummer heatwave that even the judge stripped to his shirtsleeves at one point, after allowing the increasingly shiny barristers to remove their wigs and silk gowns. Hiroko, with two lawyers sitting between her and her ex-husband, was the only one to maintain her composure. Perfectly still at seventy-nine, she sat throughout in a Chanel cream jacket draped with pearls and matching earrings, closest to the press. Next to her was one of the UK's most famous divorce lawyers.

Baroness Shackleton of Belgravia had acted for both Prince Charles and Prince Andrew in their divorce battles, and as solici-tor for Princes William and Harry. Heather Mills had poured a jug of water over her when she acted for her ex-husband, the ex-Beatle Paul McCartney,[6] and in more recent years she had acted for high-profile women, including Princess Haya of Jordan in her custody proceedings against the Emir of Dubai. A Conservative peer known for being both tough and charming, at one point in this long-running saga she wore a gold brooch in the shape of a portcullis, a symbol of strength and security and the British parliament. During the three years of this case, she had grown close to Hiroko, which was helpful as Shackleton's team had not been paid for some time. Their fees by the end of the week would have grown to more than £1 million.

Frederick sat at the other end of the front row, between a not-long-qualified paralegal, Abbie Leamon, and the lawyer he had appointed to speak for him, Marcus Dearle. While his wife had hired one of the best divorce lawyers in Britain, Frederick's man was an expert on family law and asset protection – financial advice for the very wealthy. Although now a partner at Miles Preston, Dearle had spent much of his career at Withers, a firm that had worked with the Barclay family on and off for years. He had spent much of his career in Hong Kong. Frederick had filed no statement, nor given any evidence since his wife had started the contempt proceedings, as was his right. Instead, he instructed Dearle, a thick-set man wearing a double-breasted suit, oblong glasses and tousled hair, who gave the impression of a provincial estate agent, to speak on his behalf.

The whole court rose when the judge entered. The Honourable Sir Jonathan Lionel Cohen had retired from the High Court in May 2021 at the age of seventy, just before publishing what he might have hoped would be his final ruling in the Barclay divorce case. Under judicial rules, he could still continue to sit full-time for three years, and in his first year he had already presided over several hearings in the case before him – including one to decide whether the eighty-seven-year-old man he was to judge had the mental capacity to attend court. He did.

Cohen was keen to get started. But, before anything of real substance could be heard, he would have to adjudicate on who could hear, or more properly read, all about it.

David's sons had sent more barristers to court than either their uncle or aunt – not to take part in the divorce proceedings but to prevent any reporting of it. Cohen was not regarded as a press-friendly judge, having spent most of his long career dealing with family cases involving children where no reporting was allowed. Yet Frederick's nephews faced an uphill battle. In awarding Hiroko £100 million in March 2021, the judge had overruled Frederick's initial objections to the media, saying the public had a right to know how badly he had behaved in the financial remedies dispute, if nothing else. As well as criticizing Frederick's decision to sell his super yacht and keep some of the proceeds 'for his own use' as 'reprehensible', Cohen had criticized 'flagrant' and repeated flouting of orders to answer questions or produce documents, leading at one point to a nine-month delay. Hiroko had argued that Frederick's 'behaviour has removed his right to privacy' and the judge had effectively agreed with her. After this, Frederick had tried to have the judge removed from the case, but failed.[7]

More importantly, Frederick now faced quasi-criminal proceedings. If he had appealed the amount of the £100 million court order, the hearings would most likely have stayed behind closed doors. But he had simply refused, or been unable, to pay. So Hiroko's lawyers now had to prove beyond reasonable doubt – a criminal standard of proof – whether Frederick had the money to pay the large lump sum as well as the unpaid legal fees and maintenance. At the time of the contempt proceedings, just this tranche of the money owed added up to £245,000.

Leading arguments for men referred to throughout as 'the nephews' was Heather Rogers QC, a media lawyer who had acted for them in the Ritz bugging case. Rogers was based at Doughty Street Chambers, known for lawyers of a liberal bent, and was also a director of the Campaign for Freedom of Information, the latter role sitting slightly at odds with her advocacy in this case. When Rogers had finished, Cohen asked about the practicalities of excluding the media from a case in which Frederick's finances – the key to deciding whether he should go to prison – were so closely aligned to, if not controlled by, his nephews.

Stewart Leech QC, acting for Hiroko, accused the nephews of 'censorship on the widest scale by a non-party' rather than a legitimate attempt to protect their confidential information.

Leech, a quick-witted litigator whose exasperation with this case came through with the occasional raised eyebrow and waspish tone, drew parallels with the concerns over other wealthy men flouting court orders: 'There is a real public interest [in knowing] that men in Sir Frederick Barclay's position – captains of industry, media moguls, knights of the realm – like anyone else in this country, ignore court orders at their peril.'[8]

Besides, the Barclays weren't just captains of any industry, but of a newspaper. The *Daily Telegraph* often saw fit to write about other family sagas that turned up in court.[9] Aidan, chairman of the Telegraph Media Group, had even told the Leveson Inquiry into press ethics: 'It is the role of newspapers, and their associated websites, to scrutinise those in positions of influence and power and to report in the public interest.' Courts deciding to send octogenarian billionaire knights of the realm to prison in private were not usually common in democracies.

By lunchtime on the first day, the judge ruled in favour of the press. 'To state the obvious, anything that affects Sir Frederick, and in particular his reasons not to pay . . . couldn't possibly be described as private,' he told the court.

The hands of seventy-nine-year-old Hiroko Barclay shook slightly as she took her oath on the first day of the case. She looked mainly at the judge to her right, occasionally at her ex-husband's barrister, but never directly at her ex-husband, who sat yards from her, at the foot of the short flight of stairs leading up to the witness stand. Frederick, for his part, largely looked straight ahead, into the wooden benches of the judiciary, occasionally grimacing and glancing up at his wife.

A statement in court had already revealed Hiroko's fear and confusion: 'If Frederick dies before I get my first lump sum, my monthly maintenance will stop. I will be left virtually penniless and almost certainly homeless after a relationship/marriage of close to half a century, where our standard of living was beyond extravagant.' She accused Frederick of a 'put-up sham', and of hiding his money in a conspiracy with, not just his nephews, but also their only child.[10]

When she had first met a dashing, well-dressed London hotelier on a beach in Cannes in 1973, Hiroko had no idea of the life of luxury she would go on to enjoy. Nor that when she finally decided to leave him forty-six years later, she would find herself living in rented accommodation, with nothing in her name but an overdrawn bank account and unpaid legal bills.

Born Hiroko Kuzusaka in Beijing in October 1942, in the middle of the Sino-Japanese War, she moved back to Tokyo along with her five elder sisters in 1945. Four of whom were still alive at almost eighty years later. Hiroko married Kenji Asado, but the marriage ended soon after their son Ko was born in 1967. Hiroko moved to London to live with one of her sisters, Akiko, who was four years older and had already opened one of the UK's first sushi restaurants, which she called Hiroko after her baby sister.

By all accounts, the beautiful Kuzasaka sisters were glamorous fixtures of the wealthy Japanese expat scene. An anonymous restaurant employee once told *The Times*: 'There were always at least three Rolls-Royces parked outside.'[11] Hiroko the restaurant closed in 1974, a year after the young mother had met Frederick while on holiday in the South of France, moving in with him shortly after, along with her young son.

It was a bumpy few years financially: the start of the property downturn and the brothers' inability to repay their loans from the Crown Agents. Despite this, their first marital home was close to one of the brothers' hotels, the Lowndes in Belgravia. Although the area of grand white-stucco buildings was more down-at-heel then than the chichi world of investment bankers and oligarchs it is now, their neighbours included Lord Mountbatten, cousin to the Queen.

In 1978, five years after meeting him, Hiroko gave birth to Frederick's only child, Amanda, who was nine when they eventually married on 6 May 1987. It seemed like a largely uneventful marriage. Hiroko looked after the children and enjoyed seeing her sisters and girlfriends. She spent time with David's first wife and three sons. After 1982, the Barclay brothers lived in several properties in Chester Square. The house Frederick and Hiroko moved into in 1992 was the only property she understood had been put in her name.

In 2005, soon after the youngest of their two grandchildren was born, there had been a 'blip' in the marriage and Hiroko started divorce proceedings. They reconciled, but five years later Frederick insisted that she transfer number 37 Chester Square to Amanda and her children. Hiroko accused Frederick of tricking her into signing over the rights to their marital home by saying their only child needed it more.[12] Only later did she discover how many properties Amanda could lay claim to as part of Frederick's detailed inheritance plans, she said. When it came to paperwork, she was given little choice. 'His body language said just sign it, so I can't even read it,' she told the court.

She had never needed to ask for money and had no real idea where any of it was. So their life together continued, through Frederick's separation from his twin brother and more until, on 28 March 2019, Hiroko walked out of their £30 million mansion in St James's. She only subsequently discovered, she said, that all she had in her name was a joint bank account with an overdraft approaching £6 million.[13]

Hiroko talked of always being at the sidelines during family rows, her understanding based on snatched conversations while she pottered about at home or on the yacht. Occasionally in their long marriage she had learned substantive things, such as when Frederick told her that he had agreed with his twin that if one of them died the 'power' went to the other when it came to the trusts. In cross-examination, Frederick's lawyer Charles Howard QC asked Hiroko about her understanding of the family fortune. 'It is such a complicated structure I don't understand [it], but he has power . . . whatever money he wanted, he could get it,' she said.[14]

Howard was the latest of at least four QCs who had acted for Frederick during his divorce. Without legal representation for about six months until early 2021, Frederick had even considered applying for legal aid, using the services of the under-resourced and overstretched official solicitor.[15]

He finally appointed Charles Howard, a highly experienced litigator who had been called to the bar in 1975, just a year after the seventy-two-year-old judge. In court, he was sometimes referred to as 'the Undertaker' behind his back, because of his funereal tone and often long-winded exposition, but Howard was detailed and dogged and obviously good at what he did.

The court would hear how the once close-knit Barclays were deeply divided. Not only had Frederick fallen out with his brother, his nephews and now his wife, but Hiroko no longer had any relationship with their only child, Amanda, who had severed relations with her mother in the wake of the divorce proceedings. Hiroko told the court that Amanda had come to threaten her with 'council housing' if she carried on with the contempt hearing. She said she missed her two grandchildren. Amanda had stopped paying her father's legal fees the year before, and had 'made it plain that she is unwilling to assist her mother in any way'.[16] She never appeared in her parents' divorce hearing, despite requests from the judge to do so, and was unavailable to lawyers for both sides.

As Frederick had no money, he said, his legal fees were being paid by his nephews by way of a loan. Yet, a year on from the settlement of the bugging case, relations were strained. Hiroko told the court that Aidan, the eldest son who had ended up with the biggest share when his uncle gave up half of his 50 per cent stake, had told her that he had 'no love' for either Amanda or Frederick.

Frederick's argument was that he could not pay his ex-wife anything because he had no control over the family finances. He left Charles Howard to sum it up: '[Frederick] has got no nexus at all . . . He has no locus at all to do anything . . My client is extremely stressed and worried about prison. He's eighty-seven. Why doesn't he just pay up? It just doesn't make sense.'

The case kept coming back to two issues: the search for huge sums of money in ownership structures that were still entirely opaque, and the search for the ultimate controller. It was like a sort of financial dance of the seven veils, occasionally revealing a glimpse of offshore ankle before coming down again to obscure the entire body.

The judge only had to find whether Frederick could access £100 million – meant to be a fraction of his wealth – and the £245,000 in overdue payments. But he had to be sure beyond reasonable doubt, particularly challenging given the complexities of the financial arrangements.

Hiroko, who admitted she did not understand the way the money had been managed, was sure of one thing. 'He organised all this,' she said of her husband.

To understand how much control Frederick really had, Cohen had to grapple with the offshore financing the twins had used to organize their fortune. In an earlier ruling, he had said of David and Frederick's succession planning: '[They] shared an obsession with privacy but also with avoiding tax, whether payable in their lifetime or on death.'[17] In drawing up their succession plan, the Barclay brothers had used a series of offshore trusts for each of the four children set to inherit the bulk of their empire. The structure was far more complex but the trusts were essentially fed by a series of underlying businesses divided into retail and non-retail arms (largely property and the media).

The complexity of a system in which many, many trusts and hundreds of companies in a range of jurisdictions are managed by a family treasury operation is perhaps summed up best by the fact that none of the people who gave evidence seemed to understand it. In written evidence read out in court, the main beneficiary of Frederick's plans, Amanda, had told the court: 'I really do have no idea about the loan notes . . . how they were set up and how they operate is beyond me.'[18] Frederick's solicitor, Marcus Dearle, an expert in asset protection who gave evidence on Frederick's behalf, said under cross-examination: 'I don't know exactly what the family office is. I don't understand the structure.'[19]

Frederick declined to give evidence in the contempt hearing, as was his right. Cohen had already rejected one argument that his dubious handling of the yacht sale was 'all part of an innocent muddle caused by old age'. When Frederick had given up his non-domicile status to move back to London, he'd decided that the most tax-efficient way to arrange his affairs was via loan notes held by two offshore trusts, one for both him and his daughter and one just for her. Essentially IOUs with better legal protection, loan notes have several corporate uses, but they are particularly effective for estate planning. They allow parents to make their children the principal beneficiaries of trusts in such a way that they can provide a tax-free income to themselves. After having his 25 per cent stake valued, Frederick effectively 'sold' his share in the whole empire to a trust set up for his daughter – the Amelia Trust – which 'paid' for this generosity by issuing £650 million of unsecured loan notes to a trust of which both Frederick and Amanda were beneficiaries at the start of 2014.[20] Frederick could then use the notes for his living expenses by asking for repayment – or redemption, in the jargon of loan notes.

Imagine you sell a car to someone but accept an IOU in return rather than cash, with the understanding that when you need some cash, say to buy a big-ticket item like a sofa, you can simply ask the person (or trust) who owes you money to pay you some of it back. In essence, and without other layers of complexity, this is how a loan note works. Such measures avoid the parent paying income, inheritance or capital gains. It was, in the judge's words, part of a 'major tax mitigation restructuring'. Hiroko, who was not named as a beneficiary of either of these two trusts, nor the marital home, told the court: '[Frederick's] not allowed to have assets . . . all not to pay tax in the UK.'

From 2014 to March 2019, when his wife left him, Frederick's lifestyle – that of one of the richest men in the UK – did not change. He spent a total of £128 million by redeeming some of the loan notes worth £650 million. Frederick awarded himself £800,000 a month for living expenses, gave up his lease in Monaco, and bought a house and yacht that would surpass any of his previous possessions, with the exception perhaps of Fort Brecqhou.

In 2016, he bought an apartment in Cleveland Court in St James's, within a stone's throw of Clarence House, the London home of the future King of England. Frederick paid £30 million for a 6,000-square-foot five-bedroom property occupying two floors of the grand neo-classical building with Portland stone façade close to the royal park. The property boasted a high level of security, two staff flats, a 24/7 concierge service and a garage. Frederick added a custom-built ballroom and hyperbaric oxygen chamber, which increases the amount of oxygen the blood can carry. He still danced regularly, sometimes daily, gliding gracefully with dance champions such as Anne Gleave well into his eighties.

At a time when Frederick 'simply spent as he wished. He did not seek the trustees approval',[21] he also splashed out on his own super yacht, after always previously having to share one with his twin brother. *Leander*, a seventy-five-metre vessel capable of accommodating twenty guests and a crew of twenty-eight, was already famous when Frederick bought her in 2016, having been owned by former vice admiral turned parking millionaire Sir Donald Gosling, a 'super yachting legend'. The yacht, probably the most beautiful of all the Barclay yachts, was also a favourite of the future King and Queen. Unlike the former naval man, the Barclays never allowed their yachts to be chartered. *Leander* was said to cost £375,000 a month to maintain.

Then, suddenly, six months after his wife left him, Frederick stopped being able to redeem the loan notes, by now said to be worth £545 million. Although the timing was suspicious, Frederick's legal team argued that financial troubles in the underlying businesses such as Yodel and the feud with his nephews had led to the taps being turned off. His nephews had used their majority control of 75 per cent to stop money being moved up to the offshore trusts that fed Amanda's Amelia Trust.

This money could have come in a variety of ways, not just profits or asset sales. The family had long sent cash offshore via unsecured interest-free loans. Once offshore, not only was transparency non-existent but professional trustees were paid to avoid disclosure, even when ordered to by an English High Court judge. Orders for the trustees to release the cash were simply ignored, the court was told. Frederick's legal team had been 'consistently blocked' in their efforts to access the cash by lawyers for the nephews and the trustees who 'could not have been less helpful'.

A long note of a meeting between Dearle and the protector of Frederick's trusts is telling about the attitude of professional trustees to handing over information. The protector of the trust, a man named Daniel Martineau, is reported as saying that while there was 'no effort to obfuscate or avoid' and that 'the trustees do not want to roadblock the production of all information', their concern was that 'if they were to give some information, it could be a slippery slope and that they would then be expected to provide everything.' He then explained that trustees governed by Liechtenstein laws 'should not necessarily give information even when beneficiaries are asking for it'.[22]

There was one frustratingly fleeting reference to an attempt to sell Amanda's entire share in the business, which would have been a dramatic way of ending Frederick's apparent financial woes. It came in a note made of Dearle's hour-long meeting with the protector of Frederick's main trusts in May 2021. As the nephews controlled all the major assets, getting any 'money, assets or information' had been 'impossible'. Besides, who would want to own a quarter-share in a business in which the controlling shareholders had already shown that they could switch off payments?

'They're very, very secretive, the Liechtenstein trustees,' Dearle said, almost mournfully.

'And the Barclay family are very secretive,' retorted Leech.

'And the Barclay family is secretive,' nodded Frederick's representative.[23]

One of the problems for Marcus Dearle, the solicitor appointed by Frederick to speak on his behalf, was that he had no relationship with his client's nephews. Apart from the fact, that is, that they were paying his fees. By the time he appeared in the witness box, they had already paid £888,000 to his firm, Miles Preston. By the end of that week in court, they would have spent more than £1 million on Frederick's solicitors – albeit, it was said, via a loan. And that was before paying their own legal fees, directed at trying to stop any reporting of the case.

Having reached a wall of silence over the issue of how Frederick could access the hundreds of millions of pounds that had previously been at his disposal, Cohen turned to an asset that was at least more physical: the island of Brecqhou. The court would hear how a fortress which once symbolized how much they had achieved together had also helped cause the rift.

In October 2019, a month after funds stopped flowing to his trust, Frederick had written a letter to David on Ritz-headed notepaper asking that Savills come and value his share in the island in order to meet his obligations to the court. The letter reads as though it was written by a lawyer, making it pretty clear that he was being forced to write it because of his divorce proceedings. David's reply six days later, marked 'Private and confidential', is on notepaper headed with the map of Brecqhou and a coat of arms that, tellingly, no longer sports twin emblems but solo ones.

In this, he offers 'a firm no' to the request to allow a valuation of the island. 'First, Brecqhou is my and my wife's home. It would be a serious invasion of our privacy to have Savills come to the island. As you know, we value our privacy highly,' he wrote to his equally private twin. 'Second, the only purpose of such an exercise can be to value your interest in the island. As matters stand you have half the freehold of Brecqhou, which is all but worthless given the length of the lease of over 100 years to Brecqhou Development Ltd. Third, while the trust of which you are a beneficiary may own half of the shares in BDL those shares also have no practical value because neither you nor your family have any right to live on Brecqhou. This is not a new state of affairs but one which has lasted for some years. Even before then, you rarely spent any time on the island. And I remind you of the very substantial cost of running the island each year to which neither you nor the trust have contributed.'

He ends by saying he is willing to buy out his brother's 'worthless' interest in the island for £75,000.

Asked about this letter, Hiroko called it 'hideous really . . . I think this is typical David.'

Frederick's less-than-warm relationship with David's widow, and the fact that David was buried on the island, made a fire sale of his stake unlikely.

★

While Frederick and his nephews were unable to find any money at all to pay Hiroko or her lawyers, they were happily paying other legal fees. Not only were David's sons paying to fund Frederick's divorce lawyers by way of a loan, their lawyers also attended every hearing and dealt with requests for documents. They employed Signature Litigation, whose founding partner had acted for the former Georgian oligarch Badri Patarkatsishvili.[24] All this before the cost of the three QCs to act on their behalf and police any possible privacy infringements.

Frederick had also spent an astonishing amount of money – more than £7.5 million – suing his nephews in the bugging case all while 'pleading impecuniosity' in the divorce hearings, according to the judge. The doorstep delivery order forcing Alistair to hand over his devices had been effective, but far from cheap. Apart from providing pretty incontrovertible evidence of the bugging operation, the means did not seem to justify the end result. Frederick had apparently received just £800,000 from the settlement – which, it was said, went straight to Frederick and Amanda's lawyers, Brown Rudnick.

At least the corporate cash flows had improved after the bugging case was settled in the middle of 2021. When he ordered Frederick to pay the £100 million in March 2021, Sir Jonathan Cohen had rejected that there were any problems with 'liquidity' in the underlying businesses, saying that Frederick had not produced a 'jot' of evidence that heavy debts and struggling businesses meant he could not find £100 million, particularly in the wake of the sale of the Ritz. After the ruling, the underlying businesses appeared to improve partly due to the pandemic. With more people at home, online shopping companies such as the old Littlewoods, now Very, had benefited. The company had even repaid Aidan Barclay's £125 million loan to the Very Group in full in the year to June 2020, and refinanced the loan guaranteed by him and his brother the following year.

Although Yodel was still battling a competitive market, it had also improved somewhat, benefiting from a surge in parcel deliveries during the pandemic to the extent that it even managed a small profit of £18 million in the year ending June 2021. The *Telegraph* too increased profits after a bump in digital subscribers to its online products.

Having rejected the argument about liquidity, the judge said: 'It doesn't seem to me that any evidence put forward proves the absence of liquidity . . . the issue in this case is the attitude of the nephews.'

In what was meant to be his final ruling on Thursday, 28 July 2022, Sir Jonathan Cohen was certain about at least one thing: the behaviour of Frederick's nephews. 'It is very striking that rather than assist in finding a solution to what should be a matter of honour to this family they refuse to provide information, hiding behind the walls of the trust structure,' he wrote. 'It would be beyond comprehension if the nephews are not seeking to assist in finding a solution to help meet the needs of their aunt, who has next to nothing after a very long marriage, and when it was the express agreement between their father and [Frederick] that the latter should receive 25% of the family wealth.' Instead, Cohen said, they had chosen to spend a fortune on lawyers 'to try to avert the gaze of the media'.[25]

As Frederick had not appealed the order but simply failed to pay it, he had left Hiroko having to prove beyond reasonable doubt that he had the money. Given the remaining doubts over the whereabouts and even existence of the family fortune, whether held in loan notes or not, in the end the verdict came down to a technicality over how much was in Frederick's lawyers' accounts.

Under cross-examination Dearle had admitted a gap in the correspondence with the nephews between October 2021 and February 2022, during which time £185,000 in legal fees and £60,000 for maintenance had not been paid to Hiroko. A letter from the nephews stipulating that the substantial funds they were sending had to be spent on Frederick's legal fees alone did not arrive until Frederick had already failed to pay two smaller sums which Miles Preston held in its accounts, in addition to a small 'residue' from the sale of the yacht. So Frederick was found guilty of failing to pay court orders to the value of £245,000 in total but not the £100 million plus he had so far failed to pay. 'I find that [Frederick] needed to do no more than ask for the money and he would have received it,' said the judge.[26]

When the court returned for sentencing two weeks later, Frederick had paid the £245,000.

Hiroko's lawyers still asked for a suspended prison sentence but Cohen adjourned for a further three months to give the family more time to come up with at least some of the £100 million lump sum. Again, he tried to embarrass the family into complying: 'It should be a matter a shame for Sir Frederick and his nephews that Lady Barclay is left with next to nothing by way of financial resources for the future . . . It seems to me extraordinary that every member of the family is prepared to put their hands into their pockets to help Sir Frederick avoid prison but will do nothing to help assist the greatest victim in this, namely Lady Barclay.'[27]

Ahead of the next court hearing early in 2023, Hiroko's lawyers again urged the judge to commit an elderly man to prison for six weeks, the maximum sentence. But in the position statement, Stewart Leech also issued an entirely new threat. For the first time in the four years since she had walked out of their marital home, Hiroko was considering bankruptcy proceedings. She had been left with little choice against her 'completely unrepentant' ex-husband. The underlying threat was that these proceedings would 'doubtless cause the personal guarantee he and his late brother gave in respect of the business's borrowings to come crashing down'.[28]

Throughout their careers, Frederick and David had offered

personal guarantees for the huge sums of money they usually borrowed to acquire companies – a common enough measure in the absence of physical assets to use as surety instead. In the bugging case, much had been made of huge debts raised against large personal guarantees made by the twins. The sum had been redacted, or kept private, but it was clear that a large amount was at stake. It was sometimes clear when these guarantees, usually held jointly and severally, were repaid, but mostly it was not. Held offshore, such arrangements were usually kept between the signatories and their banks, the deeds held far from the public gaze.

The Barclays would not want the banks that had extended such loans to become nervous about the state of their finances, was the suggestion in Hiroko's final statement. She was also considering hiring specialist litigation funders who would need access to all such private documents, whether they were in the public domain or not.

Immediately following Hiroko's statement, Frederick spoke to his nephew Howard and a settlement proposal was made that same day – the Friday before the planned court hearing the following Monday.

When he next arrived outside courtroom 40 the day before Valentine's Day, Frederick had eschewed his earlier jaunty scarlet and was wearing a sombre black velvet smoking jacket, blue silk tie and white polka-dot handkerchief. Waiting for the hearing to start, he sat alongside his legal team at a table that would not have looked out of place in a local authority office. This time it was Hiroko who wore red – a bright jacket, with a huge jewelled brooch that looked like a gold and many-faceted phoenix on her left breast pocket.

The two sides delayed the start of the hearing while the last-minute proposal was discussed. The judge gave them another three weeks to reach an agreement.

On 6 March 2023, it became clear that an agreement had still not been reached, almost exactly four years after Hiroko had walked out of their marital home and almost two after the judge had awarded her £100 million. Frederick's lawyer, Charles Howard, asked for another adjournment – simply, he suggested, for his client to find the cash.

Cohen, who had asked why he should have any confidence in this proposal after so many delays, instead issued a judicial summons for Aidan and Howard – controllers of the family fortune and owners of the *Daily Telegraph* – to testify about how much money a man who had built the family fortune along with their father really had. 'What they have to say about the means of their uncle and what has been made available to him, by way of resources, might provide a means of taking this forward in a more constructive way.'

When the clerk called for the court to rise, Frederick was the last to do so. He made no immediate comment. Neither did his nephews.

When she was asked why her husband had not paid the court order, Hiroko said: 'I think he's just waiting for either him or me to die.'

The life and times of the Barclay brothers should have been one of Britain's great post-war success stories. Twins born with nothing but nous and talent had built a great fortune, and used it – not only to live beyond their wildest dreams, but to gain power and influence. They guarded their fortune fiercely, arranging their affairs so that journalists, tax officials and almost everybody else found them difficult to follow. Early on in the unexpected divorce of the elderly billionaire, the presiding judge Sir Jonathan Cohen described what he saw as 'two hallmarks' of Frederick: the first, 'the desire to ensure there is no tax to pay, particularly on death' and the second, 'that of control'.[29] This desire for control spilled over into all parts of the brothers' lives, particularly concerning what could and could not be written, or even known, about them.

Yet David Barclay was so keen to have his story recorded for the ages that he talked to at least three potential biographers before he died. One of the last was a former *Daily Telegraph* diarist, Tim Walker, whom he met in private rooms at the Ritz in 2015.[30] David sent the journalist his thoughts on the world, notably his dislike of the Japanese and Europe. He failed to mention either his brother or his Japanese sister-in-law.

David had wanted to call the book *The Man Who Built a Castle*, the singular noun an early sign of just how much he had written his mirror twin out of their conjoined story. The title also underlined the importance of his own private island fortress to the mythology of the man.

Born on an island undergoing great change, David Barclay would not only gain power and influence, he would also attempt to command his own kingdom, united with his twin brother in a desire for privacy and overweening control.

In the end, he failed to agree terms with any biographer and instead wrote some chapters himself. In March 2016, David told a journalist he was writing his second book, which he would call *In my Experience What I know and What I believe* [sic], which he said was 'not for publication but for my grandchildren'. This tome – in which it is said he erased or downplayed the contribution of others such as Frederick and their younger brother Douglas – is understood to have been distributed to a tight-knit circle of men. Like so much about the Barclays, none of it has yet been published.

While David was the one interested in history and legacy, both brothers were equally keen on using the law– more than their own ingenuity or charm – to exert control. Long separated from his brother, Frederick still found himself locked in battle with a judge who had ordered him to pay £100 million, an amount believed to be a fraction of the Barclay family wealth. The problem for the judge, and by extension the entire legal system, was that after trying to follow the money through a byzantine financial structure of offshore trusts and family ownership, he could not say exactly, without reasonable doubt, where this money might be.

Frederick first said he had no money, then that the money was there but controlled by his nephews. The threat of bankruptcy led to more talks but even those failed to end in agreement. Meanwhile, his ex-wife – never consulted on any decision nor given command over their finances – relied on money from others and the prospect of launching new proceedings, using lawyers who had not yet been paid. After a forty-six-year relationship, she had nothing at all in her name. But then, having reorganized his affairs again to move back to the UK in 2014, the court had not found much in Frederick's name either.

After jointly building and controlling a vast, shared fortune, Frederick had given half his share to his more dominant brother's children. He had eventually left the island but, years later, like a banished Prospero trying to protect both himself and his daughter, he turned his anger on the men who had inherited his share in the business. The fallout from this row would test the limits of the man's ability to control the lives of others, and would help bring the whole edifice down.

Epilogue: The Crash

Aidan and Howard Barclay appeared together in Sir Jonathan Cohen's courtroom in May 2023 two months after they had been summoned, having spent the time fighting and losing an appeal against his legal command. With his dove-grey, double-breasted suit, navy tie and pale pocket handkerchief, the by-now sixty-seven-year-old Aidan had inherited his father's style, as well as his stature, receding hairline and, less explicably, his working-class London accent.

From the stand, Aidan said that he had not spoken to his uncle Frederick for several years and assumed that he was 'perfectly capable of looking after himself' given his 'properties and rents'. His uncle's failure to pay £100 million was 'not my fight', he told the court.

During their appearance in court, David's sons kept themselves apart from all but their own advisers. Including – most notably – from their uncle. Frederick may have parked his Range Rover in a bay reserved for the judiciary, but he sat waiting with everyone else in the hall outside, while his nephews were sequestered in a private room upstairs.

Aidan repeatedly distanced himself from the complicated corporate structure he sat at the head of. Shown an organogram in which the two halves of the empire flowed into nine different trusts held by himself, two of his brothers, and a cousin, he said: 'The routing of monies is a complicated affair for which I need corporation and tax advice . . . money travels up the tree but exactly how it goes and where it goes I couldn't tell you.'

The byzantine system had been put in place 'some time in the 1980s', he said, when the twins had 'decided to give everything away' rather than 'own anything'. 'They decided they wanted to live their lives in that manner and I had no say.'

Confident under cross-examination, he stumbled at a mention of his brothers before explaining that his second brother, Duncan, continued to receive a 'salary' along with other family members, even though he was not one of the main beneficiaries of the family assets.

Since 2019 'things had been difficult', he said, citing PPI claims against the retail business, the cost of the COVID-19 pandemic and wage inflation. 'It is a time of doom and gloom. It's not actually easy at the moment. We've had lots of pressures.'

When Cohen asked why the corporate structure could not be rearranged to allow one of the founding twins to pay his court-imposed divorce order, Aidan replied: 'I would do anything I can to settle this unpleasant situation but in the short term as far as businesses are concerned that's simply not realistic . . . I have quite a few restrictions on me from a banking point of view about what I can pay out. At the moment, it's difficult.'[1]

Nothing Aidan said in the witness box on 16 May 2023 gave any indication of just how difficult things were.

Aidan and his brother had been removed from a key holding company just the day before, not by a relative but by Lloyds Bank. Unable to recoup huge debts dating back nearly twenty years, the bank had finally moved to take control of a series of companies, until eventually it seized control of the *Daily Telegraph*, one of the family's most prized assets.

When António Horta-Osório and his new team had arrived at Lloyds Bank twelve years before, they were not particularly shocked at the size of the toxic debts the bank held. In early 2011, the global credit crisis had already led to the near collapse of some the world's largest banks: an overextended Lloyds had been encouraged by the then government to merge with HBOS, a bank that had lent billions of pounds without much regard for its customers' ability to pay the money back, as part of a go-for-growth land grab. Losses at the combined Lloyds HBOS were so bad that the government used £20 billion of taxpayers' money to buy 43 per cent of the merged group at the start of 2009. By the time the then chancellor George Osborne appointed his favourite banker Horta-Osório to help rescue the part-nationalized Lloyds, it was loaded with £200 billion of toxic assets and in dire straits.

So the desperate situation he found himself in was not unexpected for Horta-Osório. One of the first things he did was ask for a list of the largest outstanding toxic loans. It was that list which caused the biggest surprise, for at the top sat an astonishing £1.6 billion debt owed by David and Frederick Barclay.

It was not just the scale of the ensuing liability that came as a shock to Lloyds insiders, but the fact that the twins were two of the most highly regarded businessmen of the time, flying high on the *Sunday Times* Rich List with several prized and valuable assets. Imagine the situation: in the early 2010s the Barclay brothers were believed to be two of Britain's wealthiest men, with a slot at the top of the *Sunday Times* rich list and a reputation to match. They had survived crashes where many had foundered and made money by spotting opportunities others had not. Besides, they were still living like kings and acting like corporate predators. Just before Horta-Osório joined Lloyds, they had launched an aggressive takeover bid for three more luxury hotels, including Claridge's.

It came as no surprise that the twins had some debts. They had grown rich borrowing money to buy undervalued assets, even before doing so to buy Ellerman in the 1980s. Their early successes meant they had little difficulty persuading banks to lend them money for more purchases. By all accounts, they did this with a mixture of charm and menace and the sense that they were men who spotted opportunities that others did not and had survived while others had not.

They had found a particularly easy source of funding in a softly spoken Scot who would go on to become one of the best-known examples of the profligate lending that characterized much of the pre-crash banking system. Peter Cummings, the former head of HBOS's corporate lending division, was subsequently banned by the Financial Services Authority for failing to 'exercise due skill, care and diligence' when it came to the major loans he agreed.[2] When the Barclay brothers needed to raise an extra £400 million to guarantee their purchase of the Telegraph Media Group from Conrad Black in 2004, it was to Cummings and the then Bank of Scotland that they turned.

After the initial bridging loan lapsed, a Bank of Scotland loan was agreed in 2006 with a vehicle registered in the British Virgin Islands whose name alone – Penultimate Investment Holdings Ltd (PIHL) – suggested that it sat near the top of the Barclays' corporate structure. But that structure was seemingly inscrutable even to those who lent the business money. Documents available from PIHL suggest that the size of the facility first agreed with Cummings was, at over £800 million, more than twice the amount needed to fund the *Telegraph* purchase. The fact that it exploded to £1.6 billion just five years later suggests that a revolving credit line for the brothers to spend as they liked to make money had not been used to pay off any of their debt or accrued interest.

At Lloyds, the new boss was keen to beef up its risk team. Two months after starting, Horta-Osório appointed a man called Stephen Shelley as the chief risk officer of the commercial banking division. Talks with Aidan and Howard began almost immediately. Given the size of the debt and the bank's exposure, it is likely to have been Horta-Osório who first approached the Barclay brothers to tell them that they needed to bring the principal amount down through the disposal of some assets. But he had far more pressing issues to deal with, including mis-sold payment protection schemes and the need to leave state ownership – pressures that were so great he ended up taking a two-month leave of absence due to a mental health crisis by the end of 2011.

Horta-Osório would continue to meet Aidan and Howard once a year in his office, but it fell largely to a team led by Shelley – a chemistry graduate from Birmingham University who had trained in accountancy as well as investment banking – to renegotiate the Barclay brothers' loans. Shelley is publicity-shy, but ask anyone who has worked with him what he is like and they draw a picture of someone at the other end of any spectrum from Peter Cummings, the relationship banker who believed in partying with his clients and considered some his friends.[3] Shelley has been described by some who know him as a 'strait-laced risk officer' and 'immune to any sort of flannel or charm', as well as 'very focused on the numbers'. In this way, Shelley seems to have more in common with the lone accountant ignored at the Crown Agents and whistle-blowers in financial scandals since. Except, in Shelley's case, he was given authority to work out a plan to get some of the money back by his superiors.

Even so, it took an extraordinarily long time. Years passed, filled by various family suggestions about how they would pay back the debt and a slowly dawning realization by Lloyds itself that an insistence on repayment would not be straightforward. Even one of the UK's biggest banks, an organization that had been rescued by the British state and therefore the British taxpayer, was struggling to follow the Barclay money.

It became clear early on that not only was the Barclay debt huge but that the guarantees which could allow Lloyds to claw back the money were pretty much unenforceable. The twins had long prided themselves on doing deals on a handshake – David had once asked the Seigneur of Sark to meet without lawyers 'mano a mano'. They appear to have borrowed £1.6 billion on the basis of something 'like name lending', with the offer of a personal guarantee from the twins. David and Frederick traded on their reputation, and an era that relied on the word of rich men being taken as their bond. This all seemed to work until their main lenders, perhaps conscious of the billions of pounds spent by governments to prop them up in the wake of the credit crisis, started to ask for some of the money back.

With the Barclays' debt unpaid and increasing doubts over how it would be reduced, the bank's risk team realized that it might need to gain some leverage over cash-generating physical assets. PIHL might have sat at the top of a pyramid of companies, but the fact it was separated from cash-generating assets such as the *Telegraph* and the Ritz by several layers of other companies made the recovery of any funds difficult.

Aggressive tax planning had both moved profits out of UK-based operating businesses and structured everything in a way that avoided the use of personal names. This may have had the effect of cutting tax bills, but it also meant that, when it came to valuing personal guarantees, bankers had little to go on – especially as the business founders grew old and withdrew from management.

The agreement between the BVI-registered Penultimate Investment Holdings and Bank of Scotland, now Lloyds, had been amended several times after 2006 – sixteen times in total in the first ten years of the loan agreement to 2016[4] – and each time the bank used a failure to repay to inch closer to the physical UK-based assets rather than the offshore companies. Offshore holding companies are common in finance, but even seasoned financiers expressed surprise that a group whose business operations were all based in just one country should have so many layers in so many offshore jurisdictions. Each time repayments were missed or other deadlines passed, Lloyds is understood to have sought loan conditions to bring it closer to the Telegraph Media Group at the bottom of the pyramid, and not Penultimate Investment Holdings where its debt sat. The real battle for control had begun.

Although David was said to be involved in the early negotiations, it was subsequently left to Aidan and Howard to visit Horta-Osório and the risk team once a year, leaving their Rolls-Royce outside the bank's headquarters on 25 Gresham Street. The very fact that the meetings were not held in the Ellerman head office, or a Barclay-owned hotel, suggested that the tables had turned on the usual way of doing business. The negotiations were always described as amicable, if far from jolly. The Barclays were unfailingly polite, always ready with a plan to make more money – from the flotation of Yodel or Very to the fight for £1.2 billion from the HMRC that went all the way to the Supreme Court. There were some disposals during this time – Aidan sold Forbes House and his yacht, and some money was made when the family eventually gave up its pursuit of Claridge's – but none of the most valuable assets were sold or listed on the stock market until the acrimonious sale of the Ritz in 2020.

Meanwhile only a few people restricted by client confidentiality realized the extent of the debts, the family as a whole continued to live extraordinarily extravagant lives, giving the impression to most outsiders that their finances were in great shape. Offshore companies such as Epitome acted as a sort of family office, while Ellerman Holdings in Jersey picked up the bills not just for family members working in head office but for many others. While Frederick was spending £128 million in the five years between 2015 and 2019, buying his £30 million mansion in St James's and spending a monthly allowance of £800,000,[5] a wider circle of family members were able to charge for cars, art, servants and more. Not only did Aidan live in a home described as 'like a mansion' in the heart of St James's, as well as owning a huge chalet within a sort of family compound in Gstaad, other family members enjoyed the benefit of living in property bought by offshore holding companies. 'Ellerman picks up everyone's bills', according to someone close to the situation, referring to one of the many family businesses as a sort of 'slush fund'.

Onshore companies like Very still managed to send huge interest-free, unsecured inter-company loans up to the offshore businesses during this time. Loans from UK-based retailer Shop Direct Holdings to Jersey-based LW Corp rose after 2016, peaking at £807 million five years later. It is impossible to tell what this money was used for. However, it was not used to pay off the family's debt to Lloyds, leaving the possibility that it was either spent on other debts or on funding the family's lifestyle.

For so many to live like billionaires, the UK-based businesses on which the fortune ultimately depended needed to be generating immense amounts of income. The fact was that, with the exception of Very in the good years, few of them were doing so. The whole saga was described by people who knew about it as 'going round and round in circles with the family not doing what they needed to do and sell the assets'.

By 2017, Stephen Shelley had been made the chief risk officer for the whole of Lloyds and the government had sold the last of its shares in the bank. On leaving a previous job as head of high street behemoth Santander, Horta-Osório had been given a cartoon of himself as a knight rescuing two damsels representing two smaller banks facing bankruptcy.[6] He never said so, but could have felt that a new drawing would see him dealing this time with two knights who also found themselves in some distress.

The family had long eschewed public markets and partnerships with others such as private equity groups, but their options to refinance their debts had shrunk in the wake of the credit crisis. Hence, their use of eyebrow-raising funding from outfits like Greensill Capital.

Although pressure had been applied since 2011 for the loan repayment, it was not until sometime in 2019, eight years later, that the Barclay debt with Lloyds went into default as they missed interest payments too. The bad debt was moved to the Lloyds Business Support Unit, a special measures division, which prompted an even closer interest in company cash flows, security and protection for the bank. It was at the end of this year that a possible 'review' of assets including the Ritz and the *Telegraph* first emerged, followed by the bugging scandal as the two sides of the family failed to agree on what to sell and who to.

Investment bankers could not understand why the family had not kept control of the situation and sold when they had the chance. Years before it first emerged they were in difficulties, they had talks about the *Telegraph* with the likes of Jeff Bezos. But all such approaches came to nothing as various family members decided they just didn't want to sell. 'What's extraordinary is that it was obvious that there was just not enough money. But either because they couldn't agree or because they just couldn't bring themselves to do it or because they just kept missing the moment, they didn't sell,' said one financier. 'Every idea, every plan failed.'

By the time Horta-Osório moved on from Lloyds in 2021, the debt owed by the family had been halved to close to £800 million. While some of this was due to write-downs as the size of the loan forced the bank to make provisions, the sale of the Ritz helped pay off some loans, though mainly to Citigroup. There were debts due to other banks during this period, including Barclays and HSBC.

In the wake of the war in Ukraine and rising inflation, the cost of borrowing soared, dealing a blow to those with significant debts. The family's debt to Lloyds had risen closer to £1 billion by 2023. By this time a new chief executive had started at Lloyds, Charlie Nunn, but he was happy to allow Stephen Shelley to carry on with his audacious plan – a plan that would shock everyone, including the Barclays.

Even after Lloyds appointed receivers and took control of B.UK, a Bermuda-based company underneath Penultimate Investment Holdings Ltd, Aidan Barclay found it hard to believe that the bank would seize control of the Telegraph Media Group. Finding out only when he received a letter removing him from the board, he subsequently told those he met that he had been shocked by the bank's lack of a warning, despite negotiations that had been going on by this point for twelve years.

It is easy to imagine that the Barclays did not believe that a bank would seize control of a national newspaper, especially one so historically close to the ruling Conservative government. The financial complexity and political consequences a year before a general election must have made it seem even less likely. This had also obviously given Lloyds pause for thought. After all, the bank had been threatening to pull the plug for ten years, and had never done so.

Despite these qualms, the process began in earnest at the start of 2022, with Stephen Shelley making the decision along with the head of the commercial bank, David Oldfield. Chief executive Charlie Nunn had the final say. Lloyds had painstakingly identified the ultimate ownership structure that would allow them to take control of all relevant company boards. They called in the receivers to B.UK in May 2023. It took two weeks for a so-called cascade of letters to get down to the operating business, with Lloyds taking over one board at a time until they sent letters dismissing Aidan, Howard and the family consigliere Philip Peters as directors of Press Acquisitions, the company that effectively owned the Telegraph Media Group.

The reaction in June 2023 was largely one of surprise rather than any outrage at Lloyds' actions, partly because the bank took the highly unusual and unexpected decision of making the extent of the family's debts known. Faced with a huge hole in the accounts and the sense that every new plan to fill it disappeared like a puff of air, the bank's senior team decided to take the risk of going public about the family's debts. They did so thinking it was the most financially prudent thing to do, but also that it was the right thing.

After more than a decade of trying to recoup its loans, a failure to act would have meant almost 10 per cent of the £20 billion bailout from the UK taxpayer being used to support brothers who not only lived a lavish lifestyles but had long organized their affairs to pay as little tax as possible.

The appointment of receivers AlixPartners prompted a frenzy of speculation over the future of the Telegraph Media Group, including the *Spectator*, with several potential bidders and an auction expected to last many months. The Barclays could still find the financing to settle the debt owed to Lloyds. But a month after this shock development Howard Barclay was unable to say whether such a possibility was likely. By the time he appeared in Sir Jonathan Cohen's court in July 2023, he was ready to say that the Telegraph Media Group could be regarded as a 'distressed' asset.[7]

Born in time to ride the wave of a post-war boom that transformed a nation into home and property owners as much as it transformed their fortunes, David and Frederick Barclay came to own great monuments to wealth and power: the Ritz Hotel and the *Daily Telegraph* newspaper. They used these totems made of rock and paper to borrow increasing amounts of money from financial institutions that also recognized there was money to be made in bricks and mortar and the gaps in between. It is in these gaps that so much could also be hidden.

The story of the Barclay brothers follows the political shifts of their long lives: they made a fortune in the 'loadsamoney' decade after Margaret Thatcher came to power. So important was Britain's first female prime minister to the brothers, and so grateful were they, that they provided her with a home and final resting place. They would go on to entertain her successors – including one, Boris Johnson, who would work for them too.

Despite the high-profile nature of their friends and business empire, their influence and power was always exercised from the shadows. Their fortune, built together, was squirrelled into a complex array of trusts, which they jointly controlled and kept away from the prying eyes as well as the demands of others. A level of secrecy so great it almost appeared like a code of *omertà* was built up. The structure was so complex and the demands upon it so onerous that it led to arguments and a breakdown in relations, with one side of the family left unsure how much money there was or even how to access it. A resident of Sark once compared an attempt at understanding the Barclays' financial affairs with that of 'knitting fog', and it seems that some details were as obscure to members of the family themselves. Battles in board and courtrooms in the early 2020s showed that even their financial backers and the judiciary found themselves in the dark.

In the end, it was the Barclay brothers' battles with each other and refusal to agree the best way forward that showed how much damage could be done by the enemy within.

Tight-knit and united as any partnership could be, their own personal story also came to reflect that of the United Kingdom. Arch-Brexiteers who loathed the lack of accountability and control exerted by Brussels, David and Frederick split from each other a few years before Britain split from the European Union in 2016.

The feud, which developed and became poisonous in a way that shocked many who knew them, revealed more about these secretive men than anything had before. And that was not only because Frederick broke cover for the first time in some eighty years, furious and hurt in equal measure by what he saw as the betrayal of his brother's sons and, by association, his brother. His inability to control the family fortune also led him to lash out, using the law to do so. His efforts to assert his authority over his nephews came as he lost control of his once compliant wife.

Odd and controlling, but also described by some as generous and good to work for, the last years of the brothers' lives were marred by dark and bitter ironies. A family that had spotted opportunities to buy from owners in difficulty, like Conrad Black, or from families who could not agree on a business plan, like the descendants of John Moores, found themselves unable to pay huge debts or agree which bits of the empire to sell or how. The Barclays as a collective had forgotten one of David's favourite pieces of advice: 'Businesses are for buying and selling and don't forget the selling.'

A bank that had done so much to fuel their earlier success delivered a humiliating double blow, both by making long-shrouded debts public and by seizing control of the Telegraph Media Group. The Barclays' failure to pay their debts over almost two decades allowed the UK's biggest high street bank to seize control of one of the country's best-known newspapers, a highly unusual state of affairs in the UK.

It is perhaps the final irony that the legal system the Barclay brothers had for so long used to exert their authority and obscure their story would ultimately expose so much of their lives. By the summer of 2023, more than two years after being ordered to pay her £100 million and a year after being found in contempt for non-payment, Frederick had still not paid his wife of thirty-four years and the mother of his only child a penny of the divorce settlement. Adjourned several times in the summer of 2023, a man called Martin Clarke kept promising that the money for Hiroko would be paid into the bank very soon, or that afternoon, or the next day. Described as Frederick's 'right-hand man' and 'amanuensis' by Stuart Leech KC, a Martin Christopher Clarke was a chartered surveyor expelled by the Royal Institute of Chartered Surveyors in 2008. Clarke, who had the facial hair, girth and unlikely demeanour of a Bad Santa Claus by the time of the extended court hearings told the court that he had been friends with Frederick for 30 years. At one point he left the witness box to wait for the call to confirm arrival into Hiroko's account of an 'acceptable sum' to settle the order, but instead took a call about a builder. The increasingly exasperated Cohen called the non-appearance of the promised funds a 'charade' as his courtroom took on an air of farce. By August 2023, with hearing after hearing ending with more broken promises, Cohen himself called the proceedings a 'long running farce'. As he approached his ninetieth year, Frederick may have been facing the possibility of a prison sentence for non-payment, but after one such hearing he was photographed by several agencies leaving the court grinning and giving a thumbs up.

In court there had been little evidence of the truce agreed with his nephews after his twin brother died in January 2021. Two years after they had attempted to close the curtains that had so strangely been drawn apart, Frederick's divorce and the family's loss of control of the *Daily Telegraph* revealed that the Wizard of Oz was not the giant of everybody's imagination. It was all a long way from the joint statement Frederick and his nephews had made at the time. 'We are pleased that, as a family, we can put this difficult period behind us and now look forward to our future together,' it said. 'In these troubled times, unity within families is more important than ever.'[8]

Author Note and Acknowledgements

The Barclay brothers and the wider family have taken pains over many years to keep as much information about their lives and their businesses out of the public domain as they can. They have always argued that they are deeply private individuals, and have used legal means to deter investigations into their business affairs and lives. Yet their influence on society and their behaviour in managing their affairs is a matter of significant public interest.

I have approached several members of the Barclay family, both asking for interviews and to check facts. I also have put specific allegations to Aidan, Howard and Alistair Barclay, as well as to Amanda and Sir Frederick Barclay, both during my research for an article in Tortoise in 2019 and for this book. All of them declined to comment.

This book would not have been possible without the very many people who talked to me on and mainly off the record, and to all of them I am hugely grateful. Without their advice, knowledge and guidance, my desire to shed light on a story that spent so long in the shadows would not have been possible.

Among the few I can name are Paul Armorgie, Brian Basham, Christopher Beaumont, Philip Beresford, Conrad Black, Stephen Clapham, Michael Cole, Jeremy Deedes, Nigel Farage, Matthew Freud, Brian Groom, Charles Garside, Paddy McKillen, Peter Oborne, Ray Perman, Jeff Randall, William Rubenstein, Dan Sabbagh, John Sweeney, Gawain Towler and Linda Williams.

I owe a special thanks to many people on Sark, especially my former tutor and guide, Richard Axton, who did not live to see this book published.

I have worked hard to avoid any mistakes but those that exist are mine alone. In contrast to working in a newsroom, book writing can be a lonely experience and I am grateful to the many other journalists who kept me company during this time, from the support team at Women in Journalism – Alison Phillips, Sue Ryan and the brilliant Kate McMillan – to the man who warned me that this endeavour would see me penniless under a railway arch but who helped me anyway. Court reporting is hugely important yet sometimes undervalued by media organizations, and I am full of admiration for the skills of those who do it, as well as grateful for the knowledge and kindness of Jonathan Browning and Brian Farmer in particular.

I am also grateful for the support and encouragement of great authors such as Tom Bower, Michael Crick, Sonia Purnell and, as ever, Alan Rusbridger. The marvellous David Leigh managed to speed-read a draft and offer brilliant advice.

Although I may not have thanked him for it at all times since, this adventure started with a phone call from James Harding, and I am grateful to him as well as his brilliant team at Tortoise Media, notably Dave Taylor and Tom Goulding.

Support from the *Guardian* has also been immense. A newspaper that believes in the right of journalists to seek the truth not only helped with advice but paid for lawyers Beth Grossman and Jude Bunting to fight an attempt to gag reporters. Thanks as ever to Kath Viner, Owen Gibson, John Stuttle, Luke Hoyland, and a woman who truly is the doyen of all newspaper media lawyers, Gill Phillips.

My colleagues at City, University of London not only provided advice and library support but, along with the Marjorie Deane Foundation, gave me some invaluable time to write. I am so grateful to the foundation trustees, led and shepherded by Michael Cronk, Zanny Minton Beddoes and Anne Foley, but also for the support from Mel Bunce and the marvellous Paul Solman.

Kamal Ahmed has proved a great friend again throughout this long process, offering advice and editing brilliance. He also introduced me to a great agent, Georgina Capel, a calm voice of wisdom and support. Thanks to her and also Rachel Conway and Simon Shaps.

My publisher, Penguin, has been brilliant and brave in deciding to publish this book, and I am grateful to everyone who worked on it, including Tom Killingbeck for the first approach and Ause Abdelhaq for the first edit. I would like to thank Martina O'Sullivan for her constant support and legal mastermind Lucy Middleton in particular.

Lucia Henwood has been an invaluable fact checker and has a great future ahead of her.

I have not been the best of company during long stretches of writing this and I want to both apologize and thank friends such as Lydia, Clare, Sarah, Sue and Lisa for listening, and in particular Shevaun, who did so at the most difficult of times. I am so grateful to her and especially to Jenny, a source of support for more than forty years who literally took me away and gave me a room of my own to write in.

Finally, my beloved George, Bryher and Iona have had to endure a mother even more distracted than usual but have done so without complaint. I am so proud of them. My biggest thanks though is, as ever, to Richard, who has checked accounts and archives as well as taking on so much more than his fair share at home. He has calmed my fears, shared my sleeplessness and celebrated my excitement, and this book would have been so very much more difficult without his help, advice and love.

Notes

No Man Is an Island

1 David Watkin, *Radical Classicism: The Architecture of Quinlan Terry*, Rizzoli, 2006.
2 Letter on Brecqhou-headed notepaper, sent on 3 September 2007.
3 Charles Garside, 'Brothers in arms', *Guardian*, 26 January 2004, https://www.theguardian.com/media/2004/jan/26/thedailytelegraph.monday-mediasection

1. Early Years

1 1939 register.
2 'Sir David Barclay, Telegraph owner who with his twin Frederick built a vast business empire – obituary', *Daily Telegraph*, 12 January 2021, https://www.telegraph.co.uk/obituaries/2021/01/12/sir-david-barclay-telegraph-owner-twin-frederick-built-vast/
3 Ibid.
4 Helen Nugent, 'Is a bankrupt brother the secret behind Barclays' passion for privacy and success?' *The Times*, 18 August 2004, https://www.thetimes.co.uk/article/is-a-bankrupt-brother-the-secret-behind-barclays-passion-for-privacy-and-success-7zxf2x32dsm
5 Ibid.
6 *Mail on Sunday*, 12 January 1992.
7 Quoted in Steven Morris, 'From the school of adversity to master of business', *Guardian*, 29 January 2004, https://www.theguardian.com/business/2004/jan/19/pressandpublishing.media
8 Simon Clark and Erik Schatzker, 'Britain's billionaire Barclay twins use stealth to amass empire', Bloomberg, 29 November 2004, https://www.bloomberg.com/news/articles/2004-11-30/britain-s-billionaire-barclay-twins-use-stealth-to-amass-empire

9 Frank Kane, 'The devil on the Barclays' shoulder', *Guardian*, 25 January 2004, https://www.theguardian.com/business/2004/jan/25/thedailytelegraph.pressandpublishing2

10 Peter Rivett, *Brecqhou: A Very Private Island*, Planetesimal, 2002, p. 245.

11 Ibid., pp. 245–80.

12 *The Times*, 18 August 2004.

13 *London Gazette*, 4 November 1960.

14 Ibid.

15 Ibid.

16 Marriage certificate.

17 *Mail on Sunday*, 12 January 1992.

18 Shirley Green, *Rachman*, Joseph , 1979, p. 36.

19 Chris Sullivan, 'Lost cities: Notting Hill and Notting Dale', *Byline Times*, 9 September 2020, https://bylinetimes.com/2020/09/09/lost-cities-notting-hill-from-rachman-to-the-westway/

20 Hansard, 'Consequences of Rent Act 1957 and Property Profiteering', vol. 681, 22 July 1963, https://hansard.parliament.uk/Commons/1963-07-22/debates/da3fa08f-9bcd-493b-8bda-3dbfc86c7249/ConsequencesOfRentAct1957AndPropertyProfiteering

21 Michael Heseltine, *Life in the Jungle*, Hodder and Stoughton, 2000, pp. 39–41.

22 Green, *Rachman*.

23 Heseltine, *Life in the Jungle*, pp. 39–41, 43.

24 Green, *Rachman*, p. 12.

25 Royal Borough of Kensington and Chelsea, Virtual Museum, 'Peter Rachman', https://www.rbkc.gov.uk/vmpeople/infamous/peterrachman.asp

26 Hansard, 'Consequences of Rent Act 1957'.

27 Green, *Rachman*, p. 167.

28 Hansard, 'Consequences of Rent Act 1957'.

29 Companies House, 'Hillgate Estate Agents', https://find-and-update.company-information.service.gov.uk/company/00724781/officers

30 Email to PB, March 2019.

31 Crown Agents documents, National Archives.

2. A King's Ransom

1 A. W. Abbott, *A Short History of the Crown Agents and Their Office*, Eyre and Spottiswoode, 1959.

2 David Sunderland, 'Managing British Colonial and Post-Colonial Development: The Crown Agents, 1914–1974', 2007, p. 3.

3 Hansard, vol. 940, 1 December 1977, 'Crown Agents', cols. 734 and 742.

4 Much of the information and detail in this chapter derives from several box files of contemporaneous notes and records on the Barclay-owned businesses and the Crown Agents kept in the National Archives at Kew, some of which were not released until 2013. Other quotes and findings are to be found in Hansard before and after two judge-led reviews of the scandal. The [Judge] Fay Committee of Inquiry was set up in April 1975 and reported on 1 December 1977. The resulting furore and parliamentary debate on the Fay report in turn led to the establishment in March 1978 of a judge-led tribunal which reported in March 1982.

5 *Report by the Committee of Inquiry Appointed by the Minister of Overseas Development into the Circumstances Which Led to the Crown Agents Requesting Financial Assistance from the Government in 1974* (Fay report), Her Majesty's Stationery Office, 1977, https://assets.publishing.service.gov.uk/government/uploads/system/uploads/attachment_data/file/235323/0048.pdf, p. 398.

6 Larry Elliott, 'A brief history of British housing', *Guardian*, 24 May 2014, https://www.theguardian.com/business/2014/may/24/history-british-housing-decade

7 Fay report, p. 383.

8 http://www.scrimgeourclan.org.uk/skirmisher/skirmisher12/s12jamesscrimgeour.htm

9 Note to Alan Challis, February 1971.

10 D. Barclay letter, May 1971.

11 'How the Crown Agents manage their £1,000m', *Guardian*, August 1971.

12 David Young, 'Lessons for life from the Crash of '73', *Spectator*, 20 December 2008, https://www.spectator.co.uk/article/lessons-for-life-from-the-crash-of-73/

13 Fay report.

14 Edward Erdman, *People and Property*, Batsford, 1982, pp. 194–7.

15 'Challis quits FNFC board', *Financial Times*, 21 December 1974.

16 Tribunal report.

17 Hansard, 'Crown Agents', col. 1050.
18 *Birmingham Post*, 2 December 1977.
19 *The Times* obituary, 2 April 2020.
20 Bloomberg, 29 November 2004.
21 Companies House, 'Leslie Michael Bolsom', https://find-and-update.company-information.service.gov.uk/officers/1nZYenDaUhtCOQ3GwujvRu00-C8/appointments
22 Companies House, 'Trenport Property Holdings Limited', https://find-and-update.company-information.service.gov.uk/company/09417510
23 Paul McCann, 'BBC settles Barclay libel battle', *Independent*, 28 April 1997, https://www.independent.co.uk/news/bbc-settles-barclay-libel-battle-1269913.html
24 *Mail on Sunday*, 12 January 1992.

3. Hitting the Big Time

1 'Records of Ellerman City Line Ltd, 1901–1970s, shipowners, Glasgow, Scotland', Archives Hub, https://archiveshub.jisc.ac.uk/search/archives/e946538d-e849-36cf-b076-183f21511c42
2 Interview with author, February 2022.
3 Susan McCabe, *H. D. and Bryher: An Untold Love Story of Modernism*, Oxford University Press, 2021.
4 'Code of secrecy surrounding Britain's wealthiest kept nation in the dark', *Wales Online*, 24 May 2006, https://www.walesonline.co.uk/news/wales-news/code-secrecy-surrounding-britains-wealthiest-2340427
5 Interview with author, February 2022.
6 Peter Scott, 'The Anatomy of Britain's Interwar Super-Rich: Reconstructing the 1928/9 "Millionaire" Population,' *Economic History Review*, vol. 74, no. 3, 2021, pp. 639–65.
7 William Rubinstein, *Beyond the Dreams of Avarice: The Very Wealthy in Modern Britain*, Edward Everett Root, 2022, p. 316.
8 Tim Carroll, 'The lost tycoon,' *Sunday Times*, 22 October 2006, https://www.thetimes.co.uk/article/the-lost-tycoon-c3oh3hb7n76
9 Ibid.
10 Sir David Scott, *Window into Downing Street*, Memoir Club, 2003, pp. 212–28.
11 Ibid.
12 'Reaping a swift £44m reward', *Financial Times*, April 1984.

13 Scott, 2003.

14 Bloomberg, 29 November 2004.

15 Taki, 'My unlikely friendship with Sir David Barclay, *Spectator*, 23 January 2021, https://www.spectator.co.uk/article/my-unlikely-friendship-with-sir-david-barclay/

16 'UK company news', *Financial Times*, 18 April 1984.

17 *Financial Times*, April 1984.

18 Scott, 2003.

19 Interview with author.

20 Bloomberg, 29 November 2004.

21 *The Times*, 9 February 2007, p. 61.

22 Interview with author.

23 'Too shy for the secretive twins – Analysis of Gulf Resources bid for Imperial Continental Gas Association', *Guardian*, 4 November 1986.

24 Hansard, vol. 107, 15 December 1986, 'Pilkington Brothers Plc', https://hansard.parliament.uk/commons/1986-12-15/debates/caf58138-45ce-498f-b198-dc23d4bbc0a0/PilkingtonBrothersPlc

25 UK parliamentary papers, in a letter after 20 November.

26 Interview with author.

27 Dominic Lawson, *Sunday Times*, 13 November 2022.

28 'Margaret Thatcher estate avoids millions in inheritance tax', Barnet Wills, 18 July 2014, https://barnetwills.co.uk/2014/07/18/margaret-thatcher-estate-avoids-millions-in-inheritance-tax/

29 Charles Moore, *Margaret Thatcher: The Authorized Biography*, vol. III, Penguin, 2020, p. 817.

30 Ibid., p. 735.

31 Ibid., p. 748.

32 Ibid.

33 Rob Evans and David Hencke, 'Tax loopholes on homes benefit the rich and cost UK millions', *Guardian*, 25 May 2002, https://www.theguardian.com/money/2002/may/25/tax.politics

34 Jim Armitage, 'Margaret Thatcher's last home on sale for £35m in Belgravia', *Evening Standard*, 16 June 2014, https://www.standard.co.uk/news/london/margaret-thatcher-s-last-home-in-belgravia-on-sale-for-ps35m-9540337.html

35 Moore, 2020, p. 846.

36 Nick Sommarlad, 'Margaret Thatcher tax shock: £12m mansion where she saw out her days registered in TAX HAVEN', *Mirror*, 30 November 2013,

https://www.mirror.co.uk/news/uk-news/margaret-thatcher-tax-shock-12m-2866929

37 *Guardian*, 25 May 2002.

38 Rex A. McKenzie's Lab, https://www.researchgate.net/lab/Rex-A-McKenzie-Lab

39 Robert Booth, Helena Bengtsson and David Pegg, 'Revealed: 9% rise in London properties owned by offshore firms', *Guardian*, 26 May 2016, https://www.theguardian.com/money/2016/may/26/revealed-9-rise-in-london-properties-owned-by-offshore-firms

40 Bloomberg, 29 November 2004.

41 Ibid.

42 'Carmakers focus on Barclay twins – AFGH deal unites three secretive entrepreneurs', *Financial Times*, 18 November 1994.

43 *Financial Times* obituary, 14 July 1998.

4. *How to Buy an Island*

1 Knight, Frank and Rutley listing, *Country Life*, 26 August 1993.

2 *Barclay v Barclay*, England and Wales High Court, 28 July 2022, https://www.casemine.com/judgement/uk/6352eb0e5358106ecd0d0b97

3 *Telegraph* obituary.

4 'An interview with Leonard Matchan', Tony's Musings [blog], 18 March 2016, http://tonymusings.blogspot.com/2016/03/an-interview-with-leonard-matchan.html

5 Clive Aslet, 'The ultimate luxury', *Critic*, March 2021, https://thecritic.co.uk/issues/march-2021/the-ultimate-luxury/

6 *Encyclopaedia Britannica* 1911, vol. 3, 'Berkeley family'.

7 Rob Wilko, 'Double trouble', Press Barons [blog], 14 April 2013, https://robwilko.wordpress.com/2013/04/14/double-trouble/

8 Rivett, p. 250.

9 Contempt hearing testimony, 25 July 2022.

10 *Barclay v Barclay* court hearing, 23 May 2023.

11 Evidence in court, 25 July 2022.

12 *Barclay v Barclay*, 2022.

13 Algernon Charles Swinburne, 'A Ballad of Sark', 1884.

14 Ben Fogle, *Offshore: In Search of an Island of My Own*, Michael Joseph, 2006.

15 David Barclay, 'Fighting feudalism', *Guardian*, 23 June 1999, https://www.theguardian.com/comment/story/0,3604,288941,00.html

16 *Review of Financial Regulation in the Crown Dependencies*, prepared by Andrew Edwards, https://www.taxjustice.net/cms/upload/pdf/Edwards_1998_Report_.pdf

17 Interview with author.

18 'Barclay twins knighted in "double dubbing"', *Daily Telegraph*, 1 November 2000, https://www.telegraph.co.uk/news/uknews/1372633/Barclay-twins-knighted-in-double-dubbing.html

19 Interview with author, January 2020.

5. Ritz and Glamour

1 https://www.theritzlondon.com/about-the-ritz/history/

2 Interview with author.

3 *London Gazette*, 16 February 1945, https://www.thegazette.co.uk/London/issue/36943/page/943

4 *The Times*, 18 August 2004.

5 Erdman, pp. 194–7.

6 Ibid., p. 196.

7 Simon Jenkins, *Evening Standard*, 2004.

8 Roy Reed, 'Lord Beaverbrook's papers sold', *New York Times*, 1 July 1977, https://www.nytimes.com/1977/07/01/archives/londons-beaverbrook-papers-sold.html

9 'London Ritz is sold; new owners pledge to retain elegance', *New York Times*, 27 March 1976, https://www.nytimes.com/1976/03/27/archives/london-ritz-is-sold-new-owners-pledge-to-retain-elegance.html

10 'Sir Nigel Broackes, British magnate, dies', *Washington Post*, 11 October 1999, https://www.washingtonpost.com/archive/local/1999/10/11/sir-nigel-broackes-british-magnate-dies/05fae38d-a2e1-4eb8-b86a-408bbc817890/

11 Interview with author, July 2022.

12 'Sir Frederick Barclay confirms £1bn approaches to sell the London Ritz hotel', 5 March 2020, https://uk.news.yahoo.com/sir-frederick-barclay-confirms-1bn-124531518.html

13 https://www.bownsbest.com/theritz.htm

14 2006 accounts.

15 *Panorama: The Tax Haven Twins*, BBC documentary, 2012.

16 'Ritz drawn into corporate tax controversy', *Financial Times*, 17 December 2012, https://www.ft.com/content/351f7696-487c-11e2-a6b3-00144feab49a

6. *Bing-Bang-Bong*

1 *Trouble at Topshop*, BBC documentary, 2022.

2 'Edwardian empire', *Sunday Herald*, 13 April 2003.

3 Bloomberg, 29 November 2004.

4 Oliver Shah, *Damaged Goods: The Inside Story of Sir Philip Green, the Collapse of BHS and the Death of the High Street*, Portfolio, 2018, p. 72.

5 Ibid.

6 Stewart Lansley, *Top Man: How Philip Green Built His High Street Empire*, Aurum, 2005.

7 Ray Perman, *Hubris: How HBOS Wrecked the Best Bank in Britain*, Birlinn, 2012, p. 2.

8 Shah, p. 112.

9 'Outlook: Green/sears', *Independent*, 22 January 1999, https://www.independent.co.uk/news/business/outlook-green-sears-1075489.html

10 'Sears sells Adams to MBO for 87m', *Financial Times*, 16 July 1999.

11 Shah, p. 76.

12 Interview with author, 11 October 2022.

13 Shah, pp. 90 and 112.

14 Richard Coopey, Sean O'Connell and Dilwyn Porter, *Mail Order Retailing in Britain: A Business and Social History*, Oxford University Press, 2005.

15 'Clan warfare', *Guardian*, 8 June 1995.

16 Chris Blackhurst, 'A dynasty divided', *Independent*, 19 November 1995, https://www.independent.co.uk/news/business/a-dynasty-divided-1582568.html

17 Paul Farrelly, 'Littlewoods' catalogue of disasters', *Observer*, 17 September 2000, https://www.theguardian.com/business/2000/sep/17/theobserver.observerbusiness3

18 Accounts year to April 2002.

19 LW Finance 2003 accounts, p. 23. Corrected to state Bank of Scotland in 2004.

20 'Littlewoods stores sold to Barclay twins', *Daily Telegraph*, 5 October 2002.

21 Perman, p. 121.

22 Bloomberg, 29 November 2004.

23 'Littlewoods sells to Barclay brothers', BBC News, 4 October 2002, http://news.bbc.co.uk/2/hi/business/2300253.stm

24 'Littlewoods Under Attack; Record Since Takeover Rapped', *Liverpool Echo*, 21 February 2003.

25 Ibid.

26 'Inside the Barclay family feud that could end an empire', *The Times*, 5 July 2020, https://www.thetimes.co.uk/article/inside-the-barclay-family-feud-that-could-end-an-empire-jtscj8982

27 Richard Fletcher, 'The Barclay brothers do things other people would not dare to do', *Sunday Telegraph*, 25 January 2004, https://www.telegraph.co.uk/finance/2874967/The-Barclay-brothers-do-things-other-people-would-not-dare-to-do.html

28 'Barclay brothers "put up almost no cash" in GUS deal', *Telegraph*, 24 June 2003.

29 Littlewoods Shop Direct Group accounts ending April 2005, note 15.

30 Graham Potter, 'Littlewoods acquisition of GUS faces competition probe', *Retail Bulletin*, 25 September 2003, https://www.theretailbulletin.com/general-merchandise/littlewoods-acquisition-of-gus-faces-competition-probe-25-09-2003/

31 LSDG accounts 2005, note 12.

32 *Littlewoods Ltd and others v Commissioners for Her Majesty's Revenue and Customs*, UKSC 70, 1 November 2017, https://www.supremecourt.uk/cases/uksc-2015-0177.html

33 'Barclay twins' Ritz hotel pays no corporation tax', BBC News, 17 December 2012, https://www.bbc.co.uk/news/uk-20729430

34 Interview with author, 11 October 2022.

35 LSDG balance sheet, 30 April 2006.

36 David Leigh, 'The spiritualists, the offshore company and the case of the extra millions', *Guardian*, 25 January 2013, https://www.theguardian.com/uk/2013/jan/25/spiritualist-association-headquarters-price

37 David Leigh and Ivor Gaber, 'Barclay brothers' £1bn VAT windfall bid puts tactics in spotlight', *Guardian*, 17 December 2012, https://www.theguardian.com/media/2012/dec/17/barclay-brothers-vat-windfall-bid

38 *Arcadia and others v Telegraph*, England and Wales High Court 223, 2019, https://www.judiciary.uk/wp-content/uploads/2019/02/arcadia-v-telegraph-2019-ewhc-233-qb.pdf

39 Mark Sweney, 'Philip Green faces £3m legal bill as new abuse allegations published', *Guardian*, 8 February 2019, https://www.theguardian.com/business/2019/feb/08/philip-green-high-court-action-against-telegraph-dropped

7. 'Why then do you want to own newspapers?'

1 Tom Baistow, Lord Hartwell obituary, *Guardian*, 4 April 2001.
2 David Graves, 'Lord Hartwell, former owner of the Telegraph, dies at 89', *Daily Telegraph*, 4 April 2001, https://www.telegraph.co.uk/news/uknews/1315139/Lord-Hartwell-former-owner-of-the-Telegraph-dies-at-89.html
3 Bloomberg, 29 November 2004.
4 Email interview with author.
5 Interview with author, 11 October 2022.
6 AFP report.
7 Heather Connon, 'Private world of Britain's newest media barons', *Independent*, 8 January 1992.
8 'Mystery twins grab a piece of Maxwell', *Courier Mail*, 11 January 1992.
9 Interview with author.
10 'New European boss is bullish', *Guardian*, 9 January 1992.
11 Interview with author.
12 Ibid.
13 Peter Millar, 'Who killed the European?' *Guardian*, 7 December 1998, https://uploads.guim.co.uk/2022/12/08/Gdn_7_Dec_1998.jpg
14 Ibid.
15 Tim Walker, 'I was David Barclay's ghostwriter – until, suddenly, I wasn't', *Guardian*, 14 January 2021, http://www.theguardian.com/commentisfree/2021/jan/14/david-barclay-ghostwriter-telegraph-owner-brexit
16 Interview with author.
17 Ibid.
18 Ibid.
19 Ibid.
20 Paul McCann, 'BBC settles Barclay libel battle', *Independent*, 28 April 1997, https://www.independent.co.uk/news/bbc-settles-barclay-libel-battle-1269913.html
21 Select Committee on Communications, 1st Report of Session 2007–08, *The Ownership of the News*, Volume 1: Report, Authority of the House of Lords, 2008, https://publications.parliament.uk/pa/ld200708/ldselect/ldcomuni/122/122i.pdf
22 'Andrew Neil: He may or may not accept a role at the Telegraph. The current editor is safe, for now. And, no, the Barclays do not and will not interfere with editorial policy', interview with Tim Webb, *Independent*, 4 July 2004, https://www.independent.co.uk/news/media/andrew-neil-he-

may-or-may-not-accept-a-role-at-the-telegraph-the-current-editor-is-safe-for-now-and-no-the-barclays-do-not-and-will-not-interfere-with-editorial-policy-45722.html

23 Interview with author.

24 *Daily Telegraph*, 1 November 2000.

25 'Telegraph could back Labour, says Barclay', *Guardian*, 20 January 2004.

26 Charles Garside, 'Brothers in arms, *Guardian*, 26 January 2004, https://www.theguardian.com/media/2004/jan/26/thedailytelegraph.monday-mediasection

27 Interview with author.

28 'Scotsman building sold', *The Times*, 17 February 1998.

29 'Johnston pays £160m for Scotsman', *Financial Times*, 20 December 2005.

30 Email interview; Gregory Kirby, ' "We'll meet again": Daily Telegraph owner Sir Frederick Barclay pays tribute to twin brother Sir David – who has died aged 86 – after "great journey" from being "bombed out of our beds in Coventry" to billionaire media moguls', *Daily Mail*, 12 January 2021, https://www.dailymail.co.uk/news/article-9140841/Daily-Telegraph-owner-Sir-David-Barclay-dies-suddenly-short-illness-aged-86.html

31 *Hollinger International v Black*, 844 A.2d 1022, 1036 (Del. Ch. 2004), https://casetext.com/case/hollinger-international-v-black

32 Ibid.

33 Email interview with author.

34 *Hollinger International v Black*, 1040; *US Securities and Exchange Commission v Conrad Black, F. David Radler and Hollinger, Inc.*, US District Court for the Northern District of Illinois Eastern Division, 2004, https://www.sec.gov/litigation/complaints/comp18969.pdf

35 Jacquie McNish and Sinclair Stewart, *Wrong Way: The Fall of Conrad Black*, Allen Lane, 2004.

36 Interview with author.

37 Securities and Exchange Commission, Schedule 13D, Hollinger Inc., https://www.sec.gov/Archives/edgar/data/911707/000104746904002082/a2127358zsc13d.htm/

38 *Hollinger International v. Black*, 844 A.2d 1022, 1053 (Del. Ch. 2004).

39 *Hollinger International v Black*, 1091.

40 Ibid.

41 'Sir David Barclay's press statement', *Guardian*, 5 March 2004, https://www.theguardian.com/media/2004/mar/05/thedailytelegraph.pressandpublishing

42 Peter Walker and Amy Walker, 'Tory leadership donations: who's really backing Boris Johnson', *Guardian*, 5 July 2019, https://www.theguardian.com/politics/2019/jul/05/tory-leadership-donations-whos-really-backing-boris-johnson

43 Email interview with author.

44 McNish and Stewart.

45 Dan Milmo and Chris Tryhorn, 'Barclays win Telegraph battle', *Guardian*, 22 June 2004, https://www.theguardian.com/media/2004/jun/22/thedailytelegraph.citynews

46 Frederick and David Barclay, Personal Guarantee, Press Holdings International Ltd, 16 January 2004, https://www.sec.gov/Archives/edgar/data/911707/000104746904002082/a2127358zex-4.htm

47 Public registry in New York and paper copy.

48 Facilities Agreement, Press Holdings International Ltd and Bank of Scotland, 16 January 2004, https://www.sec.gov/Archives/edgar/data/911707/000104746904002082/a2127358zex-3.htm#ConditionsOfUtilisation

49 Interview with author.

50 Email interview with author.

51 Bloomberg, 29 November 2004.

52 'The bargain hunters who stalk owners in distress', *The Times*, 3 November 2004, https://www.thetimes.co.uk/article/the-bargain-hunters-who-stalk-owners-in-distress-037g28d86xd

53 'Times editor faces criminal proceedings', *Financial Times*, 20 April 2005.

54 'Business in brief', *The Times*, https://www.thetimes.co.uk/article/business-in-brief-3mbdomtsdr8

55 Interview with author.

56 Select Committee on Communications Minutes of Evidence, Examination of Witnesses, Andrew Marr and Dominic Lawson, 21 November 2007, https://publications.parliament.uk/pa/ld200708/ldselect/ldcomuni/122/7112103.htm

57 Alan Rusbridger, *Breaking News: The Remaking of Journalism and Why It Matters Now*, Canongate, 2018, p. 293, http://www.ktm-hdak.org.ua/doc/Rusbridger%20A.%20Breaking%20news.pdf

58 Stephen Brook, 'Lawson slams Telegraph bosses', *Guardian*, 5 September 2007, https://www.theguardian.com/media/2007/sep/05/pressandpublishing.dailytelegraph

59 Tom Lyons, 'Green Property puts Telegraph HQ on the block for €250m', *Irish Times*, 4 September 2014, https://www.irishtimes.com/business/

commercial-property/green-property-puts-telegraph-hq-on-the-block-for-250m-1.1916923

60 Serious Fraud Office, 'SFO recovers criminal assets from £740m property fraud concealed through school donation', 17 March 2023, https://www.sfo.gov.uk/2023/03/17/sfo-recovers-criminal-assets-from-740m-property-fraud-concealed-through-school-donation/

61 'China spends big on propaganda in Britain . . . but returns are low', *HKFP Voices*, 3 April 2016, https://hongkongfp.com/2016/04/03/china-spends-big-on-propaganda-in-britain-but-returns-are-low/

62 Peter Oborne, 'Why I have resigned from the Telegraph', openDemocracy, 17 February 2015, https://www.opendemocracy.net/en/opendemocracyuk/why-i-have-resigned-from-telegraph/

63 Accounts, 2012/13.

64 'Focus on Barclay brothers' debt shake-up with HSBC', *Financial Times*, 19 March 2015, https://www.ft.com/content/eb98baa4-ce49-11e4-86fc-00144feab7de

65 From the last set of accounts published by Press Acquisitions Ltd (2 January 2022).

8. *The Neighbours from Hell*

1 See, for example, 'House of cards', *The Times*, 5 July 2020.

2 Court testimony.

3 Michael Beaumont, unpublished autobiography.

4 Ibid., Appendix 8 and archives.

5 Interview with author.

6 https://www.mourant.com/profile/view/3557/Gordon-Dawes

7 Martin Fletcher, 'The Islanders the Tycoons and a War over Democracy on Sark', *The Times*, 19 April 2008, https://www.thetimes.co.uk/article/the-islanders-the-tycoons-and-a-war-over-democracy-on-sark-vp9fk9dq3b3

8 Helen Pidd, 'Barclay brothers accused of trying to silence dissent', *Guardian*, 27 June 2012, https://www.theguardian.com/uk/2012/jun/27/barclays-sark-newsletter

9 Interview with author.

10 Interviews with author.

11 Guernsey Financial Services Commission, 'About Us', https://www.gfsc.gg/commission/about-us

12 Interview with author.

13 Interview with author.

14 See also 'Alphaville spent 36 hours on the island of Sark. Here's how it went', *Financial Times*, 29 January 2019, https://www.ft.com/content/90dee53e-9535-3a69-8a75-c0ad97193ca1

15 Ibid.

16 *The Times*, 19 April 2008.

17 Ibid.

18 Sarah Lyall, 'Shedding feudalism, a Channel Island fights for its future', *New York Times*, 9 December 2008, https://www.nytimes.com/2008/12/10/world/europe/10sark.html

19 Ibid.

20 'Barclays' Sark closures under way', BBC News, 12 December 2008, http://news.bbc.co.uk/1/hi/world/europe/guernsey/7779135.stm

21 Ibid.

22 Interview with author.

23 Beaumont, Appendix 23.

24 Ibid.

25 Crown Dependencies Justice Committee, 'Conclusions and recommendations', conclusion 6, https://publications.parliament.uk/pa/cm200910/cmselect/cmjust/56/5613.htm

26 Beaumont, Part 3, p. 42.

27 *Financial Times*, 29 January 2019.

28 Kevin Delaney, 'Privacy, Secrecy or in the Public Interest?' *Sark Newsletter*, 20 January 2012.

29 *Guardian*, 27 June 2012.

30 Beaumont, Part 3, p. 106.

31 Kevin Delaney, 'No Denial – No Investigation – No Resignation', *Sark Newsletter*, July 2014.

32 *Financial Times*, 29 January 2019.

33 'Police review 50 complaints of harassment by Sark newspaper', ITV News, 21 November 2014, https://www.itv.com/news/channel/update/2014-11-21/police-review-50-complaints-of-harassment-by-sark-newspaper/

34 *Guardian*, 27 June 2012.

35 David Lowenthal, 'The scourging of Sark', *Island Studies Journal*, vol. 10, no. 2, 2015, pp. 253–8, https://islandstudiesjournal.org/files/ISJ-10-2-Lowenthal.pdf

36 *Sark News*, July 2016.

37 Interview with author.

38 *Sark News*, July 2016.
39 Interview with author.

9. *Power to the People*

1 'Leveson inquiry: Evgeny Lebedev, Aidan Barclay, John Ryley appear', *Guardian*, 23 April 2012, https://www.theguardian.com/media/2012/apr/23/leveson-inquiry-evgeny-lebedev-aidan-barclay-live

2 Leveson Inquiry, Appendix D to witness statement of Aidan Barclay, https://discoverleveson.co.uk/evidence/Appendix_D_to_Witness_Statement_of_Aidan_Barclay/6617/media

3 Leveson Inquiry, transcript of afternoon hearing on 23 April 2012, https://www.discoverleveson.com/hearing/2012-04-23/1094/?bc=1

4 Leveson Inquiry, Exhibit AB1D, https://www.discoverleveson.com/evidence/Exhibit_AB1D/6621/media

5 Leveson Inquiry, transcript, 23 April 2012,

6 James Burleigh, 'The cheating, the rows, the revenge: Liddle and Royce spill their vitriol (and manure) in public', *Independent*, 12 July 2004, https://www.independent.co.uk/news/media/the-cheating-the-rows-the-revenge-liddle-and-royce-spill-their-vitriol-and-manure-in-public-552858.html

7 Interview with author.

8 Stephen Brook, 'Boris to return to Telegraph column', *Guardian*, 15 May 2008, https://www.theguardian.com/media/2008/may/15/dailytelegraph.pressandpublishing

9 LBC interview, 20 July 2021.

10 *Guardian*, 14 January 2021.

11 Ibid.

12 Sonia Purnell, *Just Boris: A Tale of Blond Ambition*, Aurum, 2011.

13 Interview with author.

14 'EU referendum: Farage declares "independence day"', BBC News, 24 June 2016, https://www.bbc.com/news/av/uk-politics-eu-referendum-36613295

15 Interview with author, December 2022.

16 Robert Booth, 'The shambassador's reception: tycoons are spoiling Nigel Farage', *Guardian*, 24 November 2016, https://www.theguardian.com/politics/2016/nov/23/the-shambassadors-reception-tycoons-are-spoiling-nigel-farage

17 Chris York, 'Nigel Farage's Ritz party was not very anti-establishment', HuffPost UK News, 24 November 2016, https://www.huffingtonpost.co.uk/entry/nigel-farages-ritz-party_uk_5836bc33e4b0ddedcf5c1d74

18 Screenshot 21/12/22.

19 Peter Walker and Paul Lewis, 'Nigel Farage discussed fronting far-right group led by Steve Bannon', *Guardian*, 22 May 2019, https://www.theguardian.com/politics/2019/may/22/nigel-farage-discussed-fronting-far-right-group-led-by-steve-bannon

20 Jim Waterson, 'Property developer son of billionaire Daily Telegraph owner is major UKIP donor', BuzzFeed News, 19 February 2015, https://www.buzzfeed.com/jimwaterson/property-developer-son-of-daily-telegraphs-billionaire-owner

21 https://medium.com/@kobarclay; https://twitter.com/kobarclay

22 Alex Wickham and Mark Di Stefano, 'New video shows Nigel Farage courting fringe right-wing figures at a private tea party hosted at the Ritz', BuzzFeed News, 21 May 2019, https://www.buzzfeed.com/alexwickham/farage-ritz-tea-party

23 Ibid.

24 Interview with author, December 2022.

25 'It's The Sun Wot Won It', Wikipedia entry, https://en.wikipedia.org/wiki/It%27s_The_Sun_Wot_Won_It

26 Christopher Howse, 'It's Telegraph readers wot won it!', *Daily Telegraph*, 30 January 2020, https://www.telegraph.co.uk/politics/2020/01/30/telegraph-readers-wot-won/

27 @BorisJohnson, Twitter, 13 January 2021, https://twitter.com/BorisJohnson/status/1349267504020025344?lang=en

10. *The Midas Touch*

1 Dana Vachon, 'To capture Claridge's', *Vanity Fair*, 17 July 2014, https://www.vanityfair.com/news/business/2014/08/claridges-hotel-london-battle

2 *Patrick McKillen v Misland (Cyprus) Investments Ltd and 10 others*, England and Wales High Court 2343, 2012, pt 113, https://www.oeclaw.co.uk/images/uploads/documents/McKillen_Jugdment_-_APPROVED_.pdf

3 *Vanity Fair*, 17 July 2014,

4 *McKillen v Misland.*

5   *Vanity Fair*, 17 July 2014.

6   Perman, p. 130.

7   https://fullfact.org/economy/1-trillion-not-spent-bailing-out-banks/

8   'Major balance sheet interventions', obr.uk, p. 3.

9   *McKillen v Misland*.

10 *Vanity Fair*, 17 July 2014.

11 Jill Treanor, 'Saudi prince buys the Savoy', *Guardian*, 20 January 2005, https://www.theguardian.com/business/2005/jan/20/1

12 *McKillen v Misland*, p. 312.

13 Ibid.

14 Ibid.

15 Ibid.

16 Roy Greenslade, 'Panorama confronts the Barclay brothers with tax revelations', *Guardian*, 17 December 2012, https://www.theguardian.com/media/greenslade/2012/dec/17/barclay-brothers-bbc

17 *McKillen v Misland*, pp. 26, 29.

18 Simon Bowers, 'Barclay brothers sell stake in three luxury London hotels', *Guardian*, 23 April 2015, https://www.theguardian.com/media/2015/apr/23/barclay-brothers-sale-coroin-war-three-luxury-london-hotels

19 Interview with author.

20 Frederick Barclay, witness statement to the High Court, 22 February 2012, https://archive.org/stream/359406-sir-frederick-barclay-witness-statement-to-the/359406-sir-frederick-barclay-witness-statement-to-the_djvu.txt

21 Ibid.

22 *McKillen v Misland*, p. 18.

23 Ibid., p. 34.

24 Ibid., para 210.

25 Ibid., p 23.

26 Ibid.

27 Roy Greenslade, 'New Corp's phone hacking lawyer earns £3,000 an hour' *Guardian*, 28 July 2011, https://www.theguardian.com/media/greenslade/2011/jul/28/phone-hacking-newsinternational

28 Don Van Natta Jr, 'Suspicions about former editor in battle over story complicate hacking scandal', *New York Times*, 23 July 2011, https://www.nytimes.com/2011/07/23/world/europe/23telegraph.html

29 Interview with author, 2022.

30 'McKillen sued by investigator', *Sunday Times*, 13 January 2019, https://www.thetimes.co.uk/article/mckillen-sued-by-investigator-in-barclay-brothers-dispute-57b9nldc3

31 Shane Hickey, 'McKillen left with €25m legal bill after failed case against Barclays', *Independent* (Ireland), https://www.independent.ie/business/irish/mckillen-left-with-25m-legal-bill-after-failed-case-against-barclays/26896986.html

32 Cahal Milmo, 'Qatar, the tiny gulf state that bought the world', *Independent*, 11 May 2010, https://www.independent.co.uk/news/world/middle-east/qatar-the-tiny-gulf-state-that-bought-the-world-1970551.html

33 PMc says, from disclosure court documents.

34 March UK accounts, year ending April 2009, note 14.

35 Company accounts.

36 Company accounts.

37 See, for instance, https://www.youtube.com/watch?v=EsczjIYcph4

38 'UK's Yodel warns off Twitter from "defamatory" statements', *Post and Parcel*, 9 July 2012, https://postandparcel.info/48939/news/uks-yodel-warns-off-twitter-from-defamatory-statements/

39 'DPD and DPD voted top parcel delivery firms, while CitySprint and Yodel are bottom of the pile', MoneySavingExpert, January 2021, https://www.moneysavingexpert.com/news/2021/01/parcel-delivery-poll-results/

40 £112.4 million in 2013.

41 *Littlewoods Retail Ltd & Ors v Revenue & Customs*, England and Wales High Court 2622 (QB), 31 October 2008, https://www.bailii.org/cgi-bin/format.cgi?doc=/ew/cases/EWHC/QB/2008/2622.html

42 Jon Henley, 'Hotel wars: the battle for Claridge's, the Connaught, and the Berkeley', *Guardian*, 6 September 2014, https://www.theguardian.com/business/2014/sep/06/hotel-wars-claridges-connaught-berkeley

43 'McKillen scores victory as stake in hotels secured', *Belfast Telegraph*, 6 March 2014.

44 *Guardian*, 6 September 2014.

45 Rori Donaghy, 'Was a London property dispute behind a Telegraph campaign against Qatar?' *Middle East Eye*, 15 June 2015, https://www.middleeasteye.net/news/was-london-property-dispute-behind-telegraph-campaign-against-qatar

46 Robert Mendick, 'Harrods shoppers are "buying into terror"', *Daily Telegraph*, 12 October 2014, https://www.telegraph.co.uk/news/11156406/Harrods-shoppers-are-buying-into-terror.html; Robert Mendick and Tim Ross, 'Cut business ties to Qatar over Islamic state, ministers warned', *Daily Telegraph*, 11 October 2014, https://www.telegraph.co.uk/news/uknews/11156430/Cut-business-ties-to-Qatar-over-Islamic-State-ministers-warned.html

47 *Middle East Eye*, 15 June 2015.

48 Emails sent from PA on SDB's behalf.
49 *Sunday Times*, 30 March 2021.
50 Interview with author.
51 'Fight for Claridge's boiled down to a battle between two families', *Financial Times*, 1 May 2015, https://www.ft.com/content/e2ec6a94-f00a-11e4-ab73-00144feab7de
52 Interview with author.

11. *Bugged*

1 *Barclay v Barclay*, 28 July 2022, para 6.
2 Evidence in court on 25 July 2022.
3 *Barclay v Barclay*, England and Wales Family Court 117, 30 March 2021, https://www.bailii.org/cgi-bin/format.cgi?doc=/ew/cases/EWFC/HCJ/2021/117.html, paras 25–6.
4 Companies House, 'Subsea Infrastructure Limited', https://find-and-update.company-information.service.gov.uk/company/05242151
5 Companies House, 'Winkball Ltd.', https://find-and-update.company-information.service.gov.uk/company/05532874
6 Companies House, 'NowBelieve', https://find-and-update.company-information.service.gov.uk/company/06977077/filing-history
7 https://www.livefreefoundation.org.uk/
8 Aidan Barclay, evidence in court, 31 May 2023.
9 https://www.driverdb.com/drivers/alistair-barclay
10 Andrew Napier, 'Alistair Barclay-Oropeza, driver of Bentley Continental, banned for speeding near Alresford', *Hampshire Chronicle*, 4 August 2016, https://www.hampshirechronicle.co.uk/news/14662661.alistair-barclay-oropeza-driver-of-bentley-continental-banned-for-speeding-near-alresford/
11 Court evidence, 25 July 2022.
12 Companies House, '202 Clarges Estate imited', https://find-and-update.company-information.service.gov.uk/company/09106183
13 Court testimony, 25 July 2022.
14 *Barclay v Barclay*, 28 July 2022, para 11.
15 *Barclay v Barclay*, 30 March 2021, Financial Remedies Judgment note 26.
16 Evidence in court on 25 July 2022.
17 *Barclay v Barclay*, 30 March 2021, Financial Remedies Judgment note 29.

18 Evidence in court on 25 July 2022; *Barclay v Barclay*, 28 July 2022.

19 Evidence in court on 25 July 2022.

20 This and quotes that follow are from email correspondence.

21 *Evening Standard*, 14 November 2018, https://www.standard.co.uk/home sandproperty/luxury/25bedroom-london-supermansion-could-be-the-capital-s-first-ps300-million-home-a125581.html

22 *Littlewoods Ltd and others v Commissioners for Her Majesty's Revenue and Customs*, United Kingdom Supreme Court 70, 1 November 2017, https://www.bailii.org/uk/cases/UKSC/2017/70.html

23 'Supreme Court decision in Littlewoods: the conclusion to compound interest claims against HMRC?', 7 November 2017, | https://www.bclplaw.com/en-US/events-insights-news/supreme-court-decision-in-littlewoods-the-conclusion-to-compound-interest-claims-against-hmrc.html

24 Very Group accounts 2019, note 2.

25 'Wafic Saïd funded Barclay twins' hotel deal', *Sunday Times*, 23 June 2019, https://www.thetimes.co.uk/article/wafic-said-funded-barclay-twins-hotel-deal-nwvd63kdn

26 'How Lex Greensill helped sow the seeds of Carillion crisis', *Financial Times*, 9 March 2021, https://www.ft.com/content/cb7e1c50-6e38-4063-ae20-057726c6b98f

27 'Shop Direct pulls off debut bond after dropping Barclay brothers dividend', *Financial Times*, 27 October 2017, https://www.ft.com/content/269785fe-d9fb-3ddb-a512-dd185fe83d8b

28 'Mystery of Greensill and Credit Suisse loans', *The Times*, 23 March 2021, https://www.thetimes.co.uk/article/mystery-of-greensill-and-credit-suisse-loans-k65nnmh39

29 Shop Direct Holdings Ltd accounts ending 30 June 2019, note 32, p. 46.

30 Interview with author.

31 Company accounts for year to the end of 2018.

32 *Barclay v Barclay*, 30 March 2021, para 101.

33 'Alice Brudenell-Bruce's tea party', *Tatler*, 24 March 2004, https://www.tatler.com/gallery/alice-brudenell-bruces-tea-party

34 Fletcher, *The Times*, 25 October 2019, 'Telegraph newspapers put up for sale'

35 *Barclay v Barclay*, England and Wales High Court 424 (QB), 24 February 2020, https://www.bailii.org/cgi-bin/format.cgi?doc=/ew/cases/EWHC/QB/2020/424.html

36 https://www.spycraft.co.uk/spy-equipment/spy-electronics/power-socket-bugging-device/

37 *Barclay v Barclay* 2020, para 56.

38 'Ritz "sold at half price after Sir Frederick Barclay was bugged"', *The Times*, 7 May 2020, https://www.thetimes.co.uk/article/sir-frederick-barclays-nephews-bugged-1-000-private-conversations-at-the-ritz-srnzfd7m9

39 'Former Met chief Lord Stevens linked to court case over bugging of Ritz owner Sir Frederick Barclay', *The Times*, 21 June 2020, https://www.thetimes.co.uk/article/former-met-chief-lord-stevens-linked-to-court-case-over-bugging-of-ritz-owner-sir-frederick-barclay-gg5bxkm69

40 *Barclay & Anr v Barclay & Ors*, England and Wales High Court, 7 May 2020, https://www.casemine.com/judgement/uk/5eba93122c94e017e1a6acbe

41 Bloomberg, 29 November 2004.

42 Owen Bowcott, 'Frederick Barclay was secretly recorded at Ritz, High Court hears', *Guardian*, 24 February 2020, https://www.theguardian.com/uk-news/2020/feb/24/frederick-barclay-was-secretly-recorded-at-ritz-high-court-hears

43 'The great estates: who are London's 10 largest land owners by size?' *London Loves Business*, 12 October 2016, https://londonlovesbusiness.com/the-great-estates-who-are-londons-10-largest-land-owners-by-size/

44 Green Park accounts; Aidan Barclay evidence in court 23 May 2023.

45 Mark Sweney, 'Sir Frederick Barclay threatens to sue twin over Ritz London hotel', *Guardian*, 4 March 2020, https://www.theguardian.com/business/2020/mar/04/sir-frederick-barclay-threatens-sue-twin-ritz-london-hotel

46 *Barclay & Anr v Barclay & Ors*, 7 May 2020, para 23.

47 'Secretive British billionaire Barclay sues over French play', *France 24*, 13 May 2019, https://www.france24.com/en/20190513-secretive-british-billionaire-barclay-sues-over-french-play

12. *There's No Money, Your Honour*

1 *Financial Times*, print edition, 29 July 2023.

2 *Barclay v Barclay*, 30 March 2021.

3 *Barclay v Barclay*, England and Wales Family Court 40, 5 May 2021, https://www.familylawweek.co.uk/judgments/barclay-v-barclay-2021-ewfc-40/

4 *Barclay v Barclay* court hearing, 16 June 2022

5 *Akhmedova v Akhmedov and others*, High Court of Justice Family Division, 12 June 2020, https://www.familylaw.co.uk/docs/font/akhmedova-v-akhmedov-and-others-2020-ewhc-1526-(fam).pdf?sfvrsn=e1dc2a98_2

6 'Mills soaked McCartney's lawyer', BBC News, 18 March 2008, http://news.bbc.co.uk/2/hi/entertainment/7303266.stm

7 *Barclay v Barclay*, 5 May 2021.

8 Opening statements in the preliminary trial, 25 July 2023.

9 See, for example, https://www.telegraph.co.uk/news/2020/06/23/billionaire-hinduja-brothers-embroiled-high-court-dispute-family/

10 Witness statement ahead of trial, 25 July 2023.

11 *The Times*, August 2004.

12 *Barclay v Barclay*, 30 March 2021.

13 Witness statement, August 2021.

14 Most of the courtroom testimony comes from the divorce hearing which resulted in a judicial summons commenced in August 2021 and which culminated in a four-day trial and finding of contempt on 28 July 2023. Hearings over Sir Frederick's non-payment were still ongoing in August 2023.

15 Jonathan Browning, 'UK tycoon Fred Barclay wanted government money in divorce fight', Bloomberg, 16 June 2022, https://www.bloomberg.com/news/articles/2022-06-16/uk-tycoon-fred-barclay-wanted-government-money-in-divorce-fight

16 *Barclay v Barclay*, 30 March 2021, para 21.

17 Ibid., para 24.

18 Ibid., para 112, written on 12 February 2021.

19 Court appearance, 26 July 2023.

20 *Barclay v Barclay*, 30 March 2021, paras 29–36.

21 *Barclay v Barclay*, 5 May 2021.

22 Note of call with Daniel Martineau, 10 May 2021, disclosed in court evidence.

23 Witness statement, 26 July 2023.

24 'Patarkatsishvili family reaches deal over Metalloinvest stake', *Financial Times*, 14 March 2021, https://www.ft.com/content/9f667670-ab78-11e3-aad9-00144feab7de

25 *Barclay v Barclay*, 28 July 2022, para 35.

26 Ibid., paras 6–7.

27 Jane Martinson, 'Frederick Barclay avoids jail as High Court gives him three months to pay ex-wife', *Guardian*, 11 August 2022, https://www.theguardian.com/uk-news/2022/aug/11/frederick-barclay-avoids-jail-as-high-court-gives-him-three-months-to-pay-ex-wife

28 Position statement, 13 February 2023; 'Barclay threatened with bankruptcy over £100 million divorce', Bloomberg, 13 February 2023, https://www.bloomberg.com/news/articles/2023-02-13/frederick-barclay-threatened-with-bankruptcy-over-100-million-divorce

29 *Barclay v Barclay*, 30 March 2021, para 96.

30 *Guardian*, 14 January 2021.

Epilogue: The Crash

1 Aidan Barclay, court testimony, 16 May 2023.

2 Financial Services Authority, Final Notice, 12 September 2012, https://www.fca.org.uk/publication/final-notices/peter-cummings.pdf.

3 Andrew Alderson and Roya Nikkah, 'Philip Green gives £4 million party for his son't bar mitzvah . . . but no present', *Daily Telegraph*, 15 May 2005, https://www.telegraph.co.uk/news/uknews/1490030/Philip-Green-gives-4-million-party-for-his-sons-bar-mitzvah-but-no-present.html.

4 PIHL accounts, Datacorp, https://www.datocapital.vg/companies/Penultimate-Investment-Holdings-Ltd.html.

5 *Barclay v Barclay*, 30 May 2021, para 34.

6 Julia Kollewe, 'Profile: New Lloyds chief António Hora-Osório', *Guardian*, November 2010, https://www.theguardian.com/business/2010/nov/03/profile-lloyds-chief-antonio-horta-osorio.

7 Brian Farmer, 'Judge says latest stage of Sir Frederick Barclay money fight is a "charade"', *Independent*, 7 July 2023, https://www.independent.co.uk/news/uk/crime/sir-frederick-barclay-london-high-court-sunday-telegraph-buckingham-palace-b2371235.html.

8 Joint press statement to *Financial Times*, https://www.ft.com/content/86210915-28de-4db8-a8e2-888eed30781e.